C0-AUG-891

THE ELIZABETHAN PLAYHOUSE
AND OTHER STUDIES

PERFORMANCE OF THE *LIBERATIONE DI TIRRENO* IN THE DUCAL PALACE   [*Front.*
AT FLORENCE IN 1616—AFTER CALLOT'S ETCHING (*See p.* 104.)

THE ELIZABETHAN PLAYHOUSE

AND OTHER STUDIES

BY

W. J. LAWRENCE

ILLUSTRATED

TWO VOLUMES BOUND AS ONE
FIRST SERIES

NEW YORK / RUSSELL & RUSSELL

PN
2589
L32

To
WILLIAM ARCHER

81196

FIRST PUBLISHED IN 1912
REISSUED, 1963, BY RUSSELL & RUSSELL
A DIVISION OF ATHENEUM PUBLISHERS, INC.
L. C. CATALOG CARD NO: 63-15167
PRINTED IN THE UNITED STATES OF AMERICA

THE ELIZABETHAN PLAYHOUSE

AND OTHER STUDIES

FIRST SERIES

PREFACE

IN connection with the existing, actively pursued inquiry into the physical conditions and stage conventionalisms of the Elizabethan Playhouse, I lay claim with pardonable pride to the mild honours of a pioneer. Ten years ago, when I first began to publish the result of my prolonged investigations on the subject, there were no scientific workers in the field. At home and abroad, in Germany, in America, there are many now. To those who desire to see how notable has been the progress made in this department of research during the past decade I commend Professor Reynolds' critical retrospect, "What we know of the Elizabethan Stage", as published last year in *Modern Philology* at Chicago. To myself the seriousness of this advance has been vividly brought home by the circumstance that, on examination, the first fruits of my labours in this field have proved too axiomatic to bear the test of reproduction. I refer here more particularly to a paper on "Some Characteristics of the Elizabethan-Stuart Stage," contributed in 1903 to *Englische Studien,* which at least justified itself in inspiring and directing other workers. Vainglorious as this may sound, it is simply an echo of what has been publicly acknowledged.

In bringing the following papers together for republication in collected form, I have been ruled in my selection by desire to illustrate, not only the rise and progress of the Platform Stage, but in what degree the characteristics of that stage coalesced with and otherwise influenced the early Picture Stage. It will be found, I think, that these studies embody full details of the evolution of the English theatre in its primary and secondary stages, or, in other words, from its inception in the inn-yards until the close of the seventeenth century. In them some attempt has been made to indicate what features were indigenous and what derivative, a task undertaken with the view of combating the popularly accepted idea that all the salient characteristics of the Restoration playhouse were imported wholesale from France. There can be little doubt that during the first two centuries of its history the English theatre, as an institution, was highly individualised.

For courteously sanctioning the reprinting of these papers, I have to thank the editors of the various periodicals in which, with one exception, they all originally appeared. The first, third and fourth are taken from the *Jahrbuch der Deutschen Shakespeare-Gesellschaft* (1908-11), the second from *Englische Studien* (1908), the fifth—with the accompanying illustrations—from *The English Illustrated Magazine* (1903), the sixth from *The Gentleman's Magazine* (1902), and the seventh, eighth, ninth and tenth from *Anglia* (1903-9). All have been carefully revised, some amplified, and one—the paper on "Music and Song in the Elizabethan Theatre"—entirely rewritten. In view of the publication of Sir Ernest Clarke's article on "*The Tempest* as an opera" in *The Athenaeum* of August 25, 1906,—a contribution which immediately earned for its writer in some ill-informed quarters the honours of a discoverer, and whose *raison d'être* I then vigorously challenged—it is necessary to state that my paper on the same subject, now republished, originally appeared in *Anglia* in 1904 (Vol. xxvii, pp. 205 sqq.), and that the only material strengthening of the argument has been derived from my supplementary contribution on the point, published in *Notes and Queries* later in the same year (10th S., ii. 329). Irrespective of the plates which accompany the paper on "The Mounting of the Carolan Masques", all the illustrations have been newly added. They have been chosen as much for their rarity as their appositeness. One other new feature of the book remains to be commented upon, the final paper, written after the first sheets had been printed off, by way of supplement to the opening study. This addition was rendered imperative by the appearance of Monsieur Feuillerat's article in *The Daily Chronicle*, revealing preliminary proof of the existence of an earlier playhouse in the Blackfriars.

My thanks are finally due to my publisher, Mr. A. H. Bullen, for placing at my disposal in the reading of the proofs his wide knowledge of Elizabethan life and literature. It may be that I have not been apt pupil enough so to profit by his advice as to be able to disarm Criticism; but I feel assured that he has, at least, taught me how to blunt its weapons.

W. J. LAWRENCE.

DUBLIN, *March*, 1912.

CONTENTS

ILLUSTRATIONS

THE EVOLUTION AND INFLUENCE OF THE ELIZABETHAN PLAYHOUSE

The Evolution and Influence of the Elizabethan Playhouse

Within the span of Shakespeare's birth and death there took place a vital melioration of the conditions of English acting and playgoing, together with some slight improvement in the status of the player. It is true that, subject to certain reservations, the stage still remained, as it had been constituted by Act of Parliament, a banned vocation. But, if viewed with no favourable eye by the middle classes, the player had already won the countenance of the court, and taken thereby a stride towards his enfranchisement.

In 1576, or nine years before William Shakespeare arrived in London, an epoch-marking event in stage annals had taken place. This was the erection in Moore-fields, outside the city boundaries, of the Theater, a structure without prototype, ranking not only as the first permanent English playhouse but as the first organised public theatre in modern Europe. It is matter of curiosity, as well as importance, that an event which deflected the trend of Elizabethan dramaturgy and led to the immediate systemization of the player's irregular calling should have been brought about purely by force of outward circumstance. No evidence exists to show that up to the period when James Burbage solved a difficult problem by building the Theater under protection of a royal patent, either players or playgoers were otherwise than content with the primitive histrionic conditions obtaining in the several inn-yards. For years it had been customary to give performances twice or three times a week on removable stages—possibly the "boards and barrel-heads" referred to in *The Poetaster* as the later resource of "strutters"—in the yards of well-known hostells like the Cross Keys in Grace-church Street, the Bull in Bishopsgate Street, and the Bell Savage on Ludgate Hill. In divers ways these ill-regulated assemblies had given dire offence to the Puritans who constituted the Common Council. In recurrent periods of plague they were always viewed as a menace to the public health, and every outbreak was marked by prohibition of acting. Despite all protests, the players persisted in desecrating the Lord's Day by their performances. Apprentices had been distracted from their work by the allurements of Melpomene and Thalia; there had been "sundry slaughters and maimings of the Queen's subjects" by falling scaffolds and ill-handled stage ordnance; and, worst of all, young maids and good citizens' daughters had been inveigled into "privie and unmete contracts" in the rooms overlooking the yards.[1] In December, 1574, the Common Council had issued an order imposing municipal censorship of the drama, and it was only a question of time as to when the players would be expelled from the city.[2] Forewarned, however, was forearmed, and, when it came, the blow fell on well protected shoulders.

When a decision was arrived at to migrate northwards to the Liberty of Halliwell, in Shoreditch, with the view of nullifying the gravity of the situation, Burbage and his associates were forced to evolve a suitable playhouse out of their varied experiences, both in public and in private, in town and country. For the reason that the old bull- and bear-baiting amphitheatres on the Bankside potently indicated how the greatest number of spectators could be accommodated in the least possible space, the Theater was built, like them, of wood and circular or octagonal in shape. Doubtless its near neighbour of a year or so later, the Curtain, was constructed on similar lines.[3]

---

[1] Collier's *Hist. Eng. Dram. Poetry* (1831), i. p. 214 note.

[2] The expulsion probably came circa 1582, but the order is undated. Cf. Mr. E. K. Chambers's review of Ordish's *Early London Theatres* in *The Academy* for August 24, 1895.

[3] The Theater and the Curtain were two of the four "amphitheatra" referred to by Johannes de Witt. It is plain to be seen that no square-shaped playhouse existed in 1593, else of a surety Nash would not have written then in *The Unfortunate Traveller*: "I sawe a banketting house belonging to a merchant that was the meruaile of the

Burbage's house was so elaborately decorated that John Stockwood, in a sermon delivered at Paul's Cross on August 24, 1578, could refer to it as "the gorgeous playing place erected in the fields." "The painted stage" or "painted theatres" is the phrase applied to the two Shoreditch houses at different periods by Gabriel Harvey[1] in his letters, and Spenser in his *Tears of the Muses* (1591). One recalls in this connexion what Johannes de Witt wrote a few years later concerning the Swan, whose columns were "painted in such excellent imitation of marble that it might deceive even the most cunning."

In keeping with his quality as pariah, the Elizabethan player entertained no very lofty opinion of his calling, made no particular effort to keep the temple of the Muses undesecrated. The fact that neither the Theater nor the Curtain was intended solely for dramatic purposes postulated to some extent their internal arrangement. We know from Stow[2] that both were built "for the shewe of Activities, comedies, tragedies and histories for recreation." What the the word "activities" here implies can be gathered from a characteristic passage in Gosson's *Plays confuted in Five Actions* (1582), wherein it is maintained that the devil entices the eye in the play-house by sending in "garish apparell, masques, vaulting, tumbling, dauncing of gigges, galiardes, moriscoes, hobby horses, shewing of judgeling castes—nothing forgot that might serve to set out the matter with pompe, or ravish the beholders with variety of pleasure". Other side shows, such as fencing matches, were also held in the Shoreditch playhouses. The public uses to which they were put were practically without limit. Following on the heels of his visit to London in 1596, Ludwig, Prince of Anhalt, wrote a poem commemorative of his travels, in which he pointed out that

---

world . . . It was builte round of green marble like a Theater without;" &c. See the prologue to *Old Fortunatus* (1599) for indication of the circular disposition of the auditorium of the Rose.

[1] *The Letter Book of Gabriel Harvey*, 1573–80 (Camden Society 1884), p. 67.

[2] Cf. T. Fairman Ordish, *Early London Theatres*, p. 45, et seq.

the English capital boasted four theatres[1], which were
utilised, not only for dramatic purposes, but for the bait-
ing of bulls and bears and for cockfights. Most of these
cruel and debasing exhibitions demanded a clear arena :
hence probably the main reason why the inn-yard principle
of the removable stage was adopted at the Theater and the
Curtain. As a matter of fact little deviation took place at
either house from the stage conventionalities and playgoing habitudes of the inn-yard era. So insensible was the
transition that the space occupied by the groundlings (who
remained standing at all save the private theatres for long
after Shakespeare's day) inherited the old designation of
"yard."[2] That the later term "pit" was a contraction of
"cock-pit", in part confirming the statement of Ludwig,
Prince of Anhalt, is clearly indicated in Leonard Digges'
lines on *Shakespeare's Poems* (1640):

> Let but Beatrice
> And Benedicke be seen, loe in a trice
> The cock-pit, galleries, boxes, are all full,
> To hear Malvoglio that crosse-garter'd gull.

As in the inn-yards, acting in the Shoreditch theatres
took place in the afternoon by natural light. Beyond the
covering in of the circumambient galleries, the two houses
remained unroofed. Exposure to the elements having
been thitherto the normal experience of the groundling,
the perpetuation of his discomfort was accepted with
equanimity. A quarter of a century later, however, the
public theatres were to be placed at some disadvantage by
the cosiness of the covered-in private houses. One recalls
how Webster, in his "Address to the Reader", prefixed to
The White Devil, accounts for the ill-success of his play
(as probably produced at the Curtain in the harsh winter
of 1607-8), by averring it was "acted in so dull a time of

---

[1] The other two probably being the Rose and Newington Butts, both on the
south side. Cf. W. B. Rye, *England as seen by Foreigners*, p. 133.

[2] So, too, the signboard by which the playhouse was known, the system of preliminary payment at the door and secondary "gathering" in the galleries, and the three
trumpet-blasts shortly before the performance were all relics of the inn-yard period.

winter and presented in so open and black a theatre", that it failed to attract a fitting audience.

Following the old inn-yard system, the stage in our earliest theatres was a simple, rush-strewn platform, jutting out prominently into the yard. It had neither a proscenium arch nor a front curtain, both of which were essential characteristics of the picture stage and were not to be permanently adopted in England until the period of the systematic employment of scenery, a year or two after the Restoration. Under such conditions Drama could not be wholly, or even largely, an art of emotional illusion. It was simply a more or less discursive narrative put into action. The story was told rather than realised. With the stage surrounded by spectators and the player embarrassingly close to his public, acting, to be effective, had to be rhetorical and vigorous. With the bulk of the audience noisy and turbulent attention had to be gained by resoluteness of attack and a certain measure of direct appeal.

We come now to the point of departure between the physical conditions of the inn-yard stage and the stage of the first public theatres; or, in other words, to a consideration of the various improvements suggested by the shortcomings and inconveniences of the earlier system. The paramount need of a readily accessible dressing room, with wardrobe and store for properties, led at once to the creation of the "tiring-house". So far, however, from being an isolated or hidden structure, this was adroitly conjoined to the stage and made to subserve the purposes of the play. Its composite façade formed a permanent background to the action, and the whole afforded a crude resemblance to the skene of the Attic Theatre of the fifth century. Authentic details of the prime characteristics of the Shoreditch theatres are almost wholly lacking, but these can be soundly, if laboriously, deduced by collating the stage directions in the plays written for the two houses and examining the evidence thus obtained by the light of the information derivable from interior views of subsequent theatres. To some extent the aspect of the tiring-house recalled the background of the older stages in the inn-yards, but it would appear that at least one important hint had been taken from the screen of the banquetting halls in the palaces, universities and inns of court, halls in which the players had occasionally given performances. From this source came the principle of the two frontal doors, forming the normal (but not complete) method of entrance and exit.

The deft combination of platform and tiring-house was of extremely grateful utility. It permitted of the division of the circuit of action into three distinct parts. The value of this arrangement lay in the fact that, on a stage devoid of scenery, it yielded the necessary illusion of a sudden change of place. First there was the outer platform, or stage proper. To this was appended an inner stage formed by a central passage, or opening, between the two frontal doors of the tiring-house, and hidden from view, when not in use, by arras curtains suspended by rings to an iron rod and working laterally. These curtains were commonly known as "traverses". At the back of this recess was the third door of entrance, that "mid-door" of whose employ-ment we read occasionally in old stage directions.[1] This inner area came to be known in theatrical parlance as "the study"[2], probably from the nature of the scene for which it was most commonly employed. But it was utilised for a variety of other interiors, such as caves, arbours, count-ing-houses, prisons, shops, tombs, tents and (occasionally) bed-chambers. Its employment was, to some extent, restricted by the remoteness and obscurity of its position, an inconvenience which almost invariably demanded the

[1] Cf. G. F. Reynolds, *Some Principles of Elizabethan Staging* in *Modern Philology*, ii. 587, note 3. The remoter position of the third door is clearly indicated in the following stage direction from *The Second Maiden's Tragedy* (1611), iv. 3:—"Enter the Tirant agen at a farder dore, which opened, bringes hym to the Toombe wher the Lady lies buried; the Toombe here discouered ritchly set forthe." Here what took place was this. The Tyrant made his exit by one of the frontal doors and the traverses were drawn open, revealing the tomb on the inner stage. Then the Tyrant re-entered by the mid-door at the extreme back.

[2] For examples of the phrase see *Titus Andronicus*, v. 2; *Hamlet*, Q. 1. Sc. vi. 105–8; *The Woman Hater*, v. 1; *Life and death of Lord Cromwell*, iii. 1. (where the scene is an hostel).

bringing in of lights at the commencement of all inner scenes.[1] Most of the emblematic set-pieces used as aids to the imagination were placed here. One cannot speak of a fixed rule, but they were generally put into position and removed under cover of the traverses. Apart from these traverses (or curtains designed for theatrical use), the stage was also adorned with tapestry hangings or painted cloths. A sufficiency of evidence exists to show that these were changed for draperies of black when Tragedy was performed, but the prevalent idea that the stage was hung with blue for comedies, due to a curious surmise of Malone's, has no foundation in fact.[2]

The third division of the circuit of dramatic action was known as "the upper stage", or what is tersely indicated in the old stage directions as "above". It took the form of a central room on the first story of the tiring-house, immediately over the inner stage, and was fronted by a balcony, behind which hung another set of traverses. The upper stage answered indifferently for city walls, Antony's rostrum, or the lookout of a vessel. Many, but not all, upper chamber scenes were acted within this area. Some effects of the kind were more illusively procured by means of practicable windows over the two frontal entering doors.[3] At many of the theatres, when not in dramatic use, the upper stage was occupied by the musicians and boy-singers. It is matter of certitude that at all houses alike their normal position was on an elevation at the back.

Taking a hint from the habitudes of old inn-yard audiences, Burbage and the other builders of the first public theatres saw fit to make the tiring-house a source of revenue by devoting portions of it to the service of the exclusive

---

[1] Cf. *The Two Italian Gentlemen*, ii. 2 ; *Satiromastix*, i. 2 ; *The Martyr'd Souldier*, iii. 2 ; *'Tis Pitty she's a Whore*, iii. 6.

[2] See the induction to *A Warning for Faire Women* ; also Tragedy's speech preceding the second act. In *The Rape of Lucrece* (1594), we have the line, "Black Stage for Tragedies, and murthers fell". For Malone's conjecture, see C. I. Elton, *William Shakespeare, his family and friends*, p. 462.

[3] Cf. *Two Angry Women of Abington*, iii. 2 ; *The Insatiate Countess*, iii. 1 ; *Blurt, Master Constable*, iv. 3 ; *The Partiall Law*, i. 5, and ii. 5 ; *Othello*, Q. 1622, i. 1 ; *The Taming of the Shrew*, v.

playgoer. On the same level with the upper stage were constructed a few latticed boxes for spectators, one of which was distinctively known as "the lords' room". Our first definite trace of this aristocratic rendezvous is at the Rose on the Bankside in 1592, but it doubtless had earlier and other existence. In less than seventeen years, however, its use had been abandoned by the nobles to a very inferior type of playgoer, a change which was apparently brought about by the growing fashion of sitting on the stage.

At a period when the players were becoming more and more luxurious in stage attire, the sole theatrical extravagance of the Shakespearean era, it was not to be expected that they would continue to brave the elements with the fortitude and equanimity of their fellow sufferers, the stinkards in the yard. The problem was to afford them shelter from the pelting rain without unduly darkening the house, or obstructing the spectators' view from any part. It was solved by erecting over the stage, at an elevation corresponding to the ceiling of the uppermost gallery in the auditorium, a thatched (or possibly, tiled and leaded) half-roof, sloping down from the tiring-house and known indifferently as "the shadow" or "the heavens". This curious makeshift had the additional advantage of serving as a sounding-board. Proof of the presence of the heavens in Burbage's house is afforded by a quaint metaphorical conceit of Nash's, in his preface to Sidney's *Astrophel and Stella* (1591):

. . . Let not your surfeted sight, new come frō such puppet play, think scorne to turn aside into this Theater of pleasure, for here you shal find a paper stage streud with pearle, an artificial heau'n to ouershadow the faire frame, and christal wals to encounter your curious eyes, whiles the tragicommedy of loue is performed by starlight.

Surmounting the tiring-house in the early public theatres, at a slight elevation above the roofing of the galleries, was a turret, or hutch, from which the flag, bearing the symbol of the house, was hoisted an hour or so before the

AUDITORIUM OF THE PERGOLESE THEATRE, FLORENCE,
as seen from the stage (1657).

[To face p. 9.

performance. It was here, at short intervals before the entry of the Prologue, that the three Trumpet blasts were blown. As a matter of fact, the turret, so far from being purely ornamental, was put to a great variety of useful purposes. Through its apertures stage ordnance were let off, a custom that led to the destructive fire at Shakespeare's Globe. Here thunder was simulated by "roll'd bullet" and "tempestuous drum"; and here was situated the windlass, or other rude machinery whereby the "creaking throne", or the substantial deity-bearing cloud, was lowered.[1]

Something remains to be said of the arrangement of the auditorium in the Elizabethan public theatre, a portion of the house which practically attained completeness at the outset, so few and trivial are the variations that can be traced. To the first English theatre-builders must the credit be given of having originated the modern system of the three galleries, a disposition commented upon by Samuel Kiechel of Ulm as a novelty, when he visited London in 1585.[2] Apparently the lowermost and middle galleries were divided into commodious boxes and the uppermost galleries left open. Not all, if any, of the rooms and galleries were provided with seats, although in most parts stools and cushions could be procured by paying extra. Details on this point are, however, somewhat vague. All we know for certain is that the scale of prices diminished in ratio with the height of the gallery. In keeping with this system, "the gentlemen's room", or "twelve-penny room", usually the most expensive part of the house, was situated on the lowermost gallery close to the stage.

So far as can be determined, no Pre-Restoration play-house had a separate entrance to every particular section of the building. The public theatres were only provided

---

[1] Cf. Prologue to *Every Man in his Humour*; *Cymbeline*, v. 4; *Alphonsus, King of Arragon*, opening of Act i; *The Silver Age, passim*.

[2] Cf. W. B. Rye, *England as seen by Foreigners*, p. 88. This disposition was unknown in Venice c. 1609. See *Coryat's Crudities* (Glasgow 1905), ii. p. 386. The earliest known view of a modern Italian auditorium is that of the Pergolese Theatre in Florence, engraved in 1657, and reproduced on opposite page.

with two doors, one for general admission to the yard and galleries, and the other (by which the lords and the stool-holders, as well as the actors, entered), leading into the tiring-house. Writing to Sir Ralph Winwood on July 8, 1613, Chamberlain conveys intelligence of the disastrous fire at the Globe on St. Peter's Day, "which fell out by a peal of chambers (that I know not upon what occasion were to be used in the play), the tampin or stopple of one of them lighting in the thatch that covered the house, burn'd it down to the ground in less than two hours with a dwelling house adjoyning; and it was a great marvaile and fair grace of God that the people had so little harm, having but two narrow doors to get out."[1] This curious restriction of the number of entrances was due to the continuance of the inn-yard and bear-baiting system of preliminary payment at the door with subsequent "gathering" inside. "Those who go to Paris Gardens, the Bell Savage, or Theater", writes Lambard in his *Perambulation of Kent* (1596), "to behold bear-baiting, interludes, or fence-play, must not account of any pleasant spectacle, unless first they pay one penny at the gate, another at the entry of the scaffold, and a third for quiet standing". The perpetuation of this clumsy system,[2] which, subject to some modifications, lasted until considerably after the Restoration, was due to the circumstance that in the early public theatres, the proprietor rarely, if ever, leased the house to the players, preferring to take a portion of the receipts.[3] This meant prompt payment and less risk. Hence the reason why the players themselves were remunerated by shares and not by salaries, and were generally expected to find their own costumes and defray the daily charge for "hirelings". Methods of dividing the receipts varied according to the period and the playhouse. At the Theater the players received "the profitts arising from the doors", and Burbage

---

[1] Winwood's *Memorials*, iii. p. 469. Cf. *Reliq. Wotton.* (1685), p. 425, where the play is said to have been *King Henry VIII*.

[2] A somewhat similar system is still pursued in Southern Europe. For a modern Spanish analogy, see Henry Lyonnet's *Théatre en Espagne* (1897), p. 17.

[3] Cf. W. W. Greg, *Henslowe's Diary*, ii. p. 128 and p. 134 note; also Karl Mantzius, *History of Theatrical Art* (1904), iii. pp. 82, 109, 146.

the proprietor the money gathered in the galleries. But at the second Globe and the Blackfriars half a century later (when the daily charges defrayed by the sharers had considerably increased), the players received "all the commings in at the dores to themselves and halfe the galleries from the house-kepers."[1]

Except at the first performances of new plays when the ordinary rates of admission were doubled, prices at the public theatres during the strictly Shakespearean era ran from a penny to a shilling. An allusion in Nash's *Martin's Month's Mind* shows that in 1589 admission to the Theater and the Curtain was a penny. This made the playgoer free of the yard, into which one and all hurried. "In the playhouses in London", wrote Gosson[2] in 1582, "it is the fashion of youthes to go first into the yarde, and to carry their eye through every gallery; then like unto ravens, when they spye the carion, thither they flye, and press as near to the fairest as they can". Ingress to the other parts could be obtained by external staircases,[3] but an extra charge was subsequently enforced, according to the locality, the fee being collected during the performance by "gatherers", who were sometimes pressed into stage service as supernumeraries. Hence the reason why the top gallery is somewhat confusingly referred to in contemporary plays and pamphlets as "the penny gallery", "the two-penny gallery" and "the two-penny room".[4] The charge for this part would be a penny, but the preliminary payment at the door made the total cost two-pence.

Nothing is more interesting in the social life of the Elizabethan-Stuart era than to note the frequent shiftings of the centre of gravity in the theatrical world. With the erection on the Bankside of the Rose and the Swan in the last decade of the sixteenth century, the tide of fashion set in southward, much to the satisfaction and increase of the

---

[1] Halliwell-Phillipps, *Outlines,* 3rd ed. p. 549.
[2] *Plays Confuted in Five Several Actions.*
[3] Reached from the pit by the steps marked "ingressus" in van Buchell's sketch of the Swan.
[4] Collier's *Hist. Eng. Dram. Poetry* (1831), iii. pp. 343-4.

Thames watermen. Although differing materially from each other in point of magnitude, the two new houses presented no serious departure from type. One is not unmindful that the evidence of the well-known Dutch drawing of the Swan runs counter to this assertion, but, on the other hand, potent reasons exist for believing that van Buchell's sketch is not a minutely accurate mirroring of the playhouse it depicts at second hand.[1] It is, indeed, matter for regret that we have no completely satisfying view of the interior of a Pre-Restoration playhouse, nothing that corroborates or amplifies the evidence synthetically derived. The *Roxana* and *Messalina* illustrations merely tantalise. Both suffer from the grave defect that even the meagre details presented cannot be authoritatively applied to any particular theatre or kind of theatre. The more illuminative frontispiece to *The Wits, or Sport upon Sport* (1662)—so long misdescribed as a view of the Red Bull but now recognised as a view of a "private" theatre[2]—cannot be taken strictly as evidence for the Elizabethan period, even if one uses that term in its widest sense. It deals with the surreptitious performances of Cox's Drolls during the Commonwealth, or, in other words, after the general dismantling of the theatres under the repressive act of 1648.

The art and mystery of playgoing, as mordantly revealed by Dekker in *The Guls Hornbooke* in 1609, must not be too literally applied to the Bankside houses of a decennium earlier. In the intervening period the uprise and vogue of the "private" theatres had brought about certain modifications, not only of the conditions of playgoing, but of dramatic representation. We are prone to look upon all the Southwark theatres as mere summer resorts, forgetful of the fact that performances were given there at all seasons until shortly after the dawn of the new century. At the Rose or the Swan, in and about the year 1595, the per-

[1] Cf. T. F. Ordish, *Early London Theatres*, pp. 264–70 ; G. F. Reynolds, *Mod. Phil.*, ii. p. 587 ; Victor E. Albright, *The Shakespearian Stage*, p. 39 ; *The Tribune* newspaper, of Aug. 17, 1907, Mr. William Archer's feuilleton on *The Growth of the Playhouse.*
[2] Cf. Victor Albright, op. cit. pp. 40–3.

There was no provision of programmes, as, for other reasons besides the vagaries of the weather, there was seldom any absolute certainty in the Bankside houses as to what would be performed. During Shrovetide and other holiday periods the players were at the mercy of the "saylers, watermen, shoemakers, butchers, and apprentices" then enjoying an unwonted leisure, and had to give them what they demanded, or risk the destruction of the theatre.[1] But to prevent misunderstanding (the playgoer having the right to depart without payment previous to the appearance of the gatherers[2]), it was usual, at public and private theatres alike, to expose on the stage, with the opening of the doors, a titleboard indicating in text letters what piece was about to be performed. Notwithstanding this habituation of the Elizabethan audience to inscribed boards, one sees no reason for believing what has been so often averred, viz., that changes of scene were regularly indicated in a similar way. It is tolerably certain, however, that in plays like *Pericles*, where the action oscillates rapidly from country to country, as well as in plays of the Marlowean order, where the scene occasionally changes while the characters remain on the stage, resort was made to inscribed locality-boards to prevent confusion.

Whether in the theatres in the Fields or on the Bankside there was tacit obedience (probably more from force of habit than deliberate bowing to authority) to the City ordinance that "no playing be in the dark, so that the auditory may return home before sunset". This limitation of the traffic of the stage to a period of between two hours and a half and three hours largely conditioned much that was distinctive in Elizabethan dramaturgy, as well as the entire technics of the Elizabethan player. Since time had to be rigidly economised, waits of all kinds were studiously

---

[1] See the remarkably vivid description of these saturnalia in Gayton's *Festivous Notes on the History of the renowned Don Quixote* (1654).

[2] This custom, so far as applied to the boxes, long survived the Elizabethan era, and even penetrated into Ireland. It obtained in the Dublin playhouse early in the eighteenth century.

formance generally began at two o'clock in the winter and three in the summer, and lasted from two to three hours, according to the season and the duration of light.[1] Within this limit a drama in five acts, and a brief jig (otherwise a rhymed musical farce) had usually to be given. Although acting was often a matter of uncertainty and largely depended on the state of the weather, meagre bills conveying particulars of the place of performance, the play and the hour were generally posted up in the city a day or two previously.[2] But as excessive rain might occasion an eleventh-hour postponement, the intending playgoer could not be assured positively about the arrangement till he saw the flag hoisted above the theatre. Resort had to be made to the Rose or Swan betimes in order, bodily, to secure a place. For the benefit of those who, through coming early, arrived dinnerless, eatables and drinkables, including fruits, nuts, and bottled beer, were vended in the theatre. No preliminary music to wile away the time was vouchsafed these eager enthusiasts, but powdered tobacco and the latest thing in pamphlets were procurable for a consideration, and the tedium of waiting could be allayed by reading, smoking, and playing cards. Nor must one overlook, in this connexion, Gasson's vivid testimony to the early assembling of women in the galleries and to the eagerness with which hot-blooded youth sought them out. This factor in the economy of Elizabethan playgoing is particularly notable, seeing that in no continental theatre of the sixteenth century, or the first quarter of the seventeenth, was there frank and free interminglement of the sexes.[3]

[1] Three hours is the period indicated in Whetstone's *Heptameron of Civil Discourses* (1582), and Dekker's *Raven's Almanack* (1609). "The space of two hours and a half and somewhat more" is alluded to in the induction to *Bartholomew Fair*, as played at the Hope in 1614. See also the prologue to *The Lover's Progress*, and the epilogue to *The Loyal Subject*.

[2] It was also customary, at the end of every performance, to announce the next play and the day of acting. See the allusion to this practice in the lines headed "The Stationer", by H. Moseley, prefixed to the First Folio Beaumont and Fletcher (1647). It is curiously illustrative of the intense conservatism of the player-folk that this custom should have been maintained in the English theatre down to the middle of the last century.

[3] Cf. H. A. Rennart, *Life of Lope de Vega*, chap. vi; *Coryat's Crudities* (Glasgow, 1905), ii. p. 386; *Quarterly Review*, Vol. cii, p. 416.

avoided. Speech had to be at once fluent, articulate, and well modulated. Action became well-nigh continuous, and the interplay of character upon character a merry-go-round. Act-divisions were indicated rather than realised, and generally lasted no longer than it took a dumb show to pass across the stage, or Chorus to deliver a brief speech.

Although not exactly the first of its order (a select silenced playhouse having been previously established in the Singing School of St. Paul's), the Blackfriars, as built by the Burbages and opened by Henry Evans in 1597 under royal patronage, was the first "private" theatre of importance, and the exemplar of its type. As much a public theatre as any house on the Bankside, it was only private in the sense that privacy was obtained for its better class patrons by charging higher prices of admission, the cheapest seats costing six-pence. But if more was charged, more, as we shall see, was provided.

For the first six years of its history the Blackfriars was virtually a Court Theatre subsidised by the Queen. The lessees were responsible only for rent and repairs, the heavier charges for maintenance, apparel, and furniture for the Children of the Chapel, who composed the actors and singers, being borne by the royal exchequer. In other respects, the Blackfriars enjoyed a distinction beyond any other playhouse of its era. It was the first London theatre to be honoured by a visit from a reigning monarch. We know for certain that the Queen attended the performance there on Tuesday, December 29, 1601.[1] This may not have been her first visit and, doubtless, was not her last. The vogue of the young eyases caused much heartburning among the adult players, especially as Elizabeth, in furthering the interests of the petted children, sought to suppress, or restrict the other companies.

---

[1] Cf. C. W. Wallace, *The Children of the Chapel at Blackfriars*, p. 95. Several of my details concerning the Blackfriars have been derived from this valuable work, but occasionally I have been compelled to exercise an independency of judgment where the results of extended personal study and research run counter to Prof. Wallace's deductions.

By reason of the persistence of many of its characteristics, the private theatre formed the connecting link between the platform stage of Shakespeare's day and the picture stage of Dryden's. Others of the type may be briefly referred to. Paul's, reconstituted shortly after the opening of the Blackfriars, had an audience of almost equal distinction, and might have enjoyed a similar vogue, had not its repertory consisted for the most part of "musty fopperies of antiquity". Five or six years later, synchronising with the dawn of James the First's reign, the Children of the King's Revels had their private house in Whitefriars, to be known later (after its re-edification for the adult players), as Salisbury Court. About 1615 the Cockpit in Drury Lane was transformed into a private theatre and called the Phœnix, from its sign. As often as not, however, it was referred to by its earlier designation. Largely owing to the disrepute of its surroundings, the Phœnix never gained distinction of audience, and the quality of its performances was little superior to that of the average public theatre.

With the building of the Blackfriars came in many vital improvements. So rapid an advance in a single essay was remarkable, for it must be remembered that the divergency of the private from the public theatre was considerably greater than the divergency of the public theatre from the inn-yard. To begin with, the era of the roofed theatre, with acting by artificial light, had now dawned. Again, the Blackfriars was the first of the rectangular, as opposed to the circular, or octagonal, houses. It was likewise the first to possess a rectilinear auditorium.[1] Of this the shape and

---

[1] I am basing here on Prof. Wallace's plausible argument (op. cit. chap. i.), which neither admits of proof nor disproof. But if the Blackfriars' auditorium began square-shaped it ended round. In Middleton's *The Mayor of Quinborough* (1661), as certainly acted there before the Civil War, Raynulph, as Prologue says :

> "What Raynulph, monk of Chester can,
> Raise from his Polychronicon
> That raiseth him, as works do men,
> To see long-parted light agen,
> *That best may please this round fair ring,*
> *With sparkling diamonds circled in,*
> I shall produce."

general disposition were almost wholly conditioned by pre-existent circumstances. The Blackfriars was a second floor theatre, constructed in an old monastic hall some 66 feet long by 46 feet broad. Incapable of providing accommodation for more than six hundred people, it was smaller than any existing playhouse, not even excepting Henslowe's "little Rose". But within its narrow confines several innovations of practical issue were at once effected. From being the worst, the pit now became the best part of the house. No longer at the mercy of the elements, it was furnished with benches in gradually ascending rows.[1] The house had also the regulation three galleries, not, however, as in the existing public theatres, ovoid in form, but running along three sides of a rectangle. It has been asserted that the Blackfriars was the model for at least two of the later private houses[2], but it is gravely to be doubted whether the rectangular auditorium was ever repeated in any house of this order. When *Antonio's Revenge* was produced at Paul's c. November, 1599, the prologue maintained that "a sullen tragic scene" was adapted to the melancholy of the season :—

> Therefore, we proclaim,
> If any spirit breathes *within this round*
> Uncapable of weighty passion
>
> . . . .
> . . . . . . let such
> Hurry amain from our black-visaged shows.

The "sparkling diamonds", I take it, were the ladies' eyes—which oftener sparkled in the private than the public theatres. Or the reference might be to the abounding lights of "the torchy Friars."

[1] The benches of the Blackfriars are distinctly referred to by Thomas Carew in his lines to D'Avenant on *The Just Italian*, and the benches of Salisbury Court in the epilogue to *The Scholars*. Undoubtedly it was from the earlier private houses that the Restoration theatres of the picture stage order derived the principle of the amphitheatrical pit, with the benches systematically covered with green cloth, an arrangement that held good up to the eighteenth century. Abundant evidence of its existence is to hand, owing to the fact that the contemporary continental pit was invariably a standing one, and that several French travellers have testified to the superiority of the English system. Among these are Balthasar de Monconys (1663), Brunet (1676) and Misson (1698).

[2] C. W. Wallace, op. cit. p. 18 note 3 and elsewhere.

The reference here not only indicates the circular disposition of the auditorium, but disproves Professor Wallace's assertion that the Paul's theatre had no galleries. "This round"[1] could not refer to the Singing School in which the playhouse was constructed; for that, most assuredly, was rectangular. Moreover, one treads on firm ground in inferring that the Phœnix had curved galleries, seeing that it was constructed in a cockpit, and that Shakespeare in *King Henry V* makes the Chorus speak of the Globe (or was it the Curtain?) as "this cockpit" and "wooden O."

So much for the Blackfriars auditorium. On turning our attention stagewards what first strikes us is the notable advance towards the slow-coming isolation of the player and his domains. This, however, was matter of accident, not of artistic intention. It was due to the comparative smallness of the hall. So far from projecting as of old into the middle of the pit, and being surrounded on three sides by the groundlings, the stage shrank proportionately in depth and increased in breadth. It was made to extend right across the hall, a disposition that led to the devotion of some little space at either end to the service of privileged spectators.[2] Moreover, as the house was designed for strictly theatrical purposes, the stage was made permanent, boarded in below and embellished along the front with a carved balustrade. Much inconvenience must have been experienced by the players on the old removable, unpalisaded stages (of the type represented in the well-known Swan sketch), more particularly in connexion with the working of traps, always a vital factor in Elizabethan performances. Few theatres but must have had several of these traps; many plays demanded the simultaneous employment of three or

---

[1] One is always safe in taking these references literally, provided one is certain of the place of performance. Thus, in the prologue to *The Whore of Babylon*, as written for delivery at the Fortune, we have "the charmes of silence through *this square* be throwne."

[2] If this new system of stage-building was followed at all the later private theatres, as Prof. Wallace infers, then we have no authentic view of the interior of any house of the order. The *Roxana* and *Messalina* prints both show projecting stages; and the frontispiece to *The Wits*, despite presenting signs and tokens of the private theatre in the matter of artificial lighting, indicates the groundlings on two sides.

FRONTISPIECE TO *THE WITS, OR SPORT UPON SPORT* (1663).
(Usually misdescribed as the Red Bull Theatre.)

[*To face p.* 18.

four.[1] The Induction to *The Poetaster* shows that the Black-friars stage had a central trap, and the masque in *The Maid's Tragedy* indicates the use of others. Hence one reason why the stool-holders could not have sat about promiscuously, and must have been assigned a circumscribed position. It is noteworthy also that with the introduction of the permanent stage came speaking in the cellarage: instance, the ghost in *Hamlet*.[2]

Beyond the fact that there was considerable elaboration of spectacular effect[3], stage routine at the Blackfriars ruled much as in the public houses. But some modification of the old physical conditions was clearly brought about by the complete roofing and the consequent resort to wax and tallow for lighting purposes. We know that the turret and its flag disappeared; and we can assume that "the shadow" was dispensed with. No other material alteration in stage regions took place, save a vital change in the position of the two main entering doors. On the old removable stages no permanent projections beyond the straight front of the tiring-house were practicable. Accordingly the two doors with their surmounting windows had to be flush with the façade. This arrangement was more calculated to satisfy the vision of the main body of spectators than suit every possible variety of dramatic situation. Detours had to be made where passages across the stage were demanded. Scenes where the action took place at opposite upper windows in a street were impossible to visualize. Hence situations such as that in *The Devil is an Ass*, ii. 2, had to be eschewed. But on the permanent stage of the Blackfriars these difficulties and restrictions

---

[1] Cf. *The Whore of Babylon* (Fortune Theatre), the dumb show of Falsehood (ed. Pearson, ii. 243); *If It Be Not a Good Play, the Divill is in it* (Red Bull), epilogue of Hell; and *Messalina*, v. 3.

[2] Cf. *Antonio's Revenge* (1600 at Paul's), v. 2. In all public theatres preceding the Blackfriars, as well as in the Blackfriars itself, the cellarage could hardly have exceeded five feet in depth. The stage was on a level with the line of vision, and there could have been no excavation in houses where the scaffold was occasionally removed for the holding of other entertainments. This also applies to the Blackfriars but for a different reason—the peculiar location of the theatre.

[3] Note the practicable working fountain in *Cynthia's Revels*, a characteristic feature of the Court mounting of the period.

were obviated by placing the two main entering doors and
their overhanging balconies in an oblique position at either
end of the tiring-house.[1] A host of later stage directions
testify to the gratefulness of this arrangement. For example,
in *The Malcontent*, v. 2, we have "Enter from opposite
sides Malevole and Maquerelle singing."[2] The older
directions of this sort read "enter from the one door . . .
the other door." So much more satisfactory in its results
was this new oblique disposition that it was adopted in all
subsequent public and private theatres, with the possible
exception of the Hope. Not only this, but it afforded the
prototype of the proscenium doors and balconies of the
Restoration picture-stage, a conventionality that maintained
its sway in the English theatre to a period almost within
living memory.

The Blackfriars custom of sitting on the stage, so agreeable to those who carried a year's revenue on their backs,
and desired to "publish a handsome man and a new suit,"
quickly spread to the public theatres, despite the grum-
bling of the players, the girdings of Jonson, and the
vigorous protests of the groundlings. Not, indeed, until
near the middle of the eighteenth century was the stool-
holder to be wholly banished from the scene.[3] In Pre-
Restoration days the presence of these intruders militated
against the procuring of sustained scenic illusion by means
of material accessories, with the result that properties
remained in their primitive stage of symbolism. It was
only in the imitation of natural phenomena that realism

---

[1] Cf. *Shakespeare-Jahrbuch*, xliv. pp. 165-6, Mr. William Archer's reprinted article
on *The Fortune Theatre*; Albright, op. cit. pp. 47-9. The Dutch sketch of the Swan
illustrates the older method. Had this obtained at the Blackfriars, Perigot's opening
speech in the fifth act of *The Faithful Shepherdess* would have seemed absurd. Immediately on his entry he espies Clorin seated in her cabin (i. e. on the inner stage) and says :—

> "Yon is her Cabin, thus far off I'll stand
> And call her forth; for my unhallowed hand
> I dare not bring so near yon sacred place."

[2] See also *Nice Valour*, iii. 3; *Four Plays in One*, Sc. 4 (*The Triumph of Love*),
dumb show; *The Little French Lawyer*, iii. 1; *The Chances*, v. 3; *Wife for a Month*, ii. 1.
[3] Dekker discourses upon this incubus with delicious irony in *The Guls Hornbooke*.
For a vivid picture of a typical Blackfriars audience at a somewhat later period, see
H. Fitzjeffrey, *Notes from Blackfryers* (1620).

was aimed at. Thunder, lightning, rain, mists[1], blazing stars, the singing of birds, all were illusively simulated.

At "the torchy Friars" good music was a predominant characteristic. The gross afterpieces, known as "jigs", which had so long delighted the rough frequenters of the public theatres were abandoned in favour of intercalated song and dance. The high reputation for its music gained by the Blackfriars early in its first, or subsidised, period was never afterwards lost or rivalled. In the beginning this distinction was largely attained by the quality of the prelude with which it regaled its patrons for a whole hour before the play.[2] The strange thing was that, notwithstanding all these extraneous musical features, the earliest comer was not detained at the Blackfriars any longer than three hours, or about the limit of a public theatre performance.[3] This dispatch is all the more curious seeing that the necessity for undue rapidity of action had been precluded by the employment of artificial light. But it may be that strict economy ruled, wax and tallow being expensive.

It is noteworthy that the two innovative theatres of the Elizabethan era, each typical of its class, were built by James Burbage. But Burbage's death apparently took place before the Blackfriars was finished, and the work was probably completed under the superintendence of his son Richard. There is here an important continuity, for the younger Burbage constructed in 1598, largely out of the material of the demolished Theater, the never-to-be-forgotten Globe on the Bankside. All the theatrical

---

[1] Mists (as in *Arden of Faversham*, iv. 2 and 3) were effected by smoke arising from a trap. For mimic rainstorms, see *If It Be Not a Good Play, the Divell is in I* (ed. Pearson, iii. p. 326); and *The Brazen Age*, Act i, dumb show. It is impossible to divine how this effect was managed.

[2] See the important extract from the Diary of Philipp Julius, Duke of Stetten-Pomerania (1602), given by C. W. Wallace, op. cit. chap. ix. Beyond doubt the Black-friars custom formed the prototype of the "First, Second, and Third Music" of the Restoration period. Hence the tenor of the Duke's remarks is curiously iterated by later visitors, such as Sorbières (1664) and Magolotti (1669). In the belated *Travels* of the latter we read, "before the comedy begins, that the audience may not be tired with waiting, the most delightful symphonies are played ; on which account many persons come early to enjoy this agreeable amusement."

[3] The actual traffic of the stage rarely exceeded a period of two hours. See prologue to *The Two Noble Kinsmen* and to *Love's Pilgrimage*.

improvements of the age were therefore due to the enterprise of the one family, father and son. It must not be
overlooked that the Globe was in the direct line of progress. Although its auditorium had all the normal characteristics of the older public theatres, some melioration took
place in the arrangement of the stage, based on the improvements at the Blackfriars.

We have no authentic view of Shakespeare's famous
theatre on the Bankside, but we know at least that it was
circular in outline.[1] Whether or not it was the "wooden
O" referred to by the Chorus in *King Henry V*, it was
certainly the house spoken of in the prologue to *The Merry
Devill of Edmonton* in 1608 :

> We ring *this round* with our invoking spelles. [2]

Surrounded by dykes and reached by light bridges, the
Globe stood on a sort of islet. Its situation is vividly
pictured in Ben Jonson's *Execration upon Vulcan*. Over its
galleries was a thatched roofing, an arrangement that
eventually occasioned its destruction by fire. Unlike most
of the other Bankside houses, its record remained unsullied
by bull- and bear-baiting. Since it was strictly a playhouse,
we may take it that, after the manner of the Blackfriars, it
had a permanent, palisaded stage, projecting, however (as
in the earlier public houses), into the yard. That the Globe
stage was surrounded on its three sides by a low balustrade[3]
possibly with a view of resisting the encroachments of the
groundlings, can be gleaned from Middleton's allusion in
the poetical introduction to *The Blacke Booke* (1604). Lucifer,
on ascending to speak the prologue to his own play, says :

---

[1] Halliwell-Phillipps, in his *Outlines*, identifies an uninscribed, turretless playhouse
in Hondius' view of North and South London in Speed's *Theatre of the Empire of Great
Britaine* (1610), as the Globe. But Fleay (*Chron. Hist. Eng. Stage*, p. 146) traverses this
ascription in pointing out that the so-called Globe is more likely the Rose. No reliance
can be placed on the evidence of the old maps. They were based for the most part on
surveys made many years previously ; and in them the Bankside theatres are seldom
correctly located. Cf. William Martin's *The Site of the Globe Playhouse of Shakespeare*
(1910) as reprinted from *Surrey Archæological Collections*, Vol. xxiii.

[2] Cf. the lines "On Sejanus," by "Ev. B." :—

> "When in the Globe's fair ring, our world's best stage," etc.

[3] Doubtless similar to the stage rails indicated on the engraved title pages of
Roxana and *Messalina*.

And now that I have vaulted up so high,

Above the stage rails of this earthen Globe,

I must turn actor and join companies.

There seems to be no valid reason for doubting that one invariable concomitant of the permanent (as opposed to the removable) stage was the oblique entering doors. Some slight evidence exists to show that the Globe had these. In *The Merry Devill of Edmonton*, v. 2, as performed there, the scene represents two opposite inns whose signs have been mischievously stolen or transposed. Note that the host of the George refers to his rival as "mine overthwart neighbour." The situation demands two opposite doors, with or without overhanging signs, and could not be realised by two doors ranged along a straight line in the front of the tiring-house.

Shortly after the opening of the Globe, two other public theatres were built on the north side of the river, the Red Bull in St. John Street, Clerkenwell, and the Fortune in Golden Lane, Cripplegate.[1] Both appealed to much the same type of playgoer, a rough and ready type, delighting in robustious melodrama and exuberant declamation. "I have heard," writes Gayton in 1654,[2] "that the Poets of the Fortune and Red Bull had always a mouth-measure for their actors (who were terrible tear-throats) and made their lines proportionable to their compasses, which were sesquipedales—a foot and a half."

Built in 1599, after the general disposition (but not the form) of the Globe, the Fortune was a square-shaped theatre with a rectangular auditorium. It enjoys the distinction of being the only Pre-Restoration playhouse

---

[1] No authentic view of either has come down to us. Albright (op. cit. p. 45) plausibly identifies the *Messalina* illustration as a view of the Red Bull, an ascription which, at first sight, seems borne out by what Baker (*Biog. Dramatica*, 1782, i. 266) says of Thomas Jordan, viz., that he was "a performer belonging to the company at the Red Bull, and acted the part of Lepida in the tragedy of *Messalina*." But difficulties crop up on further examination. The King's Revels men shifted about from theatre to theatre, and we have no record of the house where Richards' tragedy was first produced. And even if we had, we have no evidence to show that the view on the engraved title-page represents the stage of that particular theatre.

[2] op. cit.

which can be scientifically reconstructed. Basing on its extant building contract, and supplementing the incomplete details by knowledge derived from other sources, Mr. Walter H. Godfrey, the well-known London architect, has drawn up a series of elaborate plans which visualize satisfactorily the main characteristics of the first Fortune.[1] The only seriously debatable point in connexion with this sound reconstruction is the position of the staircases, which, on due reflection, would appear to have been external.[2]

It only remains to add that within the strictly Shakespearean era a complete cycle of theatre-building took place. The last public playhouse erected in the poet's lifetime—the malodorous Hope on the Bankside—was a reversion to type. Modelled largely on the Swan, the Hope was provided with a removable stage, so that it might maintain the unsavoury traditions of the old Bear Garden which it had superseded.

In reviewing the story of the English drama and its habitat in the seventeenth century, it is impossible to draw any sharp line of demarcation. The outbreak of the Civil War simply indicates (in military phrase) a marking of time, not a dismissal. When activities were renewed it was on the old basis. The first theatres of the Restoration period were strictly of the Elizabethan order. Even when these were superseded one cannot say that the platform stage passed away and left no trace. Some of its physical characteristics and not a few of its conventionalities became the inheritance of the picture stage. So, too, many of the playgoing customs of Shakespeare's day lasted until Congreve's. The great Elizabethan impetus cannot be said to have wholly spent itself until the middle of the nineteenth century.

---

[1] For the designs, contract, and excursus, see Mr. Godfrey's article, "An Elizabethan Theatre" in *The Architectural Review* for April, 1908. Cf. *Shakespeare-Jabrbuch*, 1908, pp. 159–66, *The Fortune Theatre*. For an independent reconstruction of the Cripplegate house, by A. Forestier, see *The Illustrated London News* of August 12, 1911. This, while in some respects an improvement on Mr. Godfrey's designs, is marred by one or two unwarrantable features, such as the curtain dividing the upper stage from front to back, and the partition at the front of the yard.

[2] See my review of Mr. Godfrey's plans in the article on "The Old Fortune" in *The Tribune* newspaper of October 23, 1907.

CHRONOLOGICAL LIST OF ELIZABETHAN, AND QUASI-
ELIZABETHAN, PLAYHOUSES (1576—1663).

THE THEATER.

Unroofed theatre; situated in Moore-fields, Shoreditch; built by
James Burbage, 1576; pulled down, 1598; authentic views, none.[1]

THE CURTAIN.

Unroofed theatre ; situated in Moore-fields, Shoreditch ; built
in 1576; pulled down c. 1630; last referred to in 1627 ; authentic
views, none.

PAUL'S.

First roofed theatre ; situated in the Choir Singing School, near
the Convocation House (St. Paul's) ; built c. 1581; suppressed,
1590-6 ; last trace of, c. 1608; burnt down in Great Fire, 1666 ;
authentic views, none.

NEWINGTON BUTTS.

Unroofed theatre ; situated in Lambeth ; built c. 1586; pulled
down c. 1603; authentic views, none.

THE ROSE.

Small, unroofed theatre ; situated on the Bankside in Southwark;
built between 1587 and 1592 ; first referred to in 1592, last in
1603; authentic views : (Exterior) Norden's Map, 1593; Ryther's
Map, 1604.

THE SWAN.

Unroofed theatre ; situated in Paris Garden, Southwark ; built
1595 by Francis Langley ; pulled down c. 1635; authentic views:
(Interior) Van Buchell's sketch, after de Witt, 1596; (Exterior)
Visscher's Map, 1616 ; Manor Map, 1627.

BLACKFRIARS.

Small, roofed, second-floor theatre ; situation, Blackfriars ; built
1596, pulled down August 6, 1655; authentic views, none.

THE FIRST GLOBE.

Unroofed theatre ; situated on the Bankside ; built 1598 ; burnt
down June 29, 1613; authentic views, none.

---

[1] Cf. G. P. Baker, *The Development of Shakespeare as a Dramatist,* pp. 36, 125, 135.
Prof. Baker here reproduces the rude depictions of two buildings from Ryther's Map of
1604, which he identifies as the Theater and the Fortune, forgetful of the fact that the
two houses were never standing at the one time. Perhaps, on second thought, he would
be inclined to say that they represented the Curtain and the Fortune—a plausible
ascription. But even here there are difficulties. The supposed view of the Fortune is
more like a church than a theatre. It has a steeple surmounted by a flag. The flag does
not necessarily prove the theatre. In Hondius' view of London in 1610 (reproduced as
a frontispiece by Prof. Baker), two city churches are shown with a similar adornment.

THE FIRST FORTUNE.

Unroofed square theatre; situated in Golden Lane (afterwards Red Cross Street), Cripplegate; built 1600; burnt down December 9, 1621; authentic views, none.

RED BULL.

Unroofed theatre; situated in St. John Street, Clerkenwell; built c. 1600; enlarged in 1632; last used as playhouse 1663 (see *Pepys' Diary*, April 25, 1664); authentic views, none.

WHITEFRIARS.

Small roofed theatre; situated near Salisbury Court, Fleet Street; built c. 1603; last referred to, 1621; authentic views, none.

THE HOPE.

Unroofed theatre and Bear-baiting arena; situated on the Bankside; built 1614; pulled down 1656; authentic views: (Exterior), Visscher's Map, 1616; "Cittie of London" Map, 1646; "Londonopolis" Map, 1657.

THE SECOND GLOBE.

Unroofed theatre (on site of, but much superior to, the first house); built 1614; pulled down 1644; exterior view of, Visscher, 1616.

THE COCKPIT, OR PHŒNIX.

Small roofed theatre; constructed in the Cockpit in Drury Lane c. 1617; dismantled 1649; last used 1664.

THE SECOND FORTUNE.

Unroofed, brick theatre; erected on site of older house c. 1623; dismantled in 1649, and never afterwards used as a playhouse; serving as a secret conventicle in November, 1682; later used as a brewery. For exterior view in final stage, see Wilkinson's *Londina Illustrata*.

SALISBURY COURT.

Roofed theatre; situated in Salisbury Court, Fleet Street; built 1629; dismantled 1649; last used 1661; destroyed by Great Fire, 1666; authentic views, none.

VERE STREET.

Oblong roofed theatre; situated in Vere Street, Clare Market; built in a tennis-court; last constructed house of the Elizabethan order; opened by Killigrew and the King's Company, November, 1660; closed April, 1663; for view of ruins of, see C. W. Heckethorn, *Lincoln's Inn and the Localities Adjacent*, p. 138.

THE SITUATION OF THE LORDS' ROOM

The Situation of the Lords' Room

Writing in his *Guls Hornbooke* (1609) on "How a Gallant should behave himself in a Playhouse," Dekker addresses his pretended fledgeling in a vein of masterly irony and contrives to pillory some of the foibles of the time. "Sithence then" he says, "the place is so free in entertainment, allowing a stoole as well to the Farmers sonne as to your Templer : that your Stinkard has the selfe-same libertie to be there in his Tobacco-Fumes, which your sweet Courtier hath : and that your Car-man and Tinker claime as strong a voice in their suffrage, and sit to give judgment on the plaies life and death, as well as the prowdest *Momus* among the tribe of *Critick* : it is fit that hee, whom the most tailors bils do make roome for, when he comes, should not be basely (like a vyoll) casd up in a corner.

"Whether therefore the gatherers of the publique or private Playhouse stand to receive the afternoones rent, let our Gallant (having paid it) presently advance himselfe up to the Throne[1] of the Stage. I meane not into the Lords roome (which is now but the Stages Suburbs) : No, those boxes, by the iniquity of custome, conspiracy of waiting women and Gentlemen-Ushers, that there sweat together, and the covetousnes of Sharers, are contemptibly thrust into the reare, and much new Satten is there dambd, by being smothred to death in darknesse. But on the very Rushes where the Comedy is to daunce, yea, and under

[1] Prof. Schelling, who is much too apt to take Dekker's figurative phrasing literally, stumbles badly over this passage. See *Elizabethan Drama* i. 175. He thinks the reference was to the actual property throne which he deems accordingly almost a permanent feature of the stage. Dekker's meaning is made apparent by the Second Child's instruction to the green playgoer in the Induction to *Cynthia's Revels* : "O lord sir ! will you betray your ignorance so much? Why throne yourself in state, as other gentlemen use, sir?" Or, in other words, hire a stool and take a conspicuous position on the stage.

the state of *Cambises* himselfe must our fethered Estridge, like a piece of Ordnance, be planted valiantly (because impudently) beating downe the mewes and hisses of the opposed rascality."

Than this, no old passage dealing with the Elizabethan-Stuart stage has been more sadly misinterpreted. It is only within the last decennium that a scientific examination of early physical conditions has been entered upon, and no investigator has as yet attained sufficient knowledge to tear out the heart of Dekker's fascinating mystery. Towards that consummation the following excursus may ultimately prove helpful.

Our first business is to note that Dekker's reflections are not limited in their application. They deal, on his own showing, with both the public and the private theatre, and one cannot but assume that all the customs referred to in the chapter were common to both.[1]

The gull is instructed to seat himself on the stage at the psychological moment, or, in other words, when "the quaking prologue" is about to enter. He has come in by the tiring-house door, having duly paid the preliminary price of admission; more remains to be disbursed for a stool. The same doorway leads to the Lords' room, a resort to be avoided, as it has lost its high repute. He is not told why Rank and Fashion had abandoned these boxes to waiting women and gentlemen-ushers. It may be that they wearied of trying to execute the impossible feat of seeing the action that occasionally took place on the inner stage beneath them, and, in sheer desperation, increased the numbers of that growing body who sat on the stage itself. This would have necessitated some enlargement of the scaffold, more in breadth, probably, than in depth, but still with some deepening. The actual position of the tiring-house would not be—could not be—altered; and yet, if we assume that acting went on well to the front of

---

[1] Prof. Wallace disputes this (op. cit. chap. xi. *passim*), but his contentions have been effectively disposed of by Mr. C. R. Baskervill in his paper on "The Custom of Sitting on the Elizabethan Stage" in *Modern Philology* (Chicago), viii. No. 4, April, 1911.

the stage, the boxes at the back would be so much the more remote from the main action. Dark and ill-placed, they should no longer have been let to spectators, but the cupidity of the players induced them to turn the deserted rooms into a licentious rendezvous for the lower middle classes.

By those not profoundly versed in Dekker's pamphleteering style, it might possibly be argued that the description of the Lords' room as "now but the Stages Suburbs" implies that the position of the boxes for the nobility had recently been altered. That this was not so, seems demonstrated by the fact that no topical allusion to the Lords' room can be traced later than *The Guls Hornbooke*. What one really requires to grasp is that Dekker uses the word "suburbs" in a sinister metaphorical sense, hard to arrive at now but readily comprehended by his contemporaries. In *Lanthorn and Candle-Light* (1608), he had already devoted a whole chapter to a gruesome description of the iniquities of London's suburbs. "Would the Divell hire a villaine to spil bloud?" asks he. "There he shall finde him. One to blaspheme; there he hath choice. A Pandar that would court a matron at her praiers? hes there. A cheator that would turne his owne father a begging; He's there too: A harlot that would murder her new-borne Infant? Shee lies in there." That Dekker meant to imply by "suburbs of the stage" a disreputable and undesirable locality is shown by a quaint passage in the first chapter of *The Guls Hornbooke*, wherein we learn of "Potato-pies, and Custards" that "stood like the sinful suburbs of Cookery, and had not a wall (so much as a handfull hie) built rownd about them."[1]

As much of this interpretation appears a mere begging of the question, I hasten to advance some proof that the boxes for the nobility were originally situated aloft in the

---

[1] Cf. Nashe's *Christs Teares over Iervsalem* (1593), "*London*, what are thy Suburbs but licensed Stewes? Can it be so many brothel-houses of salary sensuality and sixe-penny whoredome (the next doore to the Magistrates) should be set up and maintained," etc., etc. See also Dekker's *Jests to Make You Merrie*, No. 59.

tiring-house, and that before 1609 the position had been abandoned.

Of the four known views of interiors of early non-scenic theatres, three show incontestably that spectators sat in elevated boxes at the back of the stage.[1] The existence of this custom at the public houses is indicated in the well-known sketch of the Swan, and at the private by the erroneously ascribed frontispiece to Kirkman's *Drolls*, which, popular acceptance to the contrary notwithstanding, does not represent the Red Bull.[2] Professor Baker, as behoves a thick-and-thin supporter of Dr. Cecil Brodmeier's individual exposition of the alternation theory, scouts the possibility of spectators sitting at the back of the stage, and opines that De Witt's sketch is largely responsible for the persistence of the idea. He tries to explain away the evidence it presents, forgetful of the fact that corroboration of its details in this respect is ample.[3] "It is by no means clear," he writes, "that the persons seen in this gallery in the print are not actors watching the scene on the front stage, so that any argument from it starts from an exceedingly weak premise. Secondly, the great majority of the Elizabethan plays call for use of the upper stage. How convenient and how probable, to turn the occupiers of the upper stage seats out when the exigencies of the play demanded! Above all, why should rational theatre-goers wish to gaze on the backs of the actors and to sit in the one part of the house where hearing would be most difficult." The prime mistake here is in supposing that the whole of the second floor in the tiring-house was given over to the upper stage. A sufficiency of pictorial and textual evidence exists to show that only a central portion of the floor was so allotted ; the

---

[1] Unfortunately the tiny view on the title-page of *Messalina* has been lopped of its fair proportions through the exigencies of engraving.

[2] The print, with its details of artificial lighting, plainly indicates a private theatre, and the Red Bull was never otherwise than a public one. The ascription was unknown to Malone and is utterly unwarranted. It dates apparently from 1809, when the plate was reproduced separately in London with a long inscription associating it with the Red Bull.

[3] See his *Development of Shakespeare as a Dramatist*, p. 75.

remainder was divided up into boxes for the musicians and for spectators. Even if some of the boxes were occasionally pressed into the service of the scene to represent windows,—a not improbable supposition—I see no reason why the spectators should not have been disturbed. Those who went there took all risks. Spectators of a similar order had to undergo a like discomfiture at a much later period. In the London theatres of the eighteenth century there were stage boxes over the two proscenium doors, and in these spectators frequently sat. It is to this arrangement Tate Wilkinson refers when he says in his *Memoirs* "whenever a Don Choleric in The Fop's Fortune, or Sir Amorous Vainwit in A Woman's a Riddle, or Charles in The Busy Body, tried to find out secrets, or plot an escape from a balcony, they always bowed and thrust themselves into the boxes over the stage, amidst the company, who were greatly disturbed, and obliged to give up their seats." Prof. Baker's query as to why rational people should desire to occupy such a generally undesirable position as that of the back boxes can be satisfactorily answered. The nobility went there in the beginning because they could enter by the tiring-house door, and be completely isolated from the mob. When the inconvenience of the locality from the mere playgoer's point of view became unbearable, the Lords' room was abandoned to the desecrations of those who made of it a mart for illicit love and bought kisses.

The earliest known reference to the Lords' room occurs in Henslowe's *Diary*, in a list of payments made for the building or repairing of the Rose circa 1592 :

> pd. for sellynge of the Rome ouer the tyerhowsse. . . . x s.
> pd. for sellinges my lords Rome. . . . xiiij s. [1]

It may be that the association of the two entries does not warrant us in assuming the propinquity of the two rooms ; but if we take it that the room over the tiring-house is represented by the garret in the Swan sketch out

---

[1] Ed. Greg (1904), p. 10. Collier makes sad hash of these details. Cf. *Hist. Eng. Dram. Poetry* (1831), iii. 317.

61196

of which the trumpeter is emerging, the Lords' room at the Rose might well have been on the lower story. That it was sub-divided is apparently indicated by Henslowe's use of the word "sellinges," and the relative payments show that it occupied a somewhat larger area than the top room.

Two important textual allusions bring into sharper perspective the evidence presented in the three interior views, and go far towards clinching my main argument. *Every Man Out of his Humour* was acted at the Globe in 1599. In Act ii. sc. i., Carlo Buffone comments upon Fastidious Brisk's boasting of his intimacy with certain courtiers thus: "There's ne'er a one of these but might lie a week on the rack, ere they could bring forth his name; and yet he pours them out as familiarly as if he had seen them stand by the fire in the presence, or ta'en tobacco with them over the stage, in the lords' room."[1] This is definite enough. "Over the stage" can only be interpreted to mean above in the tiring-house. None of the rooms in the auditorium proper could be said to be over the stage. In the Swan sketch, as well as in the so-called Red Bull frontispiece, a clear space (for the use of spectators in the yard or pit) is shown between the sides of the platform and the lowermost gallery. At the Fortune theatre, as one can readily deduce from the building contract,[2] this space formed a gap of some six feet on each side. On the *Messalina* and *Roxana* engraved title-pages (wherein the type of theatre represented cannot be satisfactorily determined) we have indications in the narrowing stage of a similar arrangement. From these facts may be safely predicated the existence of a definite rule for the public theatres. The chances are, however, that in the private houses, with their comfortably seated pits, a different system obtained. On

---

[1] Compare Webster's induction to *The Malcontent* (Globe, 1604):

    John Lowin: Good sir, will you leave the stage? I'll help you to a private room.

    Sly: Come Cuz, lets take some tobacco . . .

[2] Given in extenso, from Malone's *Shakespeare*, in Halliwell-Phillipps' *Outlines*, 3rd ed., pp. 524 ff.

Prof. Wallace's showing the stage in Burbage's Blackfriars extended right across the entire width of the hall.[1] Even conceding this, it is doubtful if the Lords' rooms during the first lustrum of this house's history were situated otherwhere than in the tiring-house. One longs to speak decisively on this point so that one might the more readily visualize that amiable habitude of Ben Jonson's at the Friars, caustically alluded to in *Satiromastix, or the Untrussing of the Humorous Poet* (1602), in that curious passage beginning, "Besides you must forswear to venture on the stage when your play is ended, and to exchange courtesies and compliments with the gallants in the Lords' rooms, to make all the house rise up in arms and to cry 'that's Horace, that's he! that's he!'" &c.

Before the period of its degradation the Lords' room was more remarkable for the conspicuousness and distinction bestowed upon its occupants than for its play-seeing conveniency. That a certain type of ruffler haunted the place is seen in an undated epigram on "Spongus the gallant" preserved in *The Dr. Farmer Chetham MS. Commonplace Book*[2]:

> He playes at Primero[3] over the stage,
> fighte for the wall, and keepes a lac'te Cloke page;
> Ryde through the streetes in glisteringe braverie
> and swallowes not the least indignitie.

To occupy a seat in the Lords' room was accordingly to place oneself where all eyes would naturally be attracted. The action had no other background than the tiring-house. That was the sense in which such a seat was "the best and most conspicuous place" according to the allusion of Sir John Davies in his *Epigrams*[4]:

> Rufus the Courtier, at the theatre,
> Leauing the best and most conspicuous place,

---

[1] op. cit. pp. 215, et. seq.

[2] Ed. Grosart (1873), pt. i. p. 104.

[3] A fashionable game at cards. "I left him at primero with the Duke of Suffolk." *King Henry VIII*, i. 2.

[4] Published at Middelburgh circa 1598.

Doth either to the stage himselfe transfer,
Or through a grate[1] doth show his doubtful face.

For that the clamorous frie of Innes of court,
Filles up the priuate roomes of greater prise;
And such a place where all may haue resort,
He in his singularitie doth despise.

Yet doth not his particular humour shunne
The common stews and brothels of the towne,
Though all the world in troupes do thither runne,
Clean and vnclean, the gentle and the clowne:

Then why should Rufus in his pride abhorre
A common seate, that loues a common whore.

As for the waiting-women and gentlemen-ushers who resorted to the Lords' room after it had fallen from its high estate, and who, according to Dekker, sweltered there in ignoble obscurity, some allusion to this well-marked and undiscriminating type of playgoer is evidently intended in Ben Jonson's lines to Fletcher on *The Faithful Shepherdess:*

The wise and many-headed bench that sits
Upon the life and death of plays and wits,
Compos'd of gamester, captain, knight, knight's man,
Lady or pusil, that wears maske or fan,
Velvet or taffata cap, rank'd in the dark
With the shops foreman, or some suche brave sparke,
(That may judge for his sixpence) had before
They saw it half, damn'd thy whole play.

One wonders whether it would be safe from this to draw the inference that the Lords' rooms, at the period of their decline and fall, were known as "sixpenny rooms". In the induction to *The Magnetick Lady* (1632), Jonson makes allusion to "the faeces or grounds of your people, that sit in the oblique caves and wedges of your house, your sixpenny mechanicks." In *The Actors' Remonstrance*, a satirical

---

[1] Grated stage boxes were sometimes pressed into the service of the scene. Cf. *The Two Noble Kinsmen*, ii. 1, the Daughter's penultimate speech. Also 1 *King Henry VI*, i. 4, where Salisbury on the upper stage talks of looking "through the Grate." In *The Picture*, iv. 2, Ubaldo, in his shirt, peeps out of a grated window in the upper part of the tiring-house.

tract published in 1643 after the silencing of the theatres, promise is made on behalf of the players that in future they will cease to admit into their "sixpenny rooms those unwholesome enticing harlots that sit there merely to be taken up by apprentices or lawyers' clerks." If it was to the harpy and her prey that the old Lords' room was given over, one can readily divine why they were content to sit there in semi-darkness, seeing little of the action, unseen of the audience.

The question naturally suggests itself, to what part of the house did the gallants resort after they had forsaken the Lords' room ? Many doubtless sat upon the stage, but this position, from its aptness to evoke "the mewes and hisses of the opposed rascality," could not have been grateful to all. Dekker in the *Proæmium* of his *Guls Hornbooke* reveals to us the position sometimes occupied by the gallant who had matriculated in "the new-found Colledge of Criticks." Addressing shallow censurers of this kidney, he writes, "I conjure you (as you come of the right *goose-caps*) staine not your hose ; but when at a new play you take up the twelve-penny rome next the stage ; (because the Lords and you may seeme to be haile fellow wel-met) there draw forth this booke, read alowd, laugh alowd, and play the *Antickes*, that all the garlike mouthd stinkards[1] may cry out, *Away with the fool.*"

As the witling could not give the impression of being hail fellow well met with the nobility without sitting in their midst, it follows that the twelvepenny room must have been the part of the house generally resorted to by the higher orders after they had forsaken the Lords' room.

Apart from the distinction of tariff between the public and the private theatres, there was apparently no uniform charge for admission to any particular part in all the houses

---

[1] A phrase commonly applied to the groundlings. One can here cite Dekker in elucidation of himself. Scoffing at the vanity of the players in his section on Winter in *Raven's Almanack*, he writes : "Ye shall be glad to play three hours for two-pence to the basest stinkards in London, whose breath is stronger than garlick, and able to poison all the twelvepenny rooms."

of any one category at any specific period.[1] But generally speaking, a shilling (or, in other words, about six or seven shillings of the present currency) was the highest charge demanded. In this connexion Collier quotes from Sir T. Overbury's *Characters* (1614), "If he have but twelvepence in his purse he will give it for the best room in the play-house." This he takes to be decisive. If then this twelve-penny room "next the stage" was the most expensive part of the house, there is every reason to believe—not only from Dekker's allusion but from other circumstances—that it was situated in the lowermost gallery. In the English theatre the rule has invariably held good (beginning with the first tier of boxes, not with the basement), the higher you go, the less you pay.

It must be said with emphasis that this twelvepenny room was no new device fashioned as a substitute for the old Lords' room. Identity of position shows that the twelvepenny room was only another name for the gentle-men's boxes, which were undoubtedly co-existent with the tiring-house room during the period it was frequented by the nobility. From the outset of its career the Globe had these gentlemen's rooms, for the Fortune was built after the manner of the Globe, and in the Fortune contract we read of "fower convenient divisions for gentlemen's roomes" in one of the galleries, the particular locality, however, remaining unspecified. But the information lacking can be obtained by a careful study of the Hope contract of 1613. In even greater degree than the Fortune was based on the Globe was the Hope constructed on the lines of the Swan. One finds it stipulated in the Hope contract that Gilbert Katherens should "also make two boxes in the lower most storie fitt and decent for gentlemen to sitt in; and shall also make the partitions betweene the roomes as they are at the saide playhouse called the Swan."

---

[1] Cf. Collier, *Hist. Eng. Dram. Poetry* (1831), iii. 341. The inflated prices at the Hope in 1614, enumerated in the induction to *Bartholomew Fair*, are accounted for by the fact that the Globe had just been burnt down. This meant less opposition and more demand for places.

We turn now to the valuable sketch of the interior of the Swan, and we find that van Buchell, acting on the instructions of his friend Johannes de Witt, has inscribed across the very portion of the lowermost story indicated by Dekker ("the twelvepenny room next the stage") the word *orchestra*.[1] This is conclusive. Neither in its original nor its latterday sense was the term here applied, but in a sense peculiar to the sixteenth and seventeenth centuries. Cotgrave in his *Dictionary*, published in 1611, defines *orchestre* as "the senators' or noblemen's places in a theatre, between the stage and the common seats." In Serlio's design for a stage and auditorium,[2] a genuine orchestra, in the classic sense, intervenes between the two, and the seats nearest the bare space are indicated as those occupied by the noblest spectators. As this was the normal arrangement on the continent throughout the sixteenth century, and as the orchestra itself was no longer made use of, the term came to be applied by natural transition to the seats occupied by the highest classes. Instances of the use of the word *orchestra* in this sense could be multiplied. Perhaps the most striking example is to be found in the *Orbis Sensualium Pictus* of Jan Amos Komensky, particularly in that edition of the book published in London in 1659, with the High Dutch portions translated into English by Charles Hoole. The Latin description of Plate Number cxxxii, entitled *Ludus Scenicus*, runs as follows. — "In Theatro (quod vestitur Tapetibus, et tegitur Sipariis) Comoediae vel Tragaediae aguntur, quibus repraesentantur memorabiles; ut hic, Historia de Filio prodigo, et Patre, ipsius, a quo recipitur, domum redux. Actores (Histriones) agunt personati; Morio dat Jocos. Spectatorum primarii, sedent in Orchestra, plebs stat in Cavea, et plaudit, si quid arridet." Hoole's translation of this reads, "In a Play-house (which is trimmed with hangings, and covered with

---

[1] Several writers have viewed the phrase with a purely modern intelligence and given it a false interpretation. Cf. Dr. Richard Wegener, *Die bühnen einrichtungen des Shakespeareschen Theaters*, p. 151; also Karl Blind's review of Gaedertz in *The Academy*, No. 840, p. 391.

[2] Serlio, *Architettura* (Paris, 1545. Book II, dealing with Perspective.)

curtains) Comedies and Tragedies are acted, wherein memorable things are represented; as here, the History of the Prodigal Son, and his Father, by whom he is entertained, being returned home. The Players act being in disguise; the Fool maketh jests. The chief of the Spectators sit in the Gallery, the Common Sort stand on the Ground, and clap their hands, if anything please them." Hoole, in rendering the passage, strives as far as possible to make it applicable to the English theatre. There is a touch of insular realism in his "trimmed with hangings, and covered with curtains." But his translation is chiefly noteworthy for the fact that "spectatorum primarii sedent in Orchestra" is rendered by "the chief of the spectators sit in the Gallery." This was probably as near as he could get to the exact truth at a time when the London theatres had long been silenced by the Puritans.

If the foregoing conclusions win any degree of acceptance from scholars, it seems to me the result must be disastrous to the alternation theory. In the latest stages of its development, that theory (as expounded by Brodmeier) calls for a central enclosure formed of curtains hanging from the front and sides of "the Heavens." To those who have full knowledge of the physical conditions of the Elizabethan stage such an arrangement is inconceivable. In creating it to bolster up their cause, the alternationists failed to take into consideration the presence of spectators at the back. Are we asked in all seriousness to believe that from first to last the occupants of the tiring-house rooms would have been content with seeing barely a moiety of the action? Possibly at a pinch we might stretch our imaginations so far as to concede that the players had the audacity to ignore the claims of the philanderers who infested these boxes in 1608 and thereabouts. But what of the years that preceded? Would the Elizabethan nobles whose patronage of the Lords' room gave it its title have suffered such indignity?

Title and Locality Boards on the Pre-Restoration Stage

Title and Locality Boards on the Pre-Restoration Stage

Side by side with the strenuous efforts that are now being made to arrive at the prime physical characteristics of the Elizabethan stage it is desirable that some one should undertake the task of thoroughly investigating the origin and influence of certain stage conventions which were either born of those physical conditions or contributed to their establishment. Moreover, the time is ripe for rigid scientific discussion of one or two principles whose existence has long been suspected but never definitely established. Of this order is the *vexata quæstio* of inscribed scene-boards, a matter on which there has been much dogmatism and very little argument. Among scientific investigators Professor Reynolds stands alone in point of making serious attempt to pluck out the heart of the mystery.[1] My purpose now is to consider the question in its broadest aspect, throwing out a wide drag-net with the hope of bringing to the surface all the available data relative to the employment of inscribed boards and inscriptions generally on the early stage. The subject permits of easy division into two sections, the one dealing with title-boards and the other with scene-boards, and it will be most convenient to discuss the former first.

So far as the general employment and persistent usage of title-boards on the Tudor and early Stuart stage are concerned, all is plain sailing. The only difficulty is to determine whether the custom was of purely native origin or derived from foreign initiative. Later on, in connexion with the masque-titles I shall discuss the point more fully, but at present I must content myself with saying that a prolonged study of early European theatrical conditions

---

[1] See his *Some Principles of Elizabethan Staging* (Chicago 1905), i. pp. 20 et seq. (= *Modern Philology*, Vol. ii. 581–614), to which I beg to express my obligations.

has imbued me with the impression that the prototype of the English title-board must be sought for in Italy, that great fount of scenic inspiration. If this theory be sound, the principle must have been introduced into the court entertainments of Henry VIII. by one or other of the Italian painters, or artificers, that we know to have been employed there.[1] The traffic of the players with the court would lead to the transference of so grateful an expedient to the popular stage.

Whether of native or foreign origin, the convention of the title-board can be traced back in private performances to 1528. Writing early in that year of a representation of *Phormio*, given by the Children of Paul's before Cardinal Wolsey, the Venetian ambassador says "the hall in which they dined, where the comedy was performed, had a large garland of box in front, in the centre of which was inscribed in gilt letters *Terentii Phormio*."[2]

Assuming for argument's sake the correctness of my theory, it is vital to approximate the period when the title-board first began to be utilised on the popular stage. We shall see later that it was not an uncommon practice for the Prologue in the closing years of Elizabeth's reign to make allusion to, or imply the presence of, the title-board; and in view of this habit it will not be unprofitable to seek in the prologues and inductions to the moralities and inter-ludes of some thirty or forty years earlier for similar allusions and implications. In *Ralph Roister Doister*, c.1551, the only reference to the title occurs in the last stanza of the Prologue:

> Our Comedy or Interlude, which we intend to play
> Is named Royster Doyster, indeed,
> Which against the vainglorious doth inveigh,
> Whose humour the roysting sort continually doth feed.

---

[1] Cf. Collier, *Annals* (1831), i. 100. Italian influence is clearly apparent on the scenic adornment of the court entertainments of Henry VIII. The trees and foliage fashioned out of silk in the great spectacle of November 10, 1528, chronicled by Hall (Collier, i. 111–2), followed the device of Girolamo Genga of Urbino. See Walker, *Historical and Critical Essay on the Revival of the Drama in Italy*, 1805, p. 202.

[2] *Venetian State Papers*, January 8, 1528, as cited by Reynolds.

Here the word "indeed" seems to suggest a simultaneous pointing to the title-board by the speaker; the only alternative is that the word was weakly demanded by the exigencies of the rhyme.[1] In Edwards's court play of *Damon and Pythias* (1564) the introductory address not only particularises the title of the piece but the scene of action, a circumstance that might be taken to imply the absence of boards of all kinds, were it not fairly well assured that title-boards (at least) were in use at court at this period. But if we restrict our examination to the moralities and interludes of the popular stage in the pre-theatrical era—or in other words before the establishment of the regular playhouses—it will be found that, generally speaking, the prologues avoid all reference to title or locality. This omission points at least to the employment of title-boards. Coming down to a slightly later period, one finds in the prologue to *The Conflict of Conscience* (c. 1581) an allusion which seems to point to the presence on the stage, or sudden exposure by the speaker, of a title-board:

> And for because we see by proofe that men do soone forget
> Those thinges for which to call them by no name at all they
>   knowe,
> Our author, for to helpe short wittes, did thinke it very meete
> Some name for this his Comedy in preface for to showe.

Clear evidence is afforded us in the Revels Accounts of the employment of title-boards at court in the meridian of Elizabeth's reign. In the Account Book for 1579-80 a payment is recorded "for the Garnyshinge of xiiij titles" in gold and silver.[2] During that period eight plays were performed at court and a ninth prepared. It is difficult to divine the possible utility of the other five titles, unless, as seems probable, they served for scene-indications. No such problem presents itself in connexion with the item of fifteen shillings noted in the Accounts for 1580-81, as

---

[1] Cf. the prol. to the Enterlude of *Respublica* (1533):
   "But nowe of thargumente to towch a worde or twayne :
   The Name of our playe ys Respublica, certaine."
The title is mentioned here that it may be fully expounded.
[2] Cunningham, *Revels Accounts* (1842), p. 162. (*Revels*, ed. Feuillerat 1908, p. 328.)

paid to William Lyzard for the "painting of ix. titles with
cop*artment*es."[1] These were apparently for actual titles
only. Reckoning the two challenges at Tilt, there were
exactly nine entertainments at court in the period comprised
by the Account Book.

So little analogy exists between the elaborate and gradually expanding scheme of mounting in the Stuart masques
and the vague and indeterminate background of the contemporary drama as presented in the ordinary playhouse, one
takes leave to think that the persistence of the inscribed
title on the proscenia of Ben Jonson's graceful fantasies
was rather the perpetuation of an old court convention
than a practice suggested by the customs of the theatre.
Although he was not without creative faculty as a scenic
artificer, Inigo Jones mainly derived his inspiration from
direct observation in Italy, and it was in tracing back some
of his fundamental principles to their source I arrived at
the conclusion that the convention of the inscribed title
originally came from that country.[2]

If we look for a moment at the rise and progress of the
ephemeral emblematic proscenium—those frontispieces, as
they were called in England, which were constructed for
a special court, or academic performance—we shall see that
the conditions which obtained in Italy in the latter half of
the sixteenth century were almost exactly paralleled in the
later Stuart Masques. Thus when the comedy of *L'Hortensio*
was presented by the Accademia degl' Intronati at Siena
in 1560 before Cosmo I., the arms of the ducal guest were
placed in the centre of the proscenium arch, and at a distance
below the insignia of the quaintly named academy. Between
the two came the inscription, "Generoso Intronato. | Thus-
corum Principi. | Intronatorum Hilaritas." Below on
niches on either side were statues of Poetry and Comedy,
each with its respective motto of "miscet utile dulci" and
"vitae speculum."[3] The period was one of fertile scenic

---

[1] op. cit. p. 169. (Feuillerat, p. 338.)

[2] It was followed in France, c. 1637. Cf. Lacroix, *Le 17ᵉ Siècle, Lettres, Sciences
et Arts*, pp. 219 and 279–80, woodcuts.

[3] Walker, *Historical and Critical Essay on the Revival of the Drama in Italy*, p. 239 note.

resource and spirited experimentation, when state rivalled state in matters of artistry, and central authority was wholly lacking. For aught we know to the contrary, it may be that at an earlier period other academies or some of the great courts had placed the title of the play at the head of the proscenium instead of these purposeless inscriptions.[1] Relatively to the number of known productions the details that have come down to us of the characteristics of specific proscenia are proportionately few. But so far as extant evidence permits one to judge, a single broad decorative scheme obtained throughout Italy; the system pursued at Siena in 1560 held good for the frontispiece of *Ermiona* at Padua in 1632.

How closely the ornate proscenia of the Stuart masques approximated to the earlier Italian method can be seen by examining the details in the *Tethys' Festival* of Samuel Daniel (1610):

First, on eyther side stood a great statue of twelve foot high, representing *Neptune* and *Nereus*, Neptune holding a Trident, with an Anchor made to it, and this Mot, *His artibus*: that is *Regendo et retinendo*, alluding to this verse of Virgill, *He tibi erunt artis*, &c. *Nereus* holding out a golden fish on a net, with this word *Industria*: the reason whereof is deliuered after, in the speech uttered by *Triton*. These Sea-Gods stood on pedestals, and were al of gold. Behinde them were two pillasters, on which hung compartments, with other deuises; and these bore up a rich Freeze, wherein were figures of tenne foot long, of flouds and Nymphes, with a number of naked children, dallying with a draperie, which they seemed to hold up, that the Scene might be seene, and the ends thereof fell downe in foldes by the pillasters. In the midst was a

---

[1] Some meagre evidence can be adduced to show the existence of a later convention of the sort among the Italians. In *Le Théâtre Italien de Gherardi*, a collection of plays presented by the Italian comedians in Paris towards the close of the seventeenth century, one finds a series of highly realistic engravings of scenes in which the play-title is frequently shown on an escutcheon in the centre of the festooned top drapery. (For some characteristic reproductions see N. M. Bernardin, *La Comédie Italienne en France*, 1902, pp. 27, 32 and 35.) It might be claimed, of course, that this was a fanciful device of the engraver simply to afford a ready means of identifying the plates, as they are not otherwise inscribed. But the intense realism and glaring theatricality of the views rebut this. Although the frontispiece to *Arlequin Protée* depicts a seascape, it is to be remarked that besides the inscribed title and top drapery, the design actually shows the four stage chandeliers. A photograph of the scene could not have been more literal.

compartment with this inscription, *Tethyos Epinicia*, Tethys feasts of triumph. This was supported with two winged boyes, and all the work was done with that force and boldnesse on the gold and silver, as the figures seemed round and not painted.

Here the only divergence from the Italian method, as known to us, was in the use of an inscribed title. Occasionally one comes across stricter parallels, as in the case of *Lovers Made Men* (otherwise known as *The Masque of Lethe*) in 1617, and in Shirley's masque of *The Triumph of Peace* in 1634. Neither of these had an exposed title, an omission contrary to the usual practice in the generality of court masques and pastorals for which Inigo Jones provided the mounting. Among productions of the sort whose books clearly indicate the use of proscenium titles are *Florimene* (1629), *Chloridia* (1631), *Tempe Restor'd* (1631), *The Temple of Love* (1635), *Corona Minervæ* (1636), *Luminalia* (1637) and *Salmacida Spolia* (1640).[1]

Apart from the regular usage of the ordinary theatres, a point on which I shall have something to say presently, there were other performances of a special or private order where the convention of the title-board was maintained. One of the earliest instances where a special proscenium was constructed in an English playhouse for a particular production was that of *Microcosmus* at Salisbury Court in 1637. We find from the book of Nabbes' masque that the frontispiece was "of a workmanship proper to the fancy of the rest, adorn'd with brasse figures of Angles and Divels, with Several inscriptions, the Title in a Escocheon supported by an Angell and a Divell." Again, in *Candia Restaurata*, a spectacle presented at Apethorpe before the Earl and Countess of Westmoreland on February 12, 1640-1, one of the features of the frontispiece was "a scroule" on which was "written in greate CANDY RESTORED."[2]

It is noteworthy that in experimenting with his primitive English operas in the ticklish times of the Common-

---

[1] In Shirley's comedy *The Bird in a Cage*, in the scene of the intercalated masque of *Jupiter and Danae*, Donella says, "Now whet your inventions and about it, imagine our scene exprest, and the new Prison, the title advanc'd in forme."

[2] British Museum, Add. MS. 34,221.

INIGO JONES'S DESIGN FOR THE PROSCENIUM FRONT AND MAIN SCENE OF THE PASTORAL OF *FLORIMENE*.

[*To face p.* 48.

wealth, D'Avenant arrived at the neat expedient of making the one central inscription answer at once for the conveyance of both title and locality. In *The Siege of Rhodes* at Rutland House in 1656, and again at the Cockpit playhouse in Drury Lane in 1659, the single word "Rhodes" was shown on a tablet over the proscenium. So too in *The Cruelty of the Spaniards in Peru* at the Cockpit in 1658, the inscription employed was merely "Peru." D'Avenant's statement concerning the special frontispiece provided for this shows that his aim was to carry forward the masque-convention, it being "designed by way of preparation to give some notice of that argument which is pursu'd in the scene."

Possibly it might have been better to discuss some of the foregoing details in strict chronological relationship with the data concerning the observance of the title-convention in the ordinary playhouses. In striving, however, to indicate the possible origin of that convention I have deemed it politic to keep the records of the court and of the playhouse apart. Moreover, to mingle details of the proscenium-title of the private, or special, performances with a consideration of the title-convention as pursued in the regular theatres (where no proscenia were ordinarily employed, and none at all known before c. 1637) would have been to confuse the issue.

One has no evidence to show whether or not the players had adopted the principle of the title-board in the inn-yard stage of their history, but the chances are—so requisite and complementary was the expedient—that the usage was common before the building of The Theater and the Curtain. At a period when programmes were not provided[1], it was vital that the casual playgoer should have some ready means of discovering the name of the play about to be presented. Bills containing little more than

---

[1] Malone's statement that programmes or playbills with casts of characters were not made use of in England until the beginning of the eighteenth century has been challenged, but not disproved. The specious Drury Lane bill of 1663 reproduced by Collier (*Annals*, iii. 384) has been proved a forgery. See *The Connoisseur*, Vol. xviii. 1907, No. lxii. pp. 222-3, art. on "Old Playbills."

this information were certainly posted about the city, but many came to the Bankside houses, attracted by the raising of the flag, or blowing of the preliminary trumpet-blasts, who had not cast eyes on these announcements. Moreover, the daybill offered no particular guarantee of the performance specified, and the non-provision of programmes facilitated a change of piece at the eleventh hour, frequently at the caprice of the assembled groundlings.[1] Consequently a title-board was necessary to acquaint the early-comer with what he was going to see. He was not asked to buy a pig in a poke; if he knew the play already and disliked it he could have his money back. This usage was common to all theatres alike, the principle of the title-board being as well recognised in private houses of the Blackfriars order as in the more popular houses on the Bankside.

Early employment of the title-board in the theatres of Shoreditch is, I think, indicated by the allusion in *The Spanish Tragedy* (c. 1587), where Hieronimo, when about to present the bye-play of *Solyman and Perseda*, says "Hang out the title; our scene is Rhodes." Later evidence for the theatrical, as contrasted with the court, usage is of a more direct and better defined order. In the later Elizabethan period one infers that the title-board was *in situ* from the very opening of the doors. Otherwise many of the allusions in the contemporary prologues are incomprehensible. The tone of most of these proems connotes early exposure of the board. Thus in *The History of Sir John Oldcastle* (1600), the Prologue says, "the doubtful title, Gentlemen, prefixt upon the argument, we have in hand may breed suspense," etc., etc.; and in the induction to *Cynthia's Revels* (1600, at the Blackfriars), the Third Child says, " first the title of this play is Cynthia's Revels, as any man that hath hope to be saved by his book can witness." In *The Poetaster* (1601), Envy as Prologue

---

[1] Cf. Gayton, *Festivous Notes on Don Quixote* (1654), as cited by R. J. Broadbent in *Stage Whispers*, p. 82. We learn here of the arbitrary and ferocious conduct of Bankside audiences at Shrovetide and other holiday periods, when the players were often compelled, "notwithstanding their bills to the contrary, to act what the major part of the company had a mind to." When they proved refractory the house was pulled down over their heads. The whole passage is very remarkable.

reads the board, but affects to see only the sub-title of *The Arraignment*. In *Wily Beguiled* (1605) an ingenious surprise is sprung upon the spectator at the outset. The Prologue and the Player enter simultaneously, and the former asks the latter "How now my honest Roague, what Play shall we have here to-night?"[1] He gets as reply, "Sir, you may look upon the Title." He glances at the board, and, more in the role of spectator than of Prologue, says, with some petulance, "What *Spectrum* once again?" Then a Juggler arrives upon the scene to stop all argument. "Marry, sir," he says, "I will show you a trick of cleanly conveyance . . . Come aloft,[2] Jack, for thy master's advantage. He's gone, I warrant ye." And then, according to the direction, "*Spectrum* is conveyed away, and *Wily Beguiled* stands in the place of it."

A difficulty arises in connexion with this curious induction which recalls a similar situation at the beginning of *The Knight of the Burning Pestle*, as performed at the Whitefriars in 1611. The Citizen says to the Prologue, "and now you call your play *The London Merchant*. Down with your title, boy! down with your title!" The difficulty in both cases is to determine what play was announced on the bills, assuming that playgoers placed serious credence in these placards. In this matter one finds oneself impaled on the horns of a dilemma. On the one hand, to have announced *Wily Beguiled* or *The Knight of the Burning Pestle* on the bills would have been to defeat the purpose of the playwright, and on the other, to baulk an audience really assembled to see *Spectrum* or *The London Merchant* might have created a riot. At best the trick was far from calculated to produce good humour, and it is noteworthy that *The Knight of the Burning Pestle* narrowly escaped damnation at the hands of its first audience. There is some reason to believe that at the period roughly

---

[1] Like Macbeth's "Amen" this "to-night" sticks in the throat. It seems to imply a court (or at least not an ordinary) performance. On the other hand, the reference to the auditorium in the epilogue (as cited in Collier's *Annals*, iii. 441) as "this circled round" shows the place of performance to have been a theatre.

[2] For "come aloft," see *Percy Society* publications, Vol. v. pp. 45 and 84 note.

indicated by the two plays, the titles of new pieces were not given on the bills in the announcements of first performances. There was always great resort to a virgin play, as betokened by the advance of prices, and it may be that it sufficed to announce the production of a new piece by a specific author without naming the title. That some omission of the sort took place on first performances seems apparent from the phrasing of the opening lines of the prologue to *The Devil is an Ass*. This would explain away the difficulty in connexion with the *premières* of *Wily Beguiled* and *The Knight of the Burning Pestle*, but we still remain mystified as to the subsequent occasions on which the two inductions would be performed. I dwell here upon the riddle, without pretending to solve it, because it seems to show that in the absence of programmes there was a tacitly understood laxity of arrangement whereby the performance could be changed at the eleventh hour. This indetermination would make the use of the title-board all the more imperative.

Possibly there was less liability to sudden changes of performance at the better class "private" theatres, where the players were not at the mercy of a rough and ready audience. As time went on, patrons of houses like the Blackfriars would place more and more dependence on the authenticity of the bills, and there would be less need for early exposure of the title-board. Indications occur in the later Stuart period showing that, so far from being hung up with the assembling of the audience, the board was not seen until borne in by the prologue-speaker. Collier has already drawn attention to the fact that, in a late revival of *The City Wit* of Brome, Sarpego, in alluding to the circumstance that the play had been written before Ben Jonson's death, says:

> Some in this round may have both seen 't and heard,
> Ere I, that bear its title, wore a beard.[1]

---

[1] *Annals*, iii. 376. Note the direction at the beginning of the masque in *Byron's Tragedie*, as at the Blackfriars c. 1607: "Mus. and a Song, above, and Cupid enters with a Table written, hung about his neck, after him two Torche-bearers." This table was probably a title-board.

When, with the opening of the first Dublin theatre in 1634, the title-board convention was carried to Ireland, the system pursued there was the personal bringing-in of the board by the speaker of the introductory address. This is indicated in the prologue [1] to James Shirley's new comedy of *Rosania; or Love's Victory* as delivered there c. 1638 :

> *Rosania ?* methinks I hear one say
> What's that ? 'Tis a strange title to a play.
> One asks his friend who late from travel came,
> What tis ? supposing it some country's name :
> Who rather than acknowledge ignorance,
> Perhaps says, 'tis some pretty town in France
> Or Italy, and wittily discloses,
> 'Twas called Rosania, for the store of roses.
> A witty comment :—others that have seen
> And fashionably observ'd the English scene,
> Say (but with less hope to be understood)
> Such titles unto plays are now the mood,
> *Aglaura, Claricilla,*—names that may
> (Being ladies) grace and bring guests to the play.
> To save this charge of wit, that you might know
> Something i' the title, which you need not owe
> To another's understanding, you may see,
> In honest English there, *Love's Victory.*

Here the speaker doubtless reversed the title-board, which he had been holding all the time, and showed the sub-title on the other side. There would have been no point in the lines if both title and sub-title were already exposed to view on a board hanging up against the tiring-house.

One other possible allusion to the bringing on of the board in this way occurs in the secondary prologue to *The Poor Man's Comfort*, as spoken at the Red Bull on May 28, 1661, and printed some years later in Thomas Jordan's undated book of verse, *A Nursery of Novelties in Variety of Poetry*.[2] In this case the speaker entered "reading the title" and began by saying :

> *The Poor Man's Comfort*, this title some will say
> Is fitter for a Pray'r book than a Play.

---

[1] Shirley's *Poems* (London, 1646), p. 148. The play is believed to be identical with *The Doubtful Heir*, as afterwards acted at the Blackfriars, and printed in quarto in 1652.

[2] p. 23.

The evidence here is doubtful as we have no clue to the position of the board, whether in the speaker's hand or already hanging on the façade of the tiring-house. But the allusion is otherwise of value, as it shows the continuance of the old title-board convention up to the very dawn of the Restoration picture stage. [1]

This marked persistence of one specific order of inscriptions points to the congruity of others, and, in the continued absence of programmes, makes out a *prima facie* case for the use of scene boards. It is difficult to see why the Elizabethan stage manager should not have resorted to these ready expedients for dissipating the recurring vagueness of the place of action, considering that both he and the dramatist were prone to rely upon inscriptions to get them out of much lesser difficulties. In Fulwell's *Like Will to Like* (c. 1568), as the text clearly shows, Lucifer came on at the beginning with his name "written on his back and in his breast." [2] No greater mistake could be made than to rate this a mere puerility peculiar to the primitive stage. Seventy years later the device is still to be found persisting. In *A Tricke to Cheat the Divell* (Act iv, as at the Cockpit in 1639), several dancers come on singly, each with his vocation or attributes inscribed on his breast thus, "I am a Scrivener," "I am a Prodigall," etc., etc. Inscribed bannerets were also utilised in processions, notably in *The Triumph of Love* and *The Triumph of Death* in Beaumont and Fletcher's *Four Plays in One*, a composite piece assigned by Fleay to the Revels boys in 1608. We see therefore there was no lack of insular precedent of a cognate order for the establishment of a scene-board convention. If we take a wider purview we shall find the actual prototype of the system in the French mysteries of the fifteenth century.[3]

---

[1] For other allusions to title-boards see the lists of properties in *The Cuck-Queanes and the Cuckolds Errants* and *The Faery Pastorall* of William Percy, (c. 1600 at Paul's); the prologues to *Believe as You List* and *Fancies Chaste and Noble* (1632 at Cockpit); and the Induction to *The Magnetic Lady* (Blackfriars, 1632).

[2] Cf. Feuillerat, *Revels Documents*, p. 20. The Greek "Woorthyes" in a Court Masque of c. 1560 had their names inscribed on their backs and breasts. In *Old Fortunatus* (1599), i. 3, Vice and Virtue bear Latin mottoes on their garments.

[3] Cf. Emile Morice, *Histoire de la Mise en Scène depuis les Mystères jusqu'à Cid* (1836), p. 82.

To the symbolical multiple scene of the early sacred drama was due the principle of the scene-boards. In no other way could the arbitrary bringing together of widely separated localities be rendered comprehensible. At the representation of *The Mystery of the Incarnation* given at Rouen in 1485, no fewer than twenty-two *mansions* symbolising various edifices and localities were ranged side by side along the back of a shallow stage some 66 metres long, each *mansion* with its distinguishing inscription.[1] A similar system obtained in *The Mystery of the Passion* as given at Valenciennes in 1547.[2] The usage in France is clearly demonstrated in a prologue to an old play cited by Jusserand,[3] wherein the spectators are acquainted concerning the various places of action—

> vous les povez cognoistre
> Par l'escritel que dessus voyez estre.

No greater service to the cause of English theatrical history has been done than Chambers' explosion of the time-honoured fallacy that the primitive English miracle play was of the processional order.[4] A vital link in the chain of dramaturgic evolution was lacking until he made clear the fact that originally the method of staging was that of the unified composite scene. Here at last the student of English mounting has a *terminus a quo*. Personally, however, I fail at the outset to find any positive evidence of the use of locality-boards (or inscriptions) in the primitive English miracle play, but feel thoroughly assured of their employment. The custom can surely be deduced from continental habitude; analogy, if legitimate at all, is permissible here. Moreover we have distinct traces of the locality-boards in the multiple setting of the early Eliza-

---

[1] Private information from Prof. Eugène Rigal of Montpellier, to whom I make my acknowledgments. The Mystery was published in 1886, with an introduction by M. Pierre de Verdier, but this I have not seen.

[2] Jusserand, *Shakespeare in France*, p. 65. The best reproductions of the miniatures in the old MS. are those of Victor Fournel, *Le Vieux Paris* (Tours, 1887, p. 21 et seq.), where the multiple scene is not only given as a whole, but also in sections, so as to demonstrate the employment of the *mansions*.

[3] *Furnivall Memorial*, p. 186.

[4] E. K. Chambers, *The Mediæval Stage*, ii. 134 and 421.

bethan secular drama, both at court and elsewhere; and it is difficult to conceive (viewing its early usage in France) that the principle was due simply to accretion.

As to the period when our nascent secular dramaturgy first began to base upon the tenets of the simultaneous scene, it may be roughly indicated by the first quarter of the sixteenth century. So early as 1535, when *The Satyre of the Three Estaitis* was performed at Cupar, the multiple setting had begun to be employed on the profane stage in Scotland. On this occasion, as on its revival at Edinburgh in 1540, Sir David Lyndsay's play was given in the open. One proof of the composite nature of the stationary scene is that the players when not in action sat in the various *mansions* or localities to which they belonged, never leaving the sight of the audience.[1]

With the transference of the multiple setting to the indoor court play came certain vital modifications of its principles. Questions of space demanded a reduction in the number of *mansions* employed and a more compact system of grouping. The maximum was now fixed at five, and the *mansions* were generally arranged in sets of three or five, according to the scenic exigencies. No longer ranged side by side along the back line of a parallelogram, they were placed symmetrically along the two sides of an equilateral triangle, the apex of which marked the position of the third or fifth *mansion*, placed parallel to the front of the stage and closing in the vista. This arrangement was a distinct advance as it admitted of the whole being constructed and painted in perspective, a device whereby a sort of pictorial homogeneity was given to the heterogeneous constituents.[2] In the "Articles and ordynaunces concernyng the office of the

---

[1] The same principle was followed in France at the same period, making the parallelism complete. Cf. Jul. Caes. Scaligeri *Poetices Libri Septem.* (1561), lib. i. chap. 21. Also the comment of Eugène Rigal, *Le Théâtre Français avant la Période classique*, p. 241. This parallelism is probably accounted for by the fact that Lyndsay derived his play from a French source. Cf. Sir Sidney Lee's *The French Renaissance in England*, p. 372 note 3.

[2] In France the transition from the mediæval mystery stage to the modern secular stage proceeded along the same lines. Cf. Rigal, op. cit. chap. vi. *passim*. It should be noted that the entries in the English *Revels Accounts* dealing with the provision of scenic appurtenances for specific court plays afford little clue to the actual staging. These items merely represented new material. Many *mansions* and other properties in stock were used again and again.

Revelles," quoted by Feuillerat from a document of the period of 1572, it is laid down that

> The cheife busynes of the office resteth speciallye in three poyntes. In makinge of garmentes In makinge of hedpeces and in payntinge.
>
> The connynge of the office resteth in skill of devise, in understandinge of historyes, in iudgement of comedies, tragedyes and shewes, in sight of perspective and architecture some smack of geometrye and other thinges.[1]

Among the changes brought about by the new system was the creation of the coulisses. Instead of remaining from first to last in full sight of the audience, the characters now came on and went off, according to the requirements. Some degree of scenic illusion had begun to exist.[2]

That the scenery at Elizabeth's court in the early part of her reign consisted of these *mansions*, or practicable constructions, and not of one surface paintings, is clearly indicated by the details in the Revels Accounts. In a royal warrant issued on June 11, 1568, for payment of £634 odd, to Sir Thomas Benger, for materials purchased and work done in connexion with seven plays and six masques, the plays in question are specified and their scenic appurtenances detailed :

> Imprimis, for seven playes ; the first namede, *as playne as canne be; the seconde, the paynfull pillgrimage; the thirde, Jacke and Jyll;* the forthe, *Six Fooles ;* the fivethe callede, *witte an will ;* the sixte callede *Prodigallitie;* the sevoenthe of *Orestes;* and a Tragedie of the *kinge of Scottes:* to ye whiche belonged diuers howses for the setting forthe of the same, as *Stratoes howse, Dobbyns howse, Orestioes howse, Rome,*[3] *the Pallace of prosperitie, Scotlande,* and a gret Castell one thothere side.[4]

---

[1] Feuillerat, *Documents relating to the Office of the Revels in the time of Queen Elizabeth* (Louvain 1908), pp. 10 ff.

[2] Exits and entrances are indicated in John Heywood's *Play of the Wether* printed in 1533.

[3] Comp. "the sittie of Rome" in the inventory taken by Henslowe "of all the properties for my Lord Admeralles men, the 10 of Marche 1598". This portion of the Diary, originally transcribed by Malone, is now missing from the MS., and the details are therefore lacking in Greg's excellent recension. Beyond the lists of properties given in Percy's plays for the Paul's boys this is the only definite clue presented to the employment of a symbolic scenic piece in the theatres of the period.

[4] Harl. MS. 146. f. 15 (*Revels Accounts*, ed. Feuillerat p. 119). Schelling misquotes this passage from some second hand source. See his *Elizabethan Drama*, i. 114.

It is doubtful whether in action all these constructions and scenic symbols would have required elucidation. The purpose of many of the houses would be clearly indicated by the business of the scene. But pictorial generalities typifying Scotland or Rome would certainly have demanded inscriptions.[1] Hence Sir Philip Sidney's allusion (c. 1583) to "Thebes written in great letters on an old doore." It is satisfactory to find this noble and gallant author making reference to the employment of locality inscriptions. Another passage in his *Apologie for Poetry*, if taken without the context, would give the impression that scene-boards were not then employed.

> But if it be so in Gorboduc, how much more in all the rest ? where you shall have Asia of the one side, and Africa of the other, and so many underkingdoms, that the player, when he comes in, must ever begin by telling where he is, or else the tale will not be conceived.

The difficulty here is to know whether Sidney is taking all contemporary stage representations into his purview, or whether his reflections have restricted application. The passage has often been cited as proof of the non-employment of scenery in Elizabethan times, but if it has any application to the court, or academic, play, the allusion must be to the difficulty of gaining an immediate sense of locality in viewing a performance where there was a considerable commingling of scenic symbols. It was only when the player emerged from a certain inscribed *mansion* or departed through a certain inscribed door that his whereabouts were fully apparent to the audience. We are speaking now in relation to all private or semi-private performances, and not of the public theatres, whose usages remain to be considered.

It is to be remarked that in *Jocasta*, as acted at Gray's Inn in 1566, where the Unity of Place was preserved, the players had to be careful as to their exits and entrances,

---

[1] A few of the stage directions in early plays with multiple setting seem to imply the use of elucidatory inscriptions. Thus in *Common Conditions* (c. 1570) we have "Here entreth Galiarbus out of Phrigia", and again "Here enter Lamphedon out of Phrigia."

now departing through "the gate called Electrae," and now through "the gate called Homoloydes." It is clear that the significance of these gates could not have been rendered to the spectators unless each were inscribed. We shall find later on that occasionally, at least, on the public stage a special significance was given to specific entrance doors, and that the actor had to exercise caution in coming in and going off.

One has only to make minute examination of the constructive system of Lyly[1] to become convinced that the multiple setting held sway at court for more than a score of years after the erection of The Theater and the Curtain. That it exercised some influence not only on the popular staging but on the dramaturgy of Shakespeare's immediate predecessors admits of no dispute. The difficulty is to know how long and at what theatres there was strict visualization of the multiple principle. One says strict visualization advisedly, for one has reason to believe—as evidenced by a curious direction of Percy's shortly to be discussed—that the spirit of the principle was more often followed than the letter. Beyond the fact that the Paul's boys made use of a modified multiple setting c. 1600 on the stage in their singing-school, it cannot be traced that other playhouses, public or private, made regular employment of these cumbrous scenic symbols. But side by side with this lack of direct evidence we have the fact, so difficult to account for, that the technique of the pre-Shakespearean theatre-dramatist was somewhat slavishly based on conventions born of the multiple principle. Analyse Marlowe, and you will be convinced of this. At least two of the distinguishing characteristics of the Elizabethan drama had their origin in the simultaneous setting, the curious system of changing the scene of action while the characters remained, and the system no less curious of completing journeys in full sight of the audience, instead of describing them or imagining them.

---

[1] The student must be warned to avoid the glosses of Mr. R. Warwick Bond, who has devoted much misplaced ingenuity to the harmful interpretation of Lyly's text by the usages of the ordinary Elizabethan theatres.

On the whole, there seems some reason to believe that
the players, either during the inn-yard phase of their history
or shortly after the building of The Theater and the Curtain,
made serious attempt to adopt the simultaneous setting in
its literality, but finding the conjunctive properties incon-
venient, began piecemeal to substitute inscribed locality
boards for the cumbersome scenic symbols. In this way the
stage would be gradually cleared of its obstructions without
much change being effected in the conventions belonging
to the original method. That there was a possibility of some
such transition in the Marlowean period is shown by the
option permitted to the Children of Paul's by William
Percy in connexion with the acting of *The Faery Pastorall
or Forrest of Elves* c. 1600. Under "Properties," Percy gives
what is virtually a scene-plot for the play, and clearly
demonstrates in so doing that the whole was to be arranged
in the simultaneous method :

Highest aloft and on the top of the Musick Tree, the Title
The Faery Pastorall, Beneath him pind on Post of the Tree the
Scene *Eluida Forrest*. Lowest of all over the Canopie *NAΠAIYBO-
ΛAION* or Faery Chappell. A Kiln of Brick. A Fowen Cott. A
Hollow Oake with vice of wood to shutt to. A lowe well with
Roape and pullye. A Fourme of Turves. A Greene Bank being
Pillowe to the Hed but. Lastly a hole to creepe in and out.

Now if it so be that the Properties of any of These, that be
outward, will not serve the turne by reason of concurse of the
People on the Stage, Then you may omitt the sayd Properties which
be outward and supplye their Places with their Nuncupations onely
in Text Letters.

Here it is to be noted we have a visualized composite
scene, with both title and locality boards. The play has
"A Prologue for the Court," indicating that it had also been
performed before the Queen, but the second paragraph of
the foregoing quotation alludes solely to the crowding of
spectators on the stage of the singing school. This particular
scene-plot is therefore of supreme importance as historical
evidence, not only because it indicates the employment of
locality boards in the performances at court, but for the

reason that it points to the existence of conflicting customs in the theatre and the consequent unpopularity there of the multiple system of staging.

Are we safe in making any deductions applicable to the other private theatres from the routine of the Paul's boys? I fear not. Everything tends to show that the stage of the singing school was a place apart.[1] Habituated to perform at court, the boys were familiarised with the usages of the multiple scene. On their own stage they were probably allowed the use of the court properties stored in the Revels Office, a concession that would cancel the question of expense. We know already that they appealed to a superior type of playgoer[2]; but if we were ignorant on that point we should be compelled to guess at the truth from the fact that Percy dared to put one of his inscriptions in Greek. Pedantry of this order would have been resented by a Bankside audience. Might it not have been to Percy's plays that Brabant senior referred in the conversation in *Jack Drum's Entertainment* dealing with the characteristics of the Paul's stage?

> Aye; and they had good plays, but they produce
> Such musty fopperies of antiquity,
> And do not suit the humorous age's back
> With clothes in fashion.

Once we depart from the atmosphere of Paul's, our quest for satisfying evidence of the employment of locality boards in the Elizabethan theatres becomes unprofitable. Now and again faint clues crop up, but they hardly permit of sound inferences, viewing the existence of rebutting details. It may be that no fixed rule obtained in all the houses of any one order at any particular period; the fact remains that never was there evidence so contradictory.

In many cases the necessity for inscriptions was obviated by the more illusive employment of sign-boards and trade symbols. Examples are to be found in *The Famous Contention*

---

[1] Prof. Feuillerat's recent discovery of an earlier children's theatre in the Blackfriars demands some qualification of this statement. See my closing paper.

[2] Cf. Collier, i, 281 and iii. 377 note.

of the Houses of York and Lancaster, and in the parallel
episode in 2 *Henry VI,* v. 2. So, too, in 1 *Edward IV,*
iv. 3, Shore's shop is indicated by the sign of the Pelican.
In *The Knight of the Burning Pestle,* iii. 4, the pole and
basin hanging before the Barber's shop are ingeniously
pressed into service during the traffic of the scene. These
two properties were utilised in the spirit of the multiple
setting. They must have been in position from the very
beginning of the act, and their continued presence was not
without its incongruity.

Again, opposite the slender amount of positive evidence
indicating the employment of locality boards can be placed
an equally slender amount of negative evidence arguing
against their use. Probably the most significant item on
this latter score is that afforded by *Every Man Out of his
Humour,* which we know to have been acted in 1599 at the
Globe.   Having arranged that certain extrinsic characters
should be on the stage as Chorus throughout the play (one
of them a supposititious friend of the author and familiar
with the text), Jonson took advantage of the presence of
this friend, Cordatus, to keep indicating the imminent
changes of scene.[1] Surely this would have been an utterly
superflous proceeding if locality boards were regularly provided. Does it not look like as if Jonson, for once, sought
to remedy the persistent vagueness of the scene? If we
concede this, the evidence can only be taken at best to apply
to the Globe theatre at the dawn of its history. Concerning
the usage at the Blackfriars, Jonson gives altogether different
testimony. At that house in 1601 was produced *The Poetaster, or the Arraignment.* In the induction one finds Envy
coming up a trap to deliver an atrabilious monologue in
which there was much covert girding at the plush-covered
gallants of the day. First she catches sight of the title-board
and gloats over the sub-title, having come to blast the
enjoyment of all present. But her joy turns to dismay when

[1] For the textual indications of the various changes of scene see the close of the
first act, of Act II. sc. ii, and of Act III. sc. ii, and Act IV. sc. iv. Note especially the ingenious indication at the beginning of Act v. sc. vii.

she finds that the author, instead of laying the scene at home, has placed it in Rome. That knowledge is evidently gained by the sight of another inscription on one or more boards :

Mark how I will begin : the scene is, ha !
Rome? Rome? and Rome ? Crack eye-strings and your balls
Drop into earth.

This passage admits of two interpretations, either that Envy reads off the one inscription from three locality boards, or that she merely sees one board and, in her ruminative agony, indulges in forceful iteration. In taking the former view, Reynolds assumes that the superscriptions were placed over three entrance ways.[1] But I cannot agree with this reading. Even if we admit for argument's sake the existence of a convention at the Blackfriars whereby three concurrent scene boards were used in plays presenting a series of widely separated localities, its employment cannot be conceded in a unified play like *The Poetaster*. However tradition-ridden the players might have been they were not likely to go to superfluous trouble. The idea of using three boards to convey the same intimation in a play of unvarying locality recalls the action of the over considerate farmer who cut two holes in his barn door, one for the hen and the other for her chickens.

But if Reynolds' theory, in its particular application, be not accepted, it cannot in its broader aspect be dismissed cavalierly. If scene-boards were used at all in the public or private theatres, there were certainly many occasions when three simultaneous boards (placed, say, over the two side doors and the central curtained passage-way) would have been a grateful expedient. There are plays which vividly recall Sir Philip Sidney's sarcasm, plays whose technique is based on the old multiple convention,

---

[1] op. cit. i. 22. Reynolds here says three doors, not three entrance ways, but in most theatres there were only two conventionally recognised doors giving on to the stage proper. The third door, of which we find occasional mention, was situated at the back of the inner stage, and would be frequently out of sight owing to the closing of the traverses.

where the scene chops and changes about with kaleidoscopic swiftness and variety; and these for their proper comprehension seem positively to demand constant resort to locality boards. Of this order are *The Wounds of Civil War*, *Pericles*, and *The Fair Maid of the West*.

In such cases one of two possible methods of scenic clarification might have been pressed into service. Single locality boards could have been used and changed with each successive transition, or the dramatist might have been limited to the maximum of three localities in any one act, all of which could have been indicated by superscriptions over the various entrance-ways. The second arrangement would on all counts have proved the more satisfactory as it permitted of better visualization of the action, and precluded the necessity of changing the boards during an entire act. To see whether the dramatist was really limited in the manner indicated one would require to analyse a considerable number of plays of the chronicle or narrative order. This I have not done. But it may be remarked that we have in *Pericles* some slight basis in support of the theory. Although six widely separated localities are utilised in this play the action is confined to a maximum of three in any one act. [1]

Only one difficulty presents itself in connexion with the triple-board theory. Where certain doors represented certain localities there could have been no laxity of exit and entrance. A character who accidentally departed for Rome when he ought to have gone to, say, Jerusalem, would have played the mischief with the plot. Everything would have had to be carefully rehearsed and nothing left to chance.

Besides proof by the law of averages of the limitation to three localities per act, to establish this theory one would require to show that the Elizabethan entrance-ways were given on occasion a localised significance akin to the old Greek convention. This should not be at all an impossible task viewing the evidence that lies ready to hand. Jonson

---

[1] On the other hand in the third act of *Antony and Cleopatra* we have thirteen "scenes" dealing with at least six different localities.

we know did not write narrative plays with an ever-changing scene, and Reynolds appositely cites Jasper Mayne's encomium of rare old Ben, setting forth that in his works "The stage was still a stage, two entrances Were not two parts o' the world, disjoin'd by seas."[1] We have already seen in connexion with *Jocasta* that as early as 1566 the academic stage had given a specialized significance to the entrance-ways. Forty years later we have evidence that something of the sort had recently been done on the public stage. Discussing "How a Gallant should behave in Powles Walk," Dekker, in the fourth chapter of his *Guls Hornbooke* (1609), gives the following curiously phrased instruction :

Your Mediterranean Ile, is then the onely gallery, wherein the pictures of all your true fashionate and complementall *Guls* are, and ought to be hung up : into that gallery carry your neat body, but take heede you picke out such an hour, when the maine Shoale of Ilanders are swimming up and downe. And first observe your doores of entrance, and your *Exit*, not much unlike the plaiers at the Theatres, keeping your Decorums, even in phantasticality. As for example : if you prove to be a Northerne Gentleman, I would wish you to passe through the North doore, more often (especially) then any of the other : and so, according to your countries, take note of your entrance.

View this passage in association with Jasper Mayne's later allusion, and the meaning becomes clear. Little, however, but disappointment ensues when one comes to search for stage directions corroborating this specialized employment of the doors. Only two plays yield us evidence of the existence of any such convention ; and it would be perilous on the strength of these to infer its diffused or continuous employment. One of the two, *The Cuck-Queanes and the Cuckolds Errants, or the Bearing Downe of the Inne* (c. 1600), I shall now have occasion to discuss in detail. In the case of the other, Nabbes' comedy of *Covent Garden* (c. 1638), one has reason to suspect the employment of an

---

[1] *Jonsonus Virbius*, 1638. Reynolds, i. 22.

elaborately constructed and illusively painted homogeneous stationary scene.

Reynolds' triple-board theory gains some measure of support from the remarkable construction of *The Cuck-Queanes and the Cuckolds Errants*. Percy's directions certainly imply the existence of some such conventionalism, and the play is sound evidence for the routine pursued at the Paul's playhouse. Symbolic simultaneous representation of three several places is clearly indicated in the scene-plot, headed "Properties," prefixed to the piece.

Harwich, in Midd of the stage *Colchester* with Image of Tarlton, Signe and Ghirlond under him also. *The Raungers Lodge*, *Maldon*, a Ladder of Roapes trussed vp neare Harwich. Highest and aloft the Title The Cuck-Queanes and Cuckolds Errants. A Long Fourme.

Here we are to suppose that Harwich and Maldon were represented by the two side entering doors. Although no mention is made of the employment of locality-boards, their presence may be inferred from the phrasing of the textual stage directions. Colchester, we note, is in the middle of the stage, and Tarleton's Ghost in entering from there to speak the prologue is instructed to play awhile "lowe on his Tabour . . . standing at entrance of doore and right under the beame." We are justified by this in surmising that the superscription of Colchester together with the image and sign-board were placed over the middle door at the back of the inner stage.[1] The only possible alternative would deny to the Paul's stage a central traverse and inner section, and substitute for the traverse a middle door. This I cannot accept.

Let us look now for a moment at some of Percy's stage directions to see the working of his treble method :

Act i. sc. 1. Doucebella, Floradin and Rofe Joice enter. Marginal note, "They enter'd from Maldon." Sc. 2. Nim and Shift

---

[1] Cf. Mr. Walter H. Godfrey's conjectural plan of the Fortune in *Shakespeare Jahrbuch* (1908), p. 160. For some evidence in support of Messrs. Archer and Godfrey's oblique side-door theory, see my extracts from Percy's textual stage directions, notably those from Act i. sc. ii. and Act iii. sc. i. But one must be careful not to confuse the characteristics of the public and the private theatres.

enter. Marginal note, "they mett from Maldon and from Harwich." Sc. 4. Four characters come on. A textual stage direction says "they enterd from Harwich all."

Act iii. sc. 1. Two characters come on. Marginal note, "They mett, Denham from Maldon, Lacy from Harwich." At the end of the scene is the instruction " they crossd Denham to Harwich, Lacy to Maldon."

Act iv. scene 1. " The Direction. Aruania, Doucebella, in their riding attyres . . . Doucebella from Maldon, Aruania from Harwich. They spake aloofe."

Whatever may have been the common practice at the private theatres towards the close of Elizabeth's reign, there is some reason to believe that at houses of this order a quarter of a century or so later, locality-boards were not hung up at the beginning of the performance. In *The Broken Heart*, as played at the Blackfriars in 1633, the prologue began by saying

> Our scene is Sparta. He whose best of art
> Hath drawn this piece calls it The Broken Heart.

One would be inclined to think here that the haste in pointing out the scene of action was occasioned by the absence of a locality-board. But the same argument might be advanced to prove the non-employment of a title-board, and the example therefore is far from conclusive. I should not have been disposed to refer to it, had it not been for my discovery of more definite evidence. In *The Cardinal*, as acted before 1641, the opening lines of the prologue run :

> The Cardinal ! 'Cause we express no scene
> We do believe most of you gentlemen,
> Are at this hour in France, and busy there—

As much as to say, "Gentlemen, owing to the vagueness of the inscription of our title-board, the chances are your minds have been dwelling on Richelieu." The whole point here would have been lost if the locality-board were already in position.

We come now to consider the question of the employment of scene-boards from a textual standpoint, particularly in relation to those unlocated scenes which puzzle the modern editor, and, by a parity of reasoning, must have befogged the mind of the average Elizabethan playgoer, if unelucidated by inscriptions. Now and again, Shakespeare presents difficulties of this order. In discussing one of these it is vital to recall that in the absence of programmes the identity of a fresh character had to be arrived at by the traffic of the scene. In *All's Well That Ends Well*, iii. 1, the Duke of Florence enters with two Frenchmen and a troop of soldiers, but the text affords no clue either to the place of action or the identity of the Duke. Another equally unlocated scene occurs at the beginning of the fifth act.[1] In both cases scene-boards are positively demanded, and only one serious objection can be proffered to their use. If placards were hung up throughout the action it hardly seems likely that the dramatist left the stage manager laboriously to deduce the various localities from the text. The simplest way would have been for the author to write in the scenic indications during the process of composition, but judging by the absence of such indications from the printed copies that course was apparently not pursued.[2] Many plays are known from internal evidence to have been printed from prompt copies, and I have heard it advanced in private discussion of this matter that scene-boards could not have been used without some reference being made to them in the marginalia of these working copies. The speaker looked upon this argument as decisive, but I am far from thinking it so. Why should it have been the prompter's business to superintend the shifting of the boards? His known duties were quite onerous enough without this added responsibility. Had he not to watch the book, to be ever ready to give the word, to call the actors, summon the incidental and inter-act music, see to the bringing in of properties, the opening of traps, the flashing of the lightning and the rolling of the thunder?[3]

---

[1] Cf. 2 *Henry VI*, iv. 9.

[2] Now and again we come across a stray indication, not only localising the action but hinting at the employment of scene boards. Note Reynolds' apt citation from *A Warning for Fair Women* (1599), "Enter Two Carpenters under Newgate."

[3] Cf. the marginal instructions in *Believe as You List*, *The Custom of the Country*, *The City Madam* and other plays printed from prompt copies.

Opposite this it might be argued that the normal position of the prompter was on the stage beside the characters—an arrangement no more incongruous than the presence of the stool-holders—and that most of his instructions were given by deputy. The same call-boy who carried messages into the tiring-house could see personally to the changing of the boards. All this sounds feasible until we come to consider the probable position of the boards, viewed by the light of the information yielded by Percy's plays. To be readily seen from all parts of the house the boards would have to have been placed centrally at the back, and at some considerable elevation. This could not have been done from below with the necessary neatness and dispatch, but, supposing the boards to have been hung out on the balustrade fronting the upper stage, could easily have been done from above. One must remember there were other officials in the theatre besides the prompter upon whom the duty might have devolved, say the stage-keeper or the tireman.[3] If it be asked how the person so appointed would have known when to make the necessary changes, I should reply that it would not be a difficult matter for the theatre copyist, when transcribing the actors' parts, to make out a scene-plot with speech or music cues. When in doubt, he had the author to appeal to.

We have seen that there is a reasonable *a priori* argument in favour of locality-boards in the Elizabethan playhouse. The point also admits of discussion *a posteriori*, but the evidence deducible by this method is not very decisive, seeing that one has difficulties in determining what particular conventionalism was perpetuated, whether of the playhouse or the court, or a fusion of both. It must suffice now to demonstrate that in the later Stuart masques, as well as in a few privately performed plays of the same period, we have clear proof of resort to locality-inscriptions, and that too in scenes which were illusively represented. In Chapman's

---

[3] For the stage-keeper see the induction to *Bartholomew Fair* and the prologue to *The Example*. According to the prologue to *Hannibal and Scipio*, he, or they (for at some theatres there were several), generally wore a sort of uniform. For some of the duties of the tiremen see the inductions to *The Malcontent* and *The Staple of News*.

Masque of the Middle Temple and Lincoln's Inn (1613), the scene showed a Silver Temple standing on an eminence and bearing inscription in golden letters, "Honoris Fanum." In Tatham's pastoral, *Love Crowns the End*, as acted by scholars at Bingham in Nottinghamshire in 1632, we have the direction at the close of the scenically mounted prologue, "Exit. A place discover'd all green mirtles, adorn'd with Roses, a Title written over 't thus : LOVERS' VALLEY." In the unnamed, anonymous masque presented by Prince Charles at Richmond on September 12, 1636, and subsequently printed at Oxford, the second scene, "a well-ordred Campe," bore the inscription *Expeditio Britomartis* "in a Compartement."

My own impression is that in these cases it was the old court conventionalism that was perpetuated. To admit as much is to suggest on the strength of the meagre evidence to hand that the same specific conventionalism imposed itself on the early scenic conditions of the new Restoration theatres. At Lincoln's Inn Fields in 1663, as well as at court, was performed a comedy called *The Slighted Maid*, a hodge-podge of pastoral, masque, and opera, evidently modelled on the hybrid court productions of Louis XIV. In the middle of Act iii we find the direction "the Scene is discovered, over which in capital Letters is writ *CAMPI ELYSII*." Again, the closing scene of the last act is thus particularised in the printed copy : "The Scene, Vulcan's Court, over it is writ, Foro del Volcane." Here the Italian inscription seems to point to a foreign source for the particular scenic effect, a not improbable supposition seeing that in the absence of native scene-painters, Italian artists were brought over from Paris shortly after the Restoration. The curious point is that no evidence exists of the employment of locality-inscriptions on the contemporary continental stage, whether public or private.

To sum up on the question of scene-boards, the really vital question of this inquiry. With a caution entirely uncharacteristic, I must content myself with the possibilities suggested on the way, and resolutely refuse to hazard the formulation of any general principles. Clearly the available data are insufficient to pontify upon ; nor can I foresee the likelihood of new evidence of moment being unearthed. No single pass-key can ever be found to unlock all the doors of the mystery, and for this reason the whole truth is never likely to be known. We have definite evidence for the employment of locality-boards at one playhouse at a specific period—Paul's c. 1600—and we have reason to suspect their employment at other houses at varying periods. Of the *modus operandi*, save in the one particular instance mentioned, we cannot be certain. Proof of the existence of a certain custom at a private theatre cannot be taken as proof of its existence at a contemporary public theatre. The Globe and the Blackfriars, although maintained so long by the one body of players, failed to follow exactly the same routine. Marston, in a note to the epilogue of his *Sophonisba*, begs the reader not to blame him "for the fashion of the Entrances and Musique of this tragedy, for know it is printed only as it was presented by youths, and after the fashion of the private theatre." Broadly speaking then, there were two fashions, that of the public theatre, apparently based upon the conventionalisms of the inn-yard, and that of the private theatre, where closer and closer approximation seems to have been made as time went on to the methods of the court. We cannot find that the public theatres of the pre-Restoration era ever proceeded beyond the scrappy symbolic mounting of the miracle plays ; but in the private theatres as early as c. 1634 some tentative use had been made of successive scenery of the primitive latter-day order. Not only is there a line of demarcation between the two, but one must remember that during the first forty years of the seventeenth century both types were in irregular process of evolution, the public theatre, however, arriving the more rapidly at its maturity. Once the investigator has grasped these facts he will have become convinced of the futility of generalisation.

MUSIC AND SONG IN THE ELIZABETHAN THEATRE

MUSIC AND SONG IN THE ELIZABETHAN THEATRE

IN the latter half of the eighteenth century, when curiosity began to be aroused as to the prime characteristics of the Elizabethan stage, someone, who permitted himself to be deceived by the fallacious evidence of the quartos, put on foot an untenable theory of wholesale continuous performance in Shakespeare's day. Malone[1] doubtless thought he had given this its quietus, but more than a century after it had been decently interred its bones have been resurrected by the alternationists[2] with the vain hope of bolstering up their equally untenable theory. The chances are that in claiming too much the alternationists have proved too little. Although continuous performance as a hard and fast principle cannot be maintained, there are some reasons to believe that on occasion certain long plays like Hamlet were given without a break, or with only a single break. In the public theatres exigencies of time would have demanded this. So intimately is the problem associated with the rise and progress of inter-act music that no apology need be made for discussing it at length in a paper devoted to a wide consideration of the fruitful topic of music and song in the Elizabethan Theatre.

For the existence of inter-act music in our earliest playhouses one readily finds sufficing precedent. Considerably before the English drama had a permanent abiding place the divisions were so indicated. One of the " wise saws " in *The School of Abuse* might well have been pointed by its author into a modern instance. "Poetrie and pyping", writes Gosson, "haue allwaies bene so vnited togither, that til the time of Melanippides, Pipers were Poets' hyerlings." Primitive English comedy was nothing if not musical.

---

[1] *Shakespeare Variorum* (ed. Boswell, 1821), iii. 111.

[2] For a lucid exposition of the alternation theory, see Mr. William Archer's article on "The Elizabethan Stage" in *The Quarterly Review* for April, 1908, p. 448. et seq.

Ralph Roister Doister vividly illustrates how large a space in Tudor days was occupied by melody and song, when no gentleman could be said to be fully educated who was incapable of singing his part at sight. [1] In a quaint onomatopœic way Udall makes Dobinet Doughtie indicate what instruments were in common use among the people in the middle of the sixteenth century:

> With euery woman is he in some loues pang,
> Then vp to our lute at midnight, twangledome twang,
> Then twang with our sonets, and twang with our dumps,
> And heyhough from our heart, as heauie as lead lumpes:
> Then to our recorder with toodleloodle poope
> As the howlet out of an yuie bushe should hoope.
> Anon to our gittern, thrumpledum, thrumpledum, thrum,
> Thrumpledum, thrumpledum, thrumpledum, thrumpledum,
>   thrum.

By the very nature of things, the musicians associated with the impermanent, plastic stage could not be assigned any well recognised conjunctive position. Textual indications clearly show that they were brought on the scene as occasion required, to figure as auxiliaries and lend modest illusion to the action. [2] In *Gammer Gurton's Needle* one finds definite allusion to the custom of playing music between the acts. At the end of the second act Diccon says:

> Into the towne, will I, my frendes to vysit there,
> And hether straight again, to see the end of this gere:
> In the mean time, felowes, pipe upp; your fiddles, I say, take
>   them,
> And let your freyndes here such mirth as ye can make them. [3]

With the dawn of English tragedy in 1562 emblematical dumb shows came to be united, in the graver drama, with the inter-act music. One doubts not that a few hints were

---

[1] Cf. Ernest Walker's *History of Music in England*, p. 58.

[2] *Ralph Roister Doister*, iii. 3, at end. In John Redford's *Moral Play of Wit and Science* (Shakespeare Society, 1848), viol players come on twice to accompany songs. Some of the music in this piece (by the author) is preserved in the British Museum. See Add. MSS. 15,223, ff. 11-28.

[3] For a quaint German analogue, see Karl Mantzius' *History of Theatrical Art* (1903), ii. pp. 150-1.

taken in the beginning from the more elaborate intermedii
of the Italians. Through this clumsy innovation careful
regulation of the music became imperative. That some
considerable pains were taken to adapt the strain to the
action can be seen from an intelligent study of the directions in *Gorboduc* and *Tancred and Gismunda*.[1] Closely as
these two plays are allied in point of time, one notes in the
latter a significant advance on the principle of the purely
symbolical dumb show. The intercalated pantomime was
performed to " a sweet noise of still pipes," and other
appropriate music, by the actual personages of the drama,
and led up smoothly without break to the opening of the
succeeding act. Here the dumb show was far from "in-
explicable," and fully justified itself by binding the action.
For once, possibly for the first time, there was unbroken
continuity. The pity of it was that where in later days the
dramatist resorted to the dumb show, either in the intervals
or during the main action, to eke out defective construction, he mostly burdened it with cloudy symbolism.[2] A few
exceptions are to be noted. While the music is playing
between the second and third acts of Marston's *What You
Will*, Rydel creeps in to observe Jacomo and the others
dress Francisco. At the end of the second act of *The Phoenix*
(1607), we have the direction, "Exeunt. Towards the close
of the musick the justices three men prepare for a rob-
berie." Prefixed to the fifth act of *Parasitaster, or the Fawne*
is the direction, "Whilst the Act is a-playing, Hercules
and Tiberio enter ; Tiberio climbs the tree, and is received
above by Dulcimel, Philocalia and a Priest : Hercules stays
beneath." This instruction, it may be noted, is evidence for
the employment of inter-act music at the Blackfriars about
the year 1605. Again, in the interval following the second
act of *The Changeling*, De Flores comes in, and hides behind
a door the naked rapier required for the sudden dispatch of
his victim in the succeeding act.

---

[1] See also *The Misfortunes of Arthur* (1588).
[2] For a comprehensive article on "Dumb Shew in Elizabethan Drama before
1620," see *Englische Studien*, xliv. (1911), p. 8.

What with the prevalence of dumb shows in the early Tudor drama and the marked taste for music, it seems probable that the first theatres made no immediate departure from precedent. Intervals of time between successive scenes and successive acts would be indicated by the playing of music. Stage directions are not wanting to show this occasional marking of the divisions between scenes by brief instrumental selections, [1] and even in some cases where the direction is lacking the playing of music is absolutely suggested by the nature of the construction. How otherwise could the break be conveyed to the audience between the third and fourth scenes of the third act of *The Jew of Malta*, each of which occurs in the same place but with an intervening lapse of time?

We have clear evidence that music was employed to adjust the mood of the spectator to the tone of the coming act, and, with equal frequency, to herald the approach of some important personage or accentuate the stress of some simulated emotion. [2] In *The Two Italian Gentlemen* of Anthony Munday, which dates from about 1584, instructions are given as to the particular kind of music to be played between the acts, "a pleasant galliard," "a solemn dump," etc. Let us not rashly assume, however, that directions of this nature invariably originated with the author of the play. Collier states rather foolishly that " Marston is very particular in his *Sophonisba* (1606), in pointing out the instruments to be played during the four intervals of the acts : 'the cornets and organ playing loud-full music,' for act i ; 'organs, mixed with recorders,' for act ii ;

---

[1] Cf. *A Looking Glasse for London* (1594), l. 558, when Remilia says "Shut close these curtaines straight and shadow me." Then "they draw the Curtaines and musick plaies." A new scene begins with the entrance of the Magi. In Middleton's *Your Five Gallants* (Blackfriars c. 1605), iv. 1, is the direction "the musicke plaies on a while, then enter Tailbee, his man after, trussing him." Their appearance marks the beginning of scene ii. In *The Fair Maid of the West*, Part 1 (1631), Act iv. the duration of the interval between the second and third scenes is indicated by the curt direction, "Hautboys long." The instruction at the end of this act, "act long," shows that the act-intervals varied in length.

[2] A song is sung whilst Bassanio ruminates over the caskets in *The Merchant of Venice* (First Folio), iii. 2. In *Messalina* (1640), Act iii. "solemne musick" is played during Montanus' speech at the banquet. Cf. Professor A. C. Bradley's *Oxford Lectures on Poetry*, p. 369.

'organs, viols and voices' for act iii; and 'a base lute and a treble viol' for act iv. In the course of act v he introduces a novel species of harmony, for we are twice told that 'infernal music plays softly.'" [1] Here we have an obvious overlooking of the fact that, in a note to the epilogue, Marston writes: "After all, let me intreat my Reader not to taxe me for the fashion of the Entrances and Musique of this tragedy, for know it is printed only as it was presented by youths, and after the fashion of the private stage." In other words, *The Wonder of Women, or the Tragedy of Sophonisba* had been produced at the Blackfriars by the Children of the Queen's Revels. Taken in conjunction with a curious passage in Webster's induction to the augmented version of *The Malcontent* (as acted by the King's players at the Globe in 1604) Marston's protest reveals the existence of a serious divergence in certain matters of routine between the public and the private theatres. In Webster's induction, William Sly asks the players how they came by the piece about to be acted, and learns from Condell that they had found it. "What are your additions?" queries Sly; and Burbage replies, "Sooth, not greatly needfull; only as your sallet to your great feast, to entertain a little more time, and to abridge the not receiv'd custom of musicke in our theatre." Whether accurate or not in all its details, Fleay's elucidation of Webster's induction throws some light on the colloquy just cited. "It further appears from the Induction," he writes, "that in 1604 (no doubt on the reconstruction of the Blackfriars boys as the Queen's Revels Children in January), they 'lost' this play, which was appropriated by the King's men in retaliation for the boys having stolen their *Jeronymo* and acted it c. 1600." [2]

Additions made "to abridge the not receiv'd custom of musicke" at the Globe must obviously have been matter substituted in place of certain internal musical features of the original play. It is vital to emphasise this, superfluous as it sounds, for, with regard to the employment of music,

---

[1] *Hist. Eng. Dram. Poetry* (1831), iii. 449.
[2] *Biog. Chron. Eng. Drama*, ii. 28, 78.

there was more than one disparity at this particular period
between the Blackfriars and the public theatres. It was customary, for example, at the Blackfriars to indulge those who
had assembled early with a long vocal and instrumental
prelude, sometimes lasting an hour.[1] On the other hand, at
no public theatre of the Pre-Restoration epoch can trace of
any overture be found. References occur to music sounding
before the play, but these were to the three trumpet blasts that
invariably preceded the performance. Since the Children of
the Chapel were primarily singers and musicians and only
secondarily actors, it became an easy matter to them to
intersperse music, dancing and song in their various plays.[2]
To follow in that course would have been a difficult matter
to the adult players of the Globe : hence Webster's allusion.
It must be recalled, moreover, that at this period song and
dance in the public theatres were almost wholly confined to
the jigs which concluded the performance. In the economy
of the private theatre these ribald afterpieces never had any
place. It was a question of appealing to a different kind of
audience.. Whatever the reason for the change, it would
seem, however, that the Globe and possibly some of the
other public theatres made occasional resort at a slightly
later period to the early Blackfriars system of musical, vocal
and terpsichorean interspersions. Assuming *Antony and
Cleopatra* to be fairly sound evidence for the famous Bankside house in 1608, one notes in Act ii. 7 that cheerful
tunes were played during the banquet on Pompey's galley
and that a dance followed. But the period of the change
and the length of its duration cannot be determined. Allied
with the fact that the evidence of the old quartos is not

---

[1] Cf. C. W. Wallace, *The Children of the Chapel of Blackfriars*, pp. 106-7. The
custom fell into desuetude there with the departure of the Child-actors in 1608, but it
was doubtless revived by them at the Whitefriars in 1610. It certainly must have persisted
somewhere, since it was the prototype of "the First, Second and Third Music" of the
Restoration Theatre (vide ante p. 21, note 2). Lack of preliminary music at the
Blackfriars in 1617 is indicated in the following distich from H. Fitz-Jeffrey's *Notes
from Black-fryers*, issued in that year :

> "Come, lets bethink ourselves, what may be found
> To deceive time with, till the second sound."

[2] For examples of these interspersements, see C. W. Wallace, op. cit. pp. 116-7.

conclusive, outer testimony as to musical interspersions in the public theatre is wholly lacking.[1] The experience of Paul Hentzner, the Brandenburg jurist, on his visit of September, 1598, goes to show that the common theatres of that time were not without their attractions of dance and song but that these were confined to the terminal jigs. "Without the city," he writes, "are some theatres where English actors represent almost every day comedies and tragedies to very numerous audiences; these are concluded with excellent music, variety of dances and the excessive applause of those that are present."[2]

Two other important divergencies remain to be noted. In lieu of the unreceived custom of the jig, which gave the public theatre audience an additional half-an-hour's entertainment, all the private theatres occupied by child-players favoured their patrons with songs and dances between the acts. This custom must have operated seriously against any internal tendency towards continuous or semi-continuous performance. Precisely where it began one cannot say, most probably at the Blackfriars. As evidence for Paul's we have the direction at the end of Act ii of Middleton's *A Mad World, My Masters:* "A song sung by the Musicians, and after the song, a country dance by the actors in their visards to a new footing." For the Whitefriars in 1611 the evidence is still more conclusive. At the close of Act i of *The Knight of the Burning Pestle,* the Citizen's Wife expresses her delight at hearing the fiddles tuning up, and cries, "but look, look! here's a youth dances." More music follows at the end of the second act (where we have an indication of the playing of Dowland's "Lachrymae"); and at the end of the third the boy again dances. That this inter-act dancing was a common feature of the private theatre performances,

---

[1] Cf. *Calendar State Papers, Venetian,* xv (1617–9), p. 67, letter of Horatio Busino, from London, to Signor Georgio Contarini, under date December 8, 1617. The experience here described (from the quality of the audience) probably took place at a private theatre. No authority exists for attributing this experience to the Fortune, as in *The Quarterly Review,* Vol. cii. p. 416. This assumption formerly led me seriously astray. Cf. *Shakespeare Jahrbuch* (1908), p. 42.

[2] *Pauli Hentznerii Itinerarium Germaniae, Angliae, Italiae, cum indice locorum, rerum atque verborum commemorabilium. Noribergae* (1629), p. 196.

at this period is indicated in Beaumont's lines to Fletcher on the failure of *The Faithful Shepherdess* c. 1609:

> Nor want there those, who, as the Boy doth dance
> Between the acts, will censure the whole Play ;
> Some like, if the wax-lights be new that day.

By way of side issue, it may be pointed out that inter-act songs formed a characteristic feature of the University drama in the first half of the seventeenth century.[1] Here they were probably not so much a following of the Private Theatre habitude as a survival of the pseudo-classic Chorus. Of the prevalence of inter-act singing on the London stage in 1633 we have sufficing testimony in Prynne's *Histrio-mastix* :[2]

> By our owne moderne experience there is nothing more frequent in all our stage-playes then amorous pastoral or obscene lascivious love-songs, most melodiously chanted out upon the stage between each several action ; both to supply that chasme or vacant interim which the tyring-house takes up in changing the actors' robes to fit them for some other part in the ensuing scene,—as likewise to please the itching eares, if not to inflame the outrageous lusts, of lewde spectators.

The impression conveyed here is that at the time of writing love-songs were sung between the acts at all theatres alike. But can we take the statement without corroboration? Had Prynne sufficient experience in promiscuous playgoing to speak with authority on the public theatres? It may have been that in his zeal he conveyed more than he had intended. Emphasis must, at any rate, be laid on the fact that at no period of Pre-Restoration stage history have we any other record of inter-act song or dance in the public theatres.

The final distinguishing custom of the early private theatre began with the child-players and may have been confined to them. This was the valedictory song at the close of the comedy. In *Westward Hoe*, as acted c. 1607 at Paul's, this was sung off the stage after the actors had

---

[1] Cf. *The Rivall Friends* of Peter Hausted, as acted at Cambridge in 1632; also Dr. Fisher's *Fuimus Troes* as at Oxford (4to 1633 ; reprinted in Dodsley).

[2] p. 262.

departed. But in *A Woman is a Weathercock*, as acted at the
Whitefriars c. 1610 by the Children of Her Majesty's
Revels, the song is bound to the action by Sir John
Worldly's closing speech beginning, "On, parson on ; and,
boy, outvoice the music."[1]

These preludes, interludes, intermezzos and terminal
songs, being clearly identified with child-players, cannot be
taken as customary at all periods of private theatre history.
For at least twenty years after its erection the Cockpit, or
Phoenix, was monopolised by adult companies. One thing,
however, is reasonably assured, viz., that inter-act music
prevailed from first to last in all the private theatres, without exception.[2] Even at Paul's, where pressure of circumstance confined the children, as we shall see, strictly to "the
two hours' traffic of the stage," intermezzos were given,
though, doubtless, they had often to be reduced to the
narrowest limits. In "a note to the Master of the Children of
Powles," appended to his extant MS. play of *Necromantes*,[3]
William Percy writes :

Memorandum, that if any of the fine and formost of these Pas-
toralls and comœdyes conteyned in this volume, shall but overeach
in length (the children not to begin before foure, after prayers,
and the gates of Powles shutting at six) the tyme of supper, that
then in tyme and place convenient, you do let passe some of the
songs, and make the consort the shorter ; for I suppose these plaies
be somewhat too long for that place. Howsoever, on your own
experience, and at your best direction be it.

"Make the consort[4] the shorter" evidently means cur-
tail the inter-act music. It could hardly have referred to
a preliminary concert, such as obtained at the Blackfriars,
which must have been precluded by the exigencies of time.
Even at the Whitefriars, where no such limitations ruled,

[1] Cf. the Fool's Jig-song at the close of *Twelfth Night*.
[2] For the Cockpit in 1635, see the prologue to Nabbes' *Hannibal and Scipio*. For
the Blackfriars in its later period, see *The City Madam* (1632), marginal instruction in
Act iv ; also *The Fatal Dowry*, end of Act ii.
[3] Collier, op. cit. (1831), iii. 377 note.
[4] Cf. the same author's *The Cuck-Queanes and Cuckolds Errants*, direction at the close
of every act, "Here they knockt up the consort" (i.e., gave the signal for the inter-act
music).

the waits between the acts were, on occasion, of the briefest. In *A Woman is a Weathercock* the music played in the first interval began before the act had ended, apparently with the penultimate speech. Apart from the stage direction, the music itself is alluded to by the last speaker. A few bars more at the close of the act would have indicated the break without causing any material delay.

It remains now to consider the possibility of occasional continuous (or quasi-continuous) performance in the public theatres. I say occasional for the reason that the idea of continuous performance as a principle cannot be entertained. It would have involved too serious a mental strain, and called for powers of concentration given to few. Moreover the possibility is precluded by the evidence for inter-act music and other division-markings. In " The Platt of the *Dead Man's Fortune*," otherwise a prompter's guide made for the Rose c. 1593, the act-divisions are indicated by marginal "musique" cues placed opposite rows of crosses.[1] In other platts of the same period made for the same theatre, where music is not indicated, either the Chorus comes on in the interval or a dumb show is presented. Again, take Yarrington's *Two Tragedies in One*, which Fleay thinks was given at the Fortune c. 1600, and which we are, at any rate, safe in assuming to be a public-theatre play. At the end of Act iii, Truth, as Chorus, comes on while Merry, with his back turned to the audience, is mutilating Beech's body. Addressing himself directly to the audience he says :

> I see your sorrowes flowe up to the brim,
> And overflowe your cheeks with brinish teares.
> But though the sight bring surfeit to the eye,
> *Delight your eares with pleasing harmonie,*
> That ears may counter checke your eyes and say,
> Why shed teares, this deed is but a playe ?

Let us next consider what would have been the necessity in the public theatre for occasional continuous, or quasi-continuous, performance. Limitation of time combined with

---

[1] Cf. W. W. Greg, *The Henslowe Papers*, ii. 127, appendix ii.

extreme length of play might now and again have demanded this heroic remedy. Where acting was by natural light and the performance did not begin until two or three o'clock [1] in the afternoon there was no possibility at any time save in the summer of extending beyond the normal limits. If one were assured that these were fully indicated in the "two hours' traffic" or "two short hours" of the prologues to *Romeo and Juliet* and *Henry VIII*, the possibility of frequent, nay, almost regular, continuous performance would have to be conceded. But there is a preponderance of evidence to show that the maximum period of performance in the public theatre was three hours. Other and later references to the shorter period all occur in prologues and epilogues spoken at private theatres. [2] As early as 1582 Whetstone, in his *Heptameron of Civil Discourses*, wrote of three hours as the complement. Dekker, in his section on Winter, in *Raven's Almanack* scoffs at the vanity of the players and tells them that "Ye shall be glad to play three hours for two pence to the basest stinkards in London, whose breath is stronger than garlick, and able to poison all the twelve-penny rooms." Ben Jonson in the induction to *Bartholomew Fair*, as acted in 1614 at the Hope, refers to the "space of two hours and a half and somewhat more." [3] Although within these three hours the public theatre players had usually to give a tragedy or comedy and a jig, it seems not unlikely that when a play of excessive length came to be represented, the jig, despite its popularity, was omitted. So far as these rhymed afterpieces were concerned, there was no question of fulfilling an advertised programme. Choice of jigs was frequently left to the audience, as indicated in the references to calling for them. [4] Evidence is almost wholly lacking as to the average duration of these gross

---

[1] The evidence, as marshalled by Collier, op. cit. (1831), iii. 376–7, points to three o'clock as the usual hour, but there must surely have been an earlier start in the winter.

[2] See the prologues to *Love's Pilgrimage*, *The Two Noble Kinsmen*, and *The Unfortunate Lovers* ; also the epilogue to *The Scholars*.

[3] For other references to "three hours," see Prologue to *The Lover's Progress*, epilogue to *The Loyal Subject*, and Timon's allusion in *Lady Alimony* (c. 1634).

[4] Cf. Collier, op. cit. iii. 379 ; also textual allusion in Shirley's *Changes, or Love in a Maze* (1631), showing that the custom had then passed out of vogue.

afterpieces, but if they approximated to the length indicated in *Tarleton's News out of Purgatory*, where gentlemen are referred to as laughing at them for an hour, all the more reason why they would have had to go by the board. Everything points in the normal condition to very brief inter-acts. Such an habituation would explain why to many of the Elizabethan dramatists an act was more an arbitrary division than a literary unit, and account for that constructive peculiarity where acts are finished off abruptly in the middle of something that demands completion. Assuredly that remarkable situation in *A Midsummer Night's Dream* where the four lovers sleep on the stage from the end of one act until the middle of the opening scene of the next would have been perilous had the wait been of any duration. [1]

Under pressure of circumstance the step from intervals of extreme brevity to a semi-continuous performance would have been of easy gradation. And it is noteworthy that of resort to semi-continuous performance we have meagre, if satisfying evidence. In Marston's *Histriomastix*,[2] Act ii, at the close, Mavortius and his company remain on the stage till Pride comes on to raise a mist [3] under cover of which they may disappear. Immediately on the departure of Mavortius the third act begins. There is again no break between the third and fourth acts, but the action apparently ceased between the first and second and the fourth and fifth. The reason, of course, for these curtailments is that the play ran to six acts and presented seven incidental songs and a dance. The final interval, if so it can be styled, was

---

[1] Cf. Mr. William Archer's article in *The Quarterly Review* for April, 1908, pp. 459–60.

[2] The alterations in this play for court performance (as indicated by the double ending, &c.) seriously confuse the issue. But, Fleay to the contrary notwithstanding, there is no reason for doubting that it had its initial production in a private theatre. (Cf. R. A. Small, *The Stage Quarrel between Ben Jonson and the so-called Poetasters*. Breslau, 1899, pp. 77 ff.) The date, c. 1598, and Marston's connexion with Paul's point to the Singing School as the source, but difficulties arise owing to the two-hours' limit which ruled there, though, of course, this would account for the semi-continuity. The only alternative is the Blackfriars.

[3] Effected by a cloud of smoke emerging from a stage trap. For other examples see *Love's Metamorphosis*, iv. 1, and the dumb show in *The Prophetess*, Act v.

brief and connective. Act v. ends with the departure of Christoganus. Then "allarmes in severall places, that brake him off thus : after a retreat sounded, the musicke playes and Poverty enters." The sixth act then begins. [1]

Middleton's *No Wit, no Help Like a Woman's*, was, on Fleay's showing, originally produced at the Hope in or about 1614. But the printed play as we now have it represents Shirley's revision of twenty years later. At the end of the fourth act one finds the direction, "Exeunt Philip Twilight, and Savourwit. Manent Widow and Mrs. Low-water." As a colloquy between the two women opens the fifth act, there was apparently no wait. In this connection it is noteworthy that the *Hamlet* of the Folio is divided only as far as Act ii. sc. 2, as if the remainder of the tragedy ran on without break. Fleay points out that this particular version is some two hundred lines short of Shakespeare's full manuscript, a circumstance that points to its being a sound acting copy. My impression is that implications of semi-continuous performance are more dependable than implications of unbroken continuity. It is difficult to divine whence sprung up that seemingly senseless practice of printing the early quartos without indication of act-divisions. It was not the mere perpetuation of an elementary principle. The *Enterlude of Respublica* (1553) and the comedy of *Roister Doister* (1566) are both divided into acts and scenes, the latter, of course, determined in the French way. It would not be a difficult matter to prove that many of the later undivided quartos represented plays that in actual performance had act-divisions. A noteworthy example is Middleton's private theatre play *The Phoenix* (4to 1607), where the breaks are indicated in the text and shown to have been signified by the playing of music. It would be probably useless to seek an explanation why all the Shakespearean quartos, save the *Othello* of 1621, are wholly undivided. Prölss [2] thinks

---

[1] Cf. C. F. Tucker Brooke, *The Shakespeare Apocrypha*, p. 180 (*The Life and Death of the Lord Cromwell*, lines 109 ff).

[2] Robert Prölss, *Von den ältesten Drucken der Dramen Shakespeares* (1905), p. 45 et seq. For Monkemeyer's reply see his *Prolegomena zu einer Darstellung der englischen Volksbühne zur Elisabeth- und Stuart-Zeit*.

the plays existed in two forms, one for the public theatre and one for the private; and he endeavours by this means to explain the discrepancies between the quartos and the folios. Monkemeyer seriously traverses this in arguing that the quartos were mostly surreptitious copies badly taken down. But one does not exactly see why even the most indifferent of stenographers should not have noted the act divisions, if they existed.

Considering the precedent set by the Children of the Chapel at Blackfriars it is not surprising to find that throughout the first half of the seventeenth century the best musicians were attached to the private theatres. When Shirley's masque, *The Triumph of Peace*, was represented at court in February, 1634, Sir Bulstrode Whitelock superintended the music, the expense of which came to about one thousand pounds. "I was so conversant with the musitians," he writes, "and so willing to gain their favour, especially at this time, that I composed an aier my selfe, with the assistance of Mr. Ives, and called it *Whitelocke's Coranto* ; which being cried up, was first played publiquely by the Blackefryars Musicke, who were then esteemed the best of common musitians in London. Whenever I came to that house (as I did sometimes in those dayes, though not often), to see a play, the musitians would presently play *Whitelocke's Coranto* ; and it was so often called for, that they would have it played twice or thrice in an afternoone. The queen hearing it, would not be persuaded that it was made by an Englishman, bicause she said it was fuller of life and spirit than the English aiers used to be ; butt she honoured the *Coranto* and the maker of it with her majestyes royall commendation." [1]

It is interesting to note that owing to the non-provision of any specified programme of inter-act music, the Elizabethan custom of calling for particular airs persisted in the theatre until the close of the eighteenth century, and, in Dublin, often proved the source of considerable trouble through the recurring demand for party tunes.

[1] Burney's *History of Music*, iii. 376.

In Chettle's *Kind-Hart's Dreame* one notes a reference to "Players and Fiddlers" who being "maisterlesse," were burnt in the ear. It is curious to find that in the theatre, where the vocations of the two were often seriously confused, players and musicians had to procure a separate license. On April 9, 1627, the musicians of the King's company had to pay Sir Henry Herbert, Master of the Revels, the sum of one pound (equal to at least £5 of the present currency) for a warrant of protection.[1] Vexatious as was this impost, it at least procured the playhouse fiddlers immunity from arrest as vagabonds when they ventured to exercise their calling elsewhere. In a whimsical passage in the tract called *The Actor's Remonstrance* (1643), written after the silencing of the theatres, we read, "Our music, that was held so delectable and precious, that they scorned to come to a tavern under twenty shillings salary for two hours, now wander with their instruments under their cloaks—I mean such as have any—into all houses of good fellowship, saluting every room where is company with 'Will you have any music, gentlemen?'"

Collier, in his section on early theatrical music, says that "Malone refers to a warrant of protection, dated 27th of December, 1624, by Sir H. Herbert, to Nicholas Underhill, Robert Pallant, John Rhodes, and seventeen others, 'all imployed by the King's Majesty's servants in their quallity of playinge as musitians, and other necessary attendants,' and a doubt must exist whether the musicians did not sometimes perform, and *vice versa*. We know that Phillippes and other actors of eminence played upon different instruments, and Pallant was a performer in the 'Plat' of the second part of the *Seven Deadly Sins*, before 1588 : possibly after he had ceased to act he became an instrumental performer in the band."[2] It is amusing to find Collier speculating upon a point which he could have easily determined by a patient examina-

---

[1] Malone's *Shakespeare* (Dublin, 1794), ii. 81.
[2] op. cit. iii. 449. Pallant merely came in as an attendant in the Second Part of the *Seven Deadly Sins* (1592), and may therefore have been primarily a musician at that period.

tion of the old quartos. We know, for example, that the musicians often came on the stage in their own character, and in that capacity were occasionally allotted a few lines. [1] Again, in situations where a great show of supernumeraries was deemed requisite, both the musicians and the gatherers were pressed into the service of the scene. [2] I am referring now to general custom, without laying any stress on the evidence deducible from plays performed at the Blackfriars, Paul's and Whitefriars by children. This precaution is necesssary, as, in all cases, the "little eyases" combined the two vocations. One other point needs to be emphasised. When songs were given on the stage (and not, as sometimes, in the music-room), the musicians almost invariably came on to play the accompaniment. [3] Much of this coming on in plays of contemporary English life was mere stage realism. It was customary for the Elizabethan spendthrift to keep a "noise" of musicians in his employ. Sometimes they did duty as servants and wore blue liveries. A scene of this order occurs in *The City Madam*, Act iii, where Goldwire, Junior, comes on disguised as a Justice of the Peace and his fiddlers as watchmen. Happily for the present day investigator, this play was printed from a well-marked prompt copy, as acted at the Blackfriars. Twenty lines before the disguised musicians appear, we have the marginal note, "Musicke come down." Similarly in the last act, occurs the direction " musicians come down to make ready for the song at the arras."

Whence, it may be asked, did they come? The question leads to a consideration of the position normally occupied

[1] Cf. *Othello*, iii. 1, where the musicians on the stage (evidently bag-pipers), talk after playing. In *Wit Without Money*, end of Act v, the musicians come on and one of them speaks. In *Monsieur Thomas*, iii. 3, a Fiddler enters and takes part in the dialogue. Afterwards he sings and plays.

[2] In Heywood's *If You Know not Me, You know Nobody*, Part ii (ed. 1874, p. 297), we have the direction "Enter Sir Thomas Ramsie, the 2 Lords, My Lady Ramsie, the Waits in Sergeants' gowns, with an Interpreter." The musicians had just played previously and now come on as disguised supernumeraries. In several other plays one finds them referred to as " the waits".

[3] Cf. *News from Plymouth* (1635 at the Globe), Act iii ; *Cymbeline*, ii. 2 ; *The Distresses*, Act i. Dancing was also sometimes similarly accompanied, e.g., *Lust's Dominion*, iii. 2, "Enter Oberon and Fairies dancing before him ; and Music with them."

by the musicians when not engaged in the traffic of the scene. It is plain to be seen at the outset, from the various duties they had to fulfil, that the position must have been somewhere within stage regions, where they could obtain ready access to the tiring-room, and not an isolated box in the auditorium. This of itself would negative Dr. Wegener's contention that the position is indicated by the word "orchestra" in the well-known Dutch sketch of *The Swan*, even if other rebutting evidence were lacking.[1] Curiously enough, Malone, more than a century ago, got within hail of the secret, but, in stating the result of his enquiries, only succeeded in rendering the problem more intricate for posterity. Writing in his "Historical Account of the Rise and Progress of the English Stage," he says "The band, which, I believe, did not consist of more than eight or ten performers, sat (as I have been told by a very ancient stage veteran, who had his information from Bowman, the contemporary of Betterton), in an upper balcony, over what is now called the stage-box."[2] Unfortunately, Malone did not know, what is well known now, that the Elizabethan theatre, unlike the theatre of his own time, had neither proscenium arch nor front curtain; otherwise he would not have conveyed his information in precisely these terms. The stage boxes in the latter half of the eighteenth century were situated on either side of the "apron," or *avant scène*, a little in front of the proscenium arch.[3] It is at least made clear to us, however, by Malone that the ancient "music-room" was in stage regions and not in the auditorium proper. Most likely, what Bowman's acquaintance meant to convey to him was that the Elizabethan musicians occupied an upper balcony at the back of the stage. Broadly speaking, this tallies with most of the evidence educible on the subject.

An important clue is afforded by *The Thracian Wonder*, "a comical history," attributed, on its first publication in 1661, to Webster and Rowley. Fleay's opinion is that this

---

[1] Vide ante p. 39.

[2] Malone's *Shakespeare* (Dublin, 1794), ii. 80. It is painful to find Dr. Brandes and others endorsing this highly confusing statement.

[3] Cf. Victor E. Albright, *The Shaksperian Stage*, plate 10.

play was acted c. 1617 by Prince Charles' company. In Act IV. i. 186, occurs the stage direction "Pythia above, behind the curtains." Four lines previously the prompter notes, "Pythia speaks in the Musick Room behind the Curtain." Here we have three significant indications : (1) the Music Room was "above" in the tiring-house ; (2) it had front curtains ; (3) and it could be used, occasionally, for dramatic purposes. All this clearly elucidates a situation in the third act of *The Late Lancashire Witches* (1634) as acted at the second Globe. Quite unconscious of their offence, the bewitched musicians have been plaguing the wedding guests with unearthly discords. Each, in fact, has been playing a different tune. They are asked to try again. "I, and lets see your faces," says Doughty, "that you play fairely with us" ; and then follows the direction, "Musitians shew themselves above."

It was in this "musick room," behind the curtains, that, when songs had to be rendered "off", the singer usually took his stand. In *Sophonisba*, Act IV (an early Blackfriars play), "a short song to soft musicke" is heard "above", and in *The Chaste Maid in Cheapside* (as at the Swan) we read at a certain juncture that "while the company seem to weep and mourn, there is a sad song in the music room." Even as late as March 23, 1661, the old custom still obtained. Recording a visit to the Red Bull on that date, Pepys comments on the vile acting, adding "and with so much disorder, amongst others, in the musique-room, the boy that was to sing a song, not singing it right, his master fell about his ears and beat him so, that it put the whole house into an uproar."

It was doubtless also in the music-room that Ariel sang when Ferdinand heard the sweet strains above him in the air. Apparently, however, no hard and fast rule existed : the ready student will have no difficulty in citing instances where music or song heard "off" was not rendered above. Thus, in *Sophonisba*, Act IV, "a treble viall and a base lute play softly within the canopy." No previous mention is made of the canopy, but the scene was the mouth of a cave, and the canopy (or traverses shrouding the inner stage) evidently covered it. This is shown by the subsequent direction, "Syphax hastneth within the canopy as to Sophonisba's bed."

Returning now to the main question, it would probably be futile to seek a single solution to the problem of exact locality. There are grave reasons for suspecting that not all theatres of either category at any given period were arranged alike. Generalisation fails to elucidate that unique direction in *Antonio's Revenge*, v. 5, "while the measure is dancing Andrugio's ghost is placed betwixt the Musick houses." To read the riddle set here would be to determine the normal position occupied by the musicians at Paul's in 1600. The ghost comes as a silent witness of the murder of Piero, a deed evidently perpetrated on the inner stage. The position is indicated by the subsequent naïve direction, "the curtaines are drawne [together], Piero departeth." This means "close the traverses, so that the inner stage may be cleared and the actor of the murdered man may go about his business." According to this reading, Andrugio's ghost must have been stationed somewhere on the side of the stage near to the front. This position would approximate very closely to the position indicated by Malone. But no rule can be safely educed from the evidence yielded by the play, and everything points to the fact that the stage of Paul's was of exceptional arrangement. There is little room to doubt that in the majority of Elizabethan playhouses a considerable portion of the central space on the second floor of the tiring-house was devoted to "the upper stage", and the residue on either side partitioned off into boxes for spectators and musicians. Irrespective of other evidence, the so-called "Red Bull" frontispiece to *Kirkman's Drolls* largely warrants this conclusion.

Some very curious details relative to the disposition of some unascertainable private theatre, and bearing directly on our subject, are to be found in Tom Killigrew's comedy, *The Parson's Wedding*, as first printed in a folio collection of his plays in 1664. This piece had its first production on the stage at the Theatre Royal, Drury Lane, in October of the same year, but it bears distinct evidence of having been written twenty-four years previously.[1] A partial proof of this is shown by the fact that while Drury Lane at this period was fully equipped with scenery, the stage directions largely refer to the arrangement and habitudes of the earlier non-scenic theatre. Killigrew's first two plays had been produced at the Cockpit c. 1636-7, and it may have been that *The Parson's Wedding* was originally intended for that house. On Fleay's showing there is some slight evidence in favour of the Blackfriars. In Act iv, Jolly says he has got the Blackfriars' music to come and play, and had been to the theatre to hire them. The crux bristles with difficulties, but one may take it that the play was designed either for the Cockpit or the Blackfriars. Here, then, are three apposite stage directions from the folio copy :

Act i. sc. 2.—"Enter Mistress Pleasant, widow Wild her aunt, and Secret her Woman, above in the musick room, as dressing her ; a glass, a table, and she in her night cloaths."

Act iv. sc. 6.—"The tyring room, curtains drawn [open] and they discourse. His chamber, two beds, two tables, looking glasses, night cloaths, waist-coats, sweet-bags, sweet meats and wine ; Wanton dressed like a chambermaid ; all above, if the scene can be so order'd . . . Enter Widow and Mrs. Pleasant, Wild and Careless ; the Widow and Mrs. Pleasant salute Wanton . . . Exeunt Wild and Careless . . . The curtains are closed."

Act v. sc. 2.—"The Fiddlers play in the tiring room, and the stage curtains are drawn, and discover a chamber, as it were, with two beds, and the ladies asleep in them ; Mr. Wild being at Mrs. Pleasant's bedside, and Mr. Careless at the widow's. The musick awakes the widow."

---

[1] Cf. Fleay, *Biog. Chron. Eng. Drama*, ii. 25. The evidence here marshalled shows the play to have been written c. 1640, but does not show, as Fleay assumes, that it had been then acted at the Blackfriars. Several indications prove that it had not been performed till seen by Pepys on October 11, 1664. In the first case the printed copy has neither prologue nor epilogue. Secondly, Sir Henry Herbert, Master of the Revels, has a record in his Office Book opposite the name of the play, at the time of the Drury Lane production, of a receipt of a licensing fee of £2. Herbert's fee for a revived play at that period was £1 and for a new play £2. This is conclusive. Cf. Malone's *Shakespeare* (Dublin, 1794), ii. p. 224.

Even to those unacquainted with Killigrew's play, it needs no demonstration to show that the terms "music-room" and "tyring-room" in these directions refer to particular parts of the playhouse, not to specific locations in the action of the piece. Both these rooms were situated aloft (proof of the position of the tiring-room will be cited later), and one at least had front curtains. Probably a curtain before the music-room is implied, as the direction from Act i. 2 indicates a discovery.[1] It would appear that this room was again utilised in the ensuing scene, where the Widow and Pleasant show themselves "above" and speak down. Before going off the "Widow shuts the curtain".

Everything points to the conclusion that the music-room and the tiring-room in the theatre for which the play was designed were situated side by side on the first storey of the tiring-house. Moreover, since the tiring-room must have occupied a very considerable space, viewing the size and number of the properties placed there at the one time, its identity with "the upper stage" seems well assured. To many inquirers this deduction will doubtless bring in its train an element of surprise. Few, however, on due reflection, will be disposed to scoff at the practicability of the arrangement. This indicated double function of the upper stage gives added point to the graphic picture of earlier theatrical times drawn in the original prologue to *The Unfortunate Lovers*, as spoken at the Blackfriars, c. May, 1638. After complaining that audiences had grown fastidious and looked for more wit in a single play than their "silly ancestors" were vouchsafed in twenty years, D'Avenant expatiates upon the complacency of former generations :

> For they, he swears, to the theatre would come,
> Ere they had din'd, to take up the best room ;
> There sit on benches, not adorn'd with mats,
> And graciously did vail their high-crown'd hats

---

[1] No thoroughgoing Elizabethan student will allow himself to be deceived for a moment by this formal "enter". Discoveries were often senselessly phrased in this manner. Cf. *'Tis Pitty She's a Whore* (4to, 1633), iii. 6 : "Enter the Friar in his study, sitting in a chayre, Annabella kneeling and whispering to him", etc.

To every half-dress'd player, as he still
Through the hangings peeped to see how the house did fill.

So, too, when the Fortune players moved to the Red
Bull in the Easter of 1640, they begged their new patrons
in a prologue written by Tatham—

> . . . to forbear
> Your wonted custom, band[y]ing tile and pear
> Against our curtains, to allure us forth ;
> I pray, take notice, these are of more worth ;
> Pure Naples silk, not worsted, . . . [1]

Conceive of the upper stage as shut off from view by
its own particular curtains, and utilised before the play as
a common tiring-room. Under such conditions it is easy
to see how the half-dressed player could peep out from
time to time to watch the filling of the house. Occasions
when the two functions of the upper stage would clash
would be very rare. Save at those brief sporadic periods
when the place was pressed into service as an illusive factor
of the scene, it could always be utilised by the players as a
dressing room. Cumbrous properties were very rarely seen
there, and scenes demanding their use were generally acted
on the inner stage. In this connexion, the elaborate mounting in *The Parson's Wedding*, iv. 6, is apparently the exception that proves the rule. Killigrew, in devising it, had
his doubts as to its practicability, and adds, "all above, if
the scene can be so order'd." Who knows ? Perhaps the
awkwardness of the arrangement contributed in some degree to the long delay in the production of the play.

[1] *Englische Studien*, Vol. xxxii. p. 43.

THE MOUNTING OF THE CAROLAN MASQUES

THE MOUNTING OF THE CAROLAN MASQUES

OWING largely to the glowing periphrastical descriptions indulged in by Ben Jonson and others, one is apt to think of the old court masques rather as the creation of Art Magick than the product of the harmonised labours of poet, scenic artificer and musician. For almost a score of years the spirit of inquiry has been striving to dissipate this nebulosity of idea, but with little result. It is right and proper that the literary history of the masque should be scientifically written, but not the soundest and most searching work of this order can yield to us a definite impression of the prime characteristics of the masque as a scenical representation.[1] What rare old Ben states ironically in his *Expostulation with Inigo Jones*, that "painting and carpentry are the soul of masque" has been said in all seriousness by another masque-poet. "In these things, wherein the only life consists in shew," writes Daniel in *Tethys' Festival*, "the art and invention of the architect gives the greatest grace, and is of the most importance ; ours the least part, *and of least note in the time of performance thereof.*" Literary history in dwelling upon the beauty of the lyrics and the fertility of imagination displayed by the poet in these graceful fantasies has reversed the proportions. Of the masque as spectacle we shall never arrive at a full and true idea until such time as the considerable number of Inigo Jones's designs for scenery, proscenia and costume, at present in the private collection of the Duke of Devonshire at Chatsworth, be published, together with a lucid exposition of his complex scenic system from someone profoundly versed in the intricacies of early Italian stage mechanism. True, an industrious German scholar,[2] like another Curtius, has

---

[1] No fault can be found with Mr. H. A. Evans's introduction to his collection of *English Masques* (1897) in *The Warwick Library* series. Within its limits it is a wholly admirable piece of work.

[2] See Dr. Rudolph Brotanek's *Die Englische Maskenspiele* (Vienna, 1902).

thrown himself heroically into the gulf; but the age of
miracles is past, and the gulf still yawns. If I, too, am equally
impotent to close the gap, circumstances have at least con-
spired to enable me to throw in a ton or two of earth.
Some practical discussion of Inigo Jones's scenic system in
the closing days of the court masque is now rendered
possible through the acquisition of four of his designs
(formerly in the Salvin collection), by the Royal Institute
of British Architects, and by the permission graciously
accorded to me by its Council to reproduce them.

Given as it was gratuitously, the normal scenically-
adorned masque of the latter Stuart period was a luxury
that few but monarchs could afford. Although the cost
might be anything from £5,000 to £20,000, the same
entertainment was rarely presented more than twice, seldom
more than once. During the period of 1612-40 it was
customary in mounting these dainty extravaganzas to pro-
vide for each a specially designed proscenium front, whose
composite ornamentation dealt emblematically with the
subject matter of the masque. This system, as we have
already seen, was subsequently followed by Sir William
D'Avenant in the earlier presentations of his operas. Hence
it may be predicated, without fear of contradiction, that the
Carolan masque, remote as it was by nature from the ordinary run of theatrical entertainment, had a modest measure
of influence upon the initial scenic system of the Restoration stage.

Although only two out of the four designs by Inigo
Jones now reproduced bear inscriptions (in the autograph
of the great architect), three of them are readily identifiable.
This is a happy circumstance, as it enables one to deal with
concrete examples, and avoid misleading generalities. Thus,
the inscription on our first reproduction "Front. Sery[s]
[? Shirley's] masque, Inns of Court, 1633," conveys the
impression that the design was made for *The Triumph of
Peace*, as performed at Whitehall on February 3, 1633-4;
and resort to the quarto of Shirley's masque turns conjecture
into certainty. Than this, few English court entertain-

INIGO JONES'S DESIGN FOR THE PROSCENIUM OF SHIRLEY'S   [*To face p.*
MASQUE *THE TRIUMPH OF PEACE* (1634).

ments have greater historical interest. Not many months previously, William Prynne, a member of Lincoln's Inn, had written a treatise against the stage, entitled *Histrio-mastix*, in which he had fulminated vehemently against all women-players. Owing to the circumstance that the English stage had not as yet begun to employ actresses, and to the unfortunate coincidence that the book came out the very morning after the Queen and her ladies had taken part in the performance of the court pastoral of *The Shepherd's Paradise*, the obnoxious passage was construed into a direct reflection upon her Majesty. There was a hollow mockery of a trial, and the luckless Puritan was sentenced to a variety of punishments, of which the most cruel and unjust was the loss of his ears. The barbarity of the decree, savouring more of savagery than a Christian community, only served to draw the attention of the sober-minded to the scandalous extravagance of the Court. Assuredly the docking of those ears counted among the factors which eventually cost the King his head. Even the masques might figure in the schedule, for the periodical emulation at Whitehall of the luxurious habits of the courts of France, Florence and the Savoy ran the King into debt, and led to insufferable taxation.

The honourable and learned members of the four Inns of Court had little sympathy with the extreme views of their maltreated brother; and by way of emphasising their disapproval of his pronouncements, they commissioned one of their number, James Shirley, the dramatist, of Gray's Inn, to write a masque for presentment by them before the Court. The result was *The Triumph of Peace*, which owed its title to the King's happy return after allaying the troubles in the north. When one comes to consider the vast expense, amounting to some £21,000, incurred by the four Inns of Court in connexion with this notable celebration, it must be borne in mind that the indoor entertainment at Whitehall was preceded by a magnificent public pageant, in which about two hundred members of the bar participated. The procession started early in the evening from Ely

House, Holborn, and, making its way down Chancery Lane, passed along to Whitehall. It consisted for the most part of a number of mounted cavaliers, attended by pages and torchbearers, and followed by trumpeters and truncheon men. At the rear of the procession came four triumphal chariots, each drawn by four horses ; and in these, we read, "were mounted the grand Masquers, one of the foure houses in every Chariot, seated within a half Ovall, with a glorious canopy over their heads, all bordered with silver fringe, and beautified with Plumes of Feathers on the top." The old quarto also tells us that the four great chariots, (there were one or two smaller ones) were all "after the Roman forme, adorned with much embossed and carved workes, and each of them wrought with silver and his severall colour. They were mounted on carriages, the Spring-trees, Pole and Axle-trees, the Charioter's seate, standers, wheels, with the fellyes, spokes and naves all wrought with silver and their severall colour." Whitelocke, who was one of the executive council, relates in his *Memorials* how there was much dispute between the grand masquers of the various Inns on the point of precedence, and that, to obviate the difficulty, it was finally decided the chariots should be of the Roman triumphal order, all designed and ornamented alike, but each with its distinctive colouring. The seats were made of "an Oval form in the back end of the chariot, so that there was no precedence in them, and the faces of all that sat in it, might be seen together." My reason for dwelling on these details is that Inigo Jones's uninscribed design for the great chariots happens to be preserved in the Salvin collection. In reproducing it now, I take all responsibility for the identification.

Having brought the learned masquers and their retinue to Whitehall, it is time to speak of the ornate frontispiece surrounding the scene. Let us then compare the description given of it in the old quarto with Inigo Jones's design.

The border of the front and sides that enclosed all the Scaene had first a ground of Arbor-worke enter-mixt with loose branches and leaves, and in this was two Niches, and in them two great

INIGO JONES'S DESIGN FOR TRIUMPHAL CHARIOTS. *[To face p*

figures standing in easy postures, in their naturall colors, and much
bigger than the life; the one, attired after the Grecian manner,
held in one hand a Scepter, and in the other a Scrowle, and a
picked antique crowne on his head, his curasse was of Gold, richly
enchased, his robe Blue and Silver, his arms and thighs bare with
buskinds enricht with ornaments of Gold, his browne locks long
and curled, his Beard thicke, but not long, and his face was of a
grave and Joviall aspect. This figure stood on a round pedestal
fained of white Marble, enricht with severall carvings; above this
in a compartiment of Gold was written MINOS. The figure on the
other side was in a Romane habit, holding a Table in one hand,
and a Pen in the other, and a white Bend or Diadem about his
head, his Robe was crimson and gold, his mantle Yellow and Silver,
his Buskins watchet trim'd with Silver, his haire and Beard long
and white, with a venerable aspect, standing likewise on a round
Pedestall answerable to the other. And in the Compartiment over
him was written NUMA. Above all this in a proportionate distance
hung two great Festons of fruites in colors which served for finishing to these sides. The upper part in manner of a large Freeze was
adorn'd with severall compartiments with draperies hanging downe,
and the ends tied up in knots, with Trophies proper to feasts and
triumphs, composed of Masking Vizards and torches. In one of the
lesser Compartiments was figured a sharpe-sighted eye, and in the
other a Golden-yoke. In the midst was a more great and rich Compartiment on the sides of which sate naked children in their naturall
colors, with Silver wings, in action of sounding Golden Trumpets,
and in this was figured a *Caduceus* with an Olive-branch, all of
which are Hierogliphicks of Peace, Justice and Law.

It should be noted that one important feature of the
stage front, referred to in the book, is lacking in the design.
We are told that the basement "was painted in rusticke
worke," and that in the middle was "a descent of staires in
two branches landing into the roome." But the design bears
indications of having been cut into sections for working
purposes, and it may be that the lower portion is missing.
On the other hand, it might be argued that Inigo Jones,
in designing proscenia, did not always trouble to sketch in
the connective front steps, seeing that they were regular
and indispensible concomitants of all scenically mounted
masques. Their common use (obscurely hinted at in Bacon's

essay "On Masques") serves to bring home to us that the
Carolan Masque, while bearing some resemblance to a
primitive Italian opera, had few of the characteristics of a
normal theatre play. So far from the picture being kept
wholly within the frame, the floor of the hall was, in a
sense, as much the scene of action as the stage. Here there
was some carrying over of old conventions, born of a period
when the masque had neither movable scenery nor a proscenium arch. When any particular compliment had to be
paid to the King or Queen, the actors came down from the
stage by the proscenium steps and made their way up to
the canopy of state at the other end of the hall before
delivering their sugared lines.[1] This custom, one takes it,
was strictly of native origin, but a second, and more important, usage of the floor of the hall was largely due to Italian
precedent. Between the stage and the State was a broad
space equivalent to the ancient orchestra, and known as "the
dancing place." This was invariably carpeted with green
cloth.[2] Here all the dances executed by the masquers
proper, distinguished as the Entry, the Main, the Revels
and the Going-out, were given.[3] On the other hand, the
dancing of the antick-masques was almost invariably confined to the stage.[4] Unlike the others, these were dances
in character, more or less relevant to the action, and executed by professionals. It is matter for regret that no
picture of a Stuart masque has come down to us, but, seeing
that the system of mounting pursued and the method of
presenting the main dances were strictly in accord with
Italian precedent, the spectacular characteristics of the
Carolan masques are satisfactorily visualized in Callot's
etching of a carnival performance at the Florentine court
in 1616, now reproduced.

[1] Cf. H. A. Evans, op. cit. pp. 106, 110 (*The Masque of Flowers,* 1614).

[2] Cf. the vivid description of a performance of Ben Jonson's *Pleasure Reconciled to Virtue* in 1618 given in Orazio Busino's translated letter in *Cal. State Papers, Venetian,* xv. pp. 110 et seq.

[3] Cf. H. A. Evans, op. cit. intro. p. xxxiv.

[4] In *Lovers Made Men* (1617), generally miscalled *The Masque of Lethe,* where the masquers and the antick-masquers are identical, the sole antick-masque was danced on the floor of the hall.

INIGO JONES'S DESIGN FOR THE PROSCENIUM OF D'AVENANT'S   [To face p.
MASQUE *THE TEMPLE OF LOVE* (1635).

At the time when Inigo Jones executed the design given here in reduced fac-simile, the masque for which it was made had not received its determinate title. Inscribed, "For the Quenes Masque of Indiands, 1634", it vividly depicts the proscenium front (or "arch triumphal," as these proscenia were sometimes called) provided for D'Avenant's masque *The Temple of Love*, as given at Whitehall by the Queen and her ladies on Shrove Tuesday, February 18, 1634-5. A comparison of the various features of the design with the following passage from the book of D'Avenant's masque will readily prove this identity :

At the lower end of the Banquetting house, opposite to the State, was a stage of six foot high, and on that was raised an Ornament of a new Invention agreeable to the subject, consisting of Indian Trophies: on the one side upon a basement sate a naked Indian on a whitish Elephant, his legges, short'ning towards the neck of the beast, his tire and bases of severall coloured feathers, representing the Indian Monarchy ; on the other side an Asiatique in the habit of an Indian borderer, riding on a Camell, his Turbant and Coat differing from that of the Turkes, figured for the Asian Monarchy ; over these hung sheild-like Compartiments; in that over the Indian was painted a Sunne rising, and in the other an halfe Moone ; these had for finishing the Capitall of a great Pillaster, which served as a ground to stick them of, and bore up a larg freeze or border with a Coronice. In this over the Indian lay the figure of an old man, with a long white haire and beard, representing the flood *Tigris* ; on his head a wreath of Canes and Seage, and leaning upon a great Vrne, out of which runne water ; by him in an extravagant posture, stood a Tyger.

At the other end of this freeze lay another naked man, representing *Meander*, the famous river of Asia, who likewise had a great silver urne, and by him lay an Unicorne.

In the midst of this border was fixed a rich Compartiment, behind which was a crimson drapery, part of it borne up by naked children, tack'd up in severall pleats, and the rest was at each end of the Freeze tyed with a great Knot, and from thence hung down in foulds to the bottom of the pedestalls ; in the midst of this Compartiment in an Ovall was written TEMPLVM AMORIS ; all these figures were in their naturall colours, bigger than the life, and the Compartiments of Gold.

Inigo Jones's rough, uninscribed sketch for a masque-scene, reproduced on the opposite page, is none the less valuable to the student of early scenic conditions because, through haziness of detail, it admits of no positive identification. It bears out, what one readily infers from records of the famous architect's life, that inspiration was largely derived from the imposing court entertainments of Florence, Ferrara and Milan.[1] Of this, its apparent incompleteness yields subtle indication. In Italy, as elsewhere, there was no such thing as irregular, or oblique, raking of the scenic backgrounds before the last decade of the seventeenth century. Practically the whole of the scene was expressed on the wings, which were so symmetrically balanced that in designing the features of the one side, Inigo Jones sufficingly indicated both. Front curtains were used in all the Stuart masques of the middle and final periods, but as they were only brought into service at the opening and the close, all the scenic changes had to be made with neatness and dispatch in full sight of the audience. No human agency was apparent, and the various mechanical transformations had their element of charm and surprise. Much on this score can be learned from a painstaking study of Inigo Jones's ground plan and sectional elevation for the scenery in D'Avenant's *Salmacida Spolia*, which, with other plans of the sort, are now preserved among the Lansdowne MSS. in the British Museum.[2] Jones's wings and flats, characteristically called "shutters", were all arranged in sets of four or five, and worked in grooves top and bottom. That is to say, there would be four double rows of wings, each provided with the component parts for four or five changes, and with the whole closed in behind by a corresponding sequence of closely grouped flats. At a considerably earlier period (notably at Oxford in 1605, when he mounted the tragedy of *Ajax Flagellifer*), Jones had adopted another

---

[1] For an account of one of these, with contemporary illustrations (Florence, 1608), see my article "A Primitive Italian Opera," in *The Connoisseur*, xv. (1906), p. 235.

[2] No. 1171. The student should be warned that the plans are not arranged in chronological order, particularly as one of them (which has been bound in upside down !) is uninscribed.

UNINSCRIBED SKETCH BY INIGO JONES FOR A MASQUE-SCENE. *[To face p.* 106.

Italian system of quick changing, that on which all the scenery was placed on perpendicular revolving triangular frames, worked from below. But owing to the fact that this system called for more stage space than could always be devoted to it, and from the more serious drawback that it only admitted of three changes, it had ultimately to be abandoned. In the Carolan masques Inigo Jones's scenery was all ranged along the two sides of an equilateral triangle, of which the base formed the proscenium opening and the apex the vanishing point, placed in the centre of the horizontal line. In accordance with this arrangement, the wings jutted out more and more in strict proportion as they receded. Not only this, but the farther they went back, the shorter they became. Each row of wings was provided with a sky-border, and as the wings grew shorter, so the borders came lower down, concealing the upper grooves. Owing to this encroachment of the top and sides upon the visual area, very little of the back flat could be seen ; in normal cases only a space of about half the measurement of the proscenium opening. Widely different, too, from latter-day principles was the equipment of the borders. These were arranged in two parts, so that they might be pulled off laterally at either end when it was desired to show one of those descending clouds, freighted with classic divinities, which were popular features of all the European court entertainments of the seventeenth century. Trivial as these points may appear, they are not without some measure of historical importance. One finds no reason to doubt that all the early Continental theatres of the public order, beginning with the Teatro di San Cassiano of Venice in 1639, for long adopted the scenic and mechanical principles which had obtained privately for at least a quarter of a century previously.[1]

It will, of course, appear incongruous to many a modern inquirer, as it did of old to Steevens, that the Jacobean

---

[1] Cf. Georges Moynet, *Trucs et Décors*, Chap. ix, "Gloires, vols et apothéoses."

stage should have lacked the illusions of painted scenery at a time when masques were mounted with decorative profusion and great mechanical ingenuity. But without the purse of Fortunatus the players could not hope to emulate the costly glories of the court. Happy was it for the well-being of English drama that the physical conditions of the stage had long been determined upon and accepted before the masque assumed new graces by the acquirement of movable scenery; happy, too, that both player and dramatist should have been tenacious in maintaining those elemental principles of dramatic construction which stimulated the imagination without glutting the eye. All lovers of literature have reason to be thankful for this truly English resoluteness, and to rejoice over the classic austerity of the old rush-strewn, tapestry-hung stage.

The Story of a Peculiar Stage Curtain

The Story of a Peculiar Stage Curtain

So scanty and perplexing is the evidence in favour of the employment of a front curtain in the ancient Greek theatre that careful inquirers are loath to make a definite pronouncement on the subject. In Greece, the usages of the curtain, if any, are purely conjectural, based on inferences and analogies. In the fifth century, when the theatre at Athens had no raised stage, and the "skene" behind the orchestra was little better than a hut or "tiring-house" for the players, material aids to the imagination were so few that a front curtain was no more requisite than in the English theatre in Elizabethan times. On the other hand, we find ourselves confronted by the circumstance that certain of the plays of Euripides, Sophocles and Aristophanes open with a scene crowded with already assembled personages. This, to Dörpfeld-Reisch, implies the sudden removal of a front curtain; but if such were employed, it is strange that in the comedies of Aristophanes changes of scene were effected while the characters remained in full view of the audience. [1]

Nothing more definite is known about the methods of the fourth century beyond the fact that the arrangements of the Greek Theatre at that period were better adapted for the use of a front curtain. The stone "skene" then adopted was furnished with "paraskenia," or projecting wings, bordering a space that could readily have been shrouded by a curtain.

When we arrive at the Hellenistic era, the well-defined usages of the early Roman theatre supply one or two illuminating analogues. It would appear that in taking over the Greek *aulaia*, the Romans merely Latinised the name by which it had been known. Still, in the Attic Theatre in its

---

[1] Awkward as was this system, it was frequently followed on the Elizabethan stage, where it was doubtless a relic of a primitive convention. For examples, see G. F. Reynolds' *Some Principles of Elizabethan Staging* (1905), Pt. ii. pp. 6-11.

final form—what with resort to revolving scenery and the absence of act divisions—there could have been little necessity for a front curtain.

In dealing with the early Roman theatre we find ourselves on much firmer ground. We are at least safe in dating from about 55 B.C. (the period of the erection of the first perfect Roman theatre of stone), the employment of a truly remarkable stage curtain,[1] remarkable not only from the peculiarity of its method of working but from the fact that it long survived the downfall of the Empire. It differed essentially from the normal theatre curtain of to-day, inasmuch as it descended beneath the stage at the opening of the play and arose when it was necessary to obscure the scene. As to the mechanism employed authorities disagree. Donaldson (who may be taken as exemplar of the old school) argues that the device was a simple curtain, drawn down through a narrow slit in the boards of the flooring, and wound up on a cylinder beneath the stage. In proof of this he gives an illustration of the small theatre at Pompeii, showing the receptacle for the curtain and its roller.[2]

To the broad theory of the reverse roller curtain an eminent theatrical architect takes serious exception. Unaware that the *aulæum* had been revived in modern times, Charles Garnier scouts the idea as utterly impracticable. Unless the cross-bar that supported the curtain was placed, he argues, at an extreme altitude, its presence would obstruct the view of the spectators on the upper seats and prove an eyesore to everybody. No matter what the altitude of the cross-bar, the great width of the stage would have necessitated five or six connecting cords between it and the curtain, so that the latter might be properly drawn up when required. With the curtain down and the action going on, these cords would divide the scene vertically, and destroy even the modicum of scenic illusion then procurable.[3]

---

[1] Besides this *aulæum*, or front curtain, there was also in the Roman theatres a *siparium*, or light inner curtain, screening only part of the stage, which could be drawn aside. Its description recalls to mind the traverses of the Elizabethan stage, and the uses of the two may have been analogous.

[2] *Theatre of the Greeks* (1875), p. 273.

[3] Charles Garnier, *Le Théâtre*, (1871), p. 233 et seq.

Mindful of these sound objections, latter-day French archæologists incline to the opinion that the *aulæum* was not so much a curtain as a screen, and that it was concealed in the double wall dividing the basement from the orchestra. According to this theory, it was at best but a makeshift, as when raised between the acts it merely served to obscure the stage from the patricians in the lower seats. The plebeians above could see over it. Recent minute examination of the two theatres of Pompeii tends to confirm the accuracy of this concept without making clear what was the precise system of working employed. In discussing the later investigations in the large theatre Herr Mau writes :

The room underneath the stage was divided into several parts. Between the front wall and that just back of it was the place for the curtain, which, as in Roman theatres, was let down at the beginning of the play, and raised at the end. The space between the parallel walls must have been covered, leaving only a narrow slit for the curtain ; otherwise it would not have been easy to go upon the stage from the steps in the orchestra. Underneath the place for the curtain is a low passage, on the vaulted roof of which are two rows of holes, cut in blocks of basalt, and evidently designed to hold upright timbers. The passage has in recent years been entirely cleared. In the floor directly under the openings in the vaulted roof and corresponding with them were square holes. In those nearer the front of the stage were remains of timbers and of square pieces of iron fitted to the ends of these, a larger and a smaller piece for each hole. It seems likely that, as Mazois suggested, hollow upright beams were set in the holes, and in them smaller hollow beams were placed, in which were still smaller poles or iron rods ; by the sliding of these up and down, the long horizontal pole on which the curtain was hung could be raised or lowered. The use of the inner row of poles has not been satisfactorily explained.[1]

Some allusions in the old poets and satirists enable us to arrive roughly at the characteristics of the Roman *aulæum*. Thanks to the clue as to its pictorial nature provided in Virgil's *Georgics* (iii. 25), we are in a position to read the riddle set in Ovid's *Metamorphoses* (iii. 111-4) :

[1] August Mau, *Pompeii, Its Life and Art* (1902), p. 140.

> Sic, ubi tolluntur festis aulaea theatris,
> Surgere signa solent, primumque ostendere vultus,
> Cetera paullatim, placidoque educta tenore
> Tota patent, imoque pedes in margine ponunt.

The reference here is to the raising of the curtain at the close of an act, when the figures embroidered upon it would gradually come into view, as if springing up from the earth.

Conversely, Horace (in whose time, by the way, act-divisions first came into vogue) has an allusion [1] to the *aulæum* being down while the performance is going on :

> Quattuor aut plures aulaea premuntur in horas,
> Dum fugiunt equitum turmae peditumque catervae.

Hitherto it has been generally assumed that the only kind of front curtain employed on the modern stage before the introduction of the upper-working roller curtain (c. 1620), was of the double order, draperies pulling up or drawing away on either side. Undoubtedly, from the simplicity of their working, these were the curtains employed on all primitive European stages, where curtains were employed at all. But the fact has been lost sight of that, owing to the tidal wave of classic influence which swept over Renaissant Italy, the *aulæum* was revived on the academic stage, and, travelling far, held its place for upwards of a century. It was not deemed sufficient to restore Plautus and Terence to the stage, and to constitute them models of form and style ; some approximation to the physical conditions of the old Roman theatre had to be made as well.

The earliest clue to the employment of the *aulæum* on the modern stage is afforded in the *Orlando Furioso* of Ariosto, the first forty cantos of which were published in 1515. In the description of the reception given to Melissa at the castle of Tristano,[2] the poet writes :

> Quale al cader de la cortine suole
> Parer, fra mille lampade, la scena,
> D'archi, et di più d'una superba mole
> D'oro, e di statue e di pitture piena.

---

[1] 2 Epist. i. 189.
[2] Canto xxxii. stanza 80.

Seeing that the first forty cantos of the poem were written at Ferrara, where Ariosto had been for some years court dramatist, and that the stanza cited crystallizes the characteristics of Renaissance stage mounting, one is safe in assuming that the falling curtain therein referred to had been for some time employed in the theatrical performances at the Ferrarese court. All doubt on this score is removed when, within the space of a few years, we find the *aulæum* in use in other Italian States.

It is curious what stumbling blocks these allusions to the old reverse curtain in ancient and modern poets have proved to the translators. Out of the difficulty presented by the passage in Ovid, Addison only extricated himself by a paraphrase based on a popular analogy. To the translators of Ariosto's stanza no such expedient was possible, and the result was that Harington, Huggins, and Hoole all stumbled over this falling curtain. Among English renderings of the quatrain, the following, in point of neatness and finish, easily ranks first :

> Thus, at the curtain's gradual fall we spy,
> Amidst a thousand lamps, a prospect fair,
> Triumphal arcs, proud piles that threat the sky,
> Statues, and fretted gold and pictures rare.

About four years after the first instalment of *Orlando Furioso* was written, or on March 6, 1519 (being the Sunday of the Carnival), *I Suppositi*, one of Ariosto's Ferrarese comedies, was presented in Rome before Leo X in the apostolic palace of Cardinal Innocenzo Cibo, the Pope's nephew. An interesting account of the performance has been preserved in a letter written two days later to the Duke of Ferrara by his envoy, Alfonso Paolucci.[1] His Holiness stationed himself at the door to regulate the admission of the guests, giving his benediction to those whom he selected—about two thousand in all. The auditorium was arranged amphitheatrically, and the Pope's throne was placed in the middle of the fifth step from the floor. The

[1] Cf. Campori, *Notizie inedite di Raffaello da Urbino*, pp. 126–129.

pictorial curtain and the scenery had been provided by the divine Rafael. On the curtain was depicted a quaint conceit : Fra Mariano, the Pope's Dominican Jester, engaged in frolic, with a weird assembly of demons. Above was the legend *Questi sono li capricci di Fra Mariano*. When all had assembled, the curtain descended to the music of the pipers, revealing a striking scene of the city of Ferrara, which the Pope minutely examined through his spy-glass, marvelling meanwhile over its beauties.

In celebration of the marriage of Dom Francesco di Medici to Joan of Austria in 1565, *La Cofanaria*, a new comedy, with intermedii, from the pen of Gio Battista Cini was performed amidst gorgeous surroundings in the Great Hall of the Ducal Palace at Florence on St. Stephen's Day. Vasari who superintended the production, afterwards wrote a pamphlet detailing its main features.[1] The stage was adorned with an *aulæum*, 16 braccia in height and 20 braccia wide, on which Federigo Zucchero had painted a fine hunting scene. According to Vasari[2] this fell at the beginning, revealing to the gaze of the astounded audience a view of Paradise, with angels seated on clouds, and indulging in vocal and instrumental harmony.[3]

Of the persistence in Italy of the *aulæum* until at least the second decade of the seventeenth century, we have clear evidence in Lodovico's pastoral *Dell' Origine di Vicenza*, as performed at Vicenza on March 5, 1612, and printed there later in the year. In the description of the prologue we read, "al cader della Cortina si discoperse la scena ornata ed illuminata con bellissimo artificio : dalla parte destra vi si vedeva il Monte Berico : dalla sinistra alcune selve ombrose." By this period force of Italian example had carried the *aulæum* to France and England, where, as in Italy, its

---

[1] *Descrizione dell' apparato della Comedia et Intermedii d'essa recitata in Firenze il giorno di S. Stefano l'anno* 1565, etc., etc. (*In Fiorenza, MDLXVI*). See Brit. Museum, press mark "604 b 20 " or " 143 a 27."

[2] John Addington Symonds fails to grasp the significance of Vasari's " al cascar della tela," and states that the curtain rose at the beginning of the performance (*Shakspere's Predecessors*, 1884, p. 327).

[3] For another example of the employment of the *aulæum* in Florence at this period, see *La Gelosia*, comedy, by A. F. Grazini (Florence, Giunti, 1568, p. 11).

use was restricted to court, or private performances. One doubts, indeed, if the principle of the reverse roller curtain was ever put into practice in any modern public theatre. In England trace of it begins with Ben Jonson's *Masque of Blackness*, as given at Whitehall on Twelfth Night, 1605. In the first printed copy of three years later we read: "First for the scene [1] was drawn a landtschap consisting of small woods, and here and there a void place filled with huntings; which falling, an artificial sea was seen to shoot forth as if it flowed to the land," &c.

As Inigo Jones was scenic artificer of this masque, the chances are that he brought the principle of the *aulæum* straight from Italy and now utilised it in England for the first time. It is noteworthy that a copy of the masque in the calligraphy of its author, differing essentially in minor detail from the quarto, now forms one of the literary treasures of the British Museum.[2] Since it bears no distinguishing title, this was evidently a first draft of the entertainment. In it the analogous description to the one quoted reads :

In the end of the designd place, there is drawne uppon a downe right cloth, straynd for the scene, a devise of landtscope, wch openinge in manner of a curtine, an artificiall sea is seene to shoote foorth it self abroade the roome, as if it flowed to ye land.[3]

Two years later one has indication of the employment of an *aulæum* in Marston's unnamed masque as presented by Lord and Lady Huntingdon at Castle Ashby in honour of the visit of the Countess of Derby.[4] In the description it figures merely as a traverse, and, according to my reading of the following passages, must have been drawn down and up at least twice :

[1] Scene = front curtain in early masque descriptions. Cf. *The Masque of Hymen* (1606), "The scene being drawn, there was *first* discovered an altar," &c.

[2] Printed by the Shakespeare Society, under title *The Twelvth Night's Revells*, in its volume on *Inigo Jones*, issued in 1848 (pp. 99–107).

[3] Since the present tense is used in the MS. in all the descriptions and the past tense in the quarto, it would appear that the MS. was prepared for presentation to the King immediately before the performance. For allusions to this practice, see *No Wit, No Help like a Woman's*, scene of the introduced *Masque of the Elements ; The Constant Maid*, iv. 3, and *The Lover's Melancholy*, iii. 3.

[4] First printed in 1801 in the fifth vol. of Todd's *Milton*. Cf. Nichols' *Progresses of King James the First*, ii. 145.

At the approach of the Countesse into the great Chamber, the hoboyes played untill the room was marshaled, which once ordered, a travers slyded away; presently a cloud was seen move up and downe almost to the topp of the great chamber, upon which Cynthia was discovered ryding . . . . Suddenly, upon this Songe, the cornets were winded, and the travers that was drawn before the Masquers sanke downe. The whole shewe presently appeereth, which presented itself in this figure; the whole body of it seemed to be the syde of a steepely assending wood, on the top of which, in a fayre oak, sat a goulden eagle, under whose wings satt in eight severall thrones the eight Masquers.

As late as 1618, when Jonson's *Pleasure Reconciled to Virtue* was given once or twice at Whitehall, the *aulæum*, in its modern conception, was still in existence at the English court. In a vivid account of the second performance of the masque, given by Orazio Busino, chaplain to the Venetian Ambassador, we read, after a description of the Banquetting Hall and of the assembling of the spectators :

In an instant a large curtain dropped, painted to represent a tent of gold cloth with a broad fringe; the background was of canvas painted blue, powdered all over with golden stars. This became [? was] the front arch of the stage, forming a drop scene, and on its being removed there appeared first of all Mount Atlas, whose enormous head was alone visible up aloft under the very roof of the theatre; it rolled up its eyes and moved its head very cleverly. [1]

In mounting the Carolan masques Inigo Jones abandoned the old *aulæum* in favour of a curtain that rose at the beginning and fell at the close. This reads as if he had then introduced the normal roller curtain of later times—a principle which, as we shall presently see, was already known of and practised in Italy. As a matter of fact, although Malone[2] long ago credited him with that innovation, we have as yet no conclusive evidence on the subject. All we know for certain is that in Shirley's *Triumph of Peace* (1634), Carew's *Cœlum Britannicum* (1634) and D'Avenant's *Salmacida Spolia*

---

[1] *Cal. State Papers, Venetian*, xv. (1617–9), p. 110. I suspect the accuracy of this translation. Clearly the curtain could not have become the front arch after it fell. Note also the mis-identification of the masque as *The Vision of Delight*.

[2] Malone's *Shakespeare*, (Dublin, 1794), ii. 55.

(1640), as well as in the pastoral of *Florimene* (1635) and other court entertainments, the curtain, at the beginning, "flew up on the sudden" or was "suddenly drawne up."[1] If the curtain employed was the Italian roller curtain of the period, working with pulleys or counterweights, it is curious that in Inigo Jones' designs for the staging of *Florimene* and *Salmacida Spolia*, preserved in the Lansdowne MSS. in the British Museum, no indications are given as to the method of operation. When one finds that only a meagre space of 18 inches intervened between the proscenium arch and the first pair of wings, one suspects that here at any rate the curtain was not situated behind the proscenium. Curiously enough, in the opening descriptions of one or two masques mention is made of the drawing of the curtain before the proscenium came into sight, showing that in these cases it was situated in front, and probably of the double, or tableau, order. Thus in Kynaston's *Corona Minervæ* (1636) we read:

A Curtaine being drawne, there is discovered a Frontispiece, wheron the Image of Minerva is seene sitting upon a stone, placed betweene two returns of a broken arch, supported by two brass statues of Mars and Mercury, standing in neeches of Corinthian worke; under, within a prospective is seen, a pav'd gallery invironed on either side, and terminated with Doricke columnes, which flying away, Minerva presents herselfe attired in her proper habit. Over the entrance, in a square, was written CORONA MINERVAE.[2]

Even at this period employment of the *aulæum* had not been wholly abandoned. On June 15, 1633, when Charles I made his state entry into Edinburgh, his advent was signalised by sundry open-air spectacles of an allegorical nature, given on stationary stages, each with its triumphal arch. When the royal cavalcade reached one particular scaffold,

---

[1] These frequent references in the Carolan masques to the curtain "flying up" seemingly indicate that it was of the double order. Grobert dwells upon the rapidity of the tableaux curtains, it being evident that if the height is equal to the breadth of the proscenium opening, "la toile qui parcourt la moitié de l'espace pour disparoitre fait une dépense de temps, moindre de moitié, que celle qui s'élève sur la totalité de la hauteur." (*De L'Exécution Dramatique, Considérée dans ses rapports avec le matériel de la Salle et de la Scène,* 1809, p. 100.)

[2] Cf. the *Tethys' Festival* of Daniel (1610). On the other hand, the elaborate opening description in *Albion's Triumph* (1632), clearly indicates that the frontispiece was in view before the curtain was "suddenly drawne up."

"a courten falling, the theatre discovered a lady attired in tissue, her haire was dressed like a cornucopia," &c., &c.[1]

Although France doubtless employed the *aulæum* at least as early as England, our first trace of it there is in 1617 in the court ballet, *La Délivrance de Renaud,* as given in the hall of the Petit-Bourbon. A painted curtain representing a palace in perspective fell at the beginning, revealing a mountain top.[2]

Whatever may have been the mechanical difficulties presented in the working of the *aulæum* in ancient times, no such difficulties had to be surmounted at the period of the Renaissance. The conditions were entirely reversed, for whereas the stage in the old Roman theatres was characterised by its extreme width, in the primitive court theatres it was remarkable for its narrowness. Some details as to the *modus operandi* of the *aulæum* in the final period of its history are given in Sabattini's curious treatise on scenery and stage mechanism, published at Ravenna in 1638.[3] According to this sound authority, three kinds of curtains were then employed in Italy. There was the primitive kind, for which he had little liking, the double curtain pulling up in loops on either side. Then there were the curtain which rolled up above and the curtain which rolled up below. Between these there was not much to choose, but in working the latter care had to be taken that the curtain did not fall upon the actors or the flambeaux (? footlights), contingencies that were apt to create panic and disorder. The curtain which rolled up was somewhat of a novelty in Sabattini's day, but seeing that it was little liable to accident, he is inclined to give it the preference. In that he foreshadows the practice of later times. But whether the seventeenth century roller curtain was of the upper or lower order, the mechanism was much the same. It consisted of a roller connected with two lateral pulleys, and worked by a rope passing over a third pulley which turned it either way. Sometimes the

---

[1] Jackson's *History of the Scottish Stage* (Edinburgh, 1793), Appendix i. p. 5.
[2] Cf. Ludovic Celler, *Les Décors, les Costumes, et la Mise en Scène au Dix-Septième Siècle,* p. 7.
[3] *Pratica di fabricar scene e Machine ne' Teatri* (1638). Bk. 1. Chap. 37.

third pulley was above, sometimes below, accordingly as it was desired to raise or pull down the curtain.

At what period the normal ascending curtain of to-day first came into use in the English theatre it would be difficult to say. Before one has examined all the pros and cons one is inclined to jump to the conclusion that the period synchronised with the introduction and regular employment of scenery, say somewhere about 1664. But the cautious investigator, confronted by disturbing data, will hesitate to advance an opinion. There is some reason to believe that the double curtains, pulling up on either side, were the first employed in the English scenic theatre and that the principle obtained until at least the second decade of the eighteenth century. In Mrs. Centlivre's first play, the tragedy of *The Perjur'd Husband*, as performed at Drury Lane in 1700, the opening direction reads, "The Curtains fly up, and discover a Mask in Pizalto's house". One recalls also that in the description given by "Charles Easy" in *The Spectator* of December 5, 1711 (No. 240), of the beau who aired his figure on the stage, it is told how he went "behind the curtain and obliged us with several views of his person from every opening."

EARLY FRENCH PLAYERS IN ENGLAND

Early French Players in England

Viewing the fact that England had experienced considerably over four centuries of French acting before hostility to the foreign player finally exhausted itself in the famous "Monte Christo" riot of 1848, the stage historian might at first sight be disposed to think that a clue to the persistency of racial antipathies on the part of audiences from Garrick's early time onwards could possibly be found by sedulous seeking in the sociological records of remoter ages. Indeed, one has only to dwell upon the characteristic stubbornness of the British mind in maintaining a prejudice, its inborn capacity for what Matthew Arnold called provinciality of thought, to lend colour to a specious solution. This would lie in the abortive attempts made in the twelfth century to impose upon the conquered Anglo-Saxon populace the Norman-French miracle-plays. But one should consider much too curiously to consider so. No unbroken tradition of hostility on the part of the commonalty can be traced from the Norman period onwards. For long the grudge, if it existed, had nothing to feed upon. No appeal was made in the beginning by foreign players to the people at large. The story of French acting in England in the first two centuries of its course is well-nigh inextricably associated with the intrigues of the crown and the traffic of the court. Riotous demonstrations in the mid-eighteenth century over the visits of foreign players, although primarily conditioned by transient national feeling, were largely due to the fact that the fight in the open for a free hearing had been too long delayed.

As indicated there was a curious intermingling of the fortunes of the Early French players in England with the vicissitudes of the British crown, and the rise and fall of dynasties. The exile of a Tudor and a Stuart had much to do with the fostering of a taste for foreign acting among the English nobles. To the politic lingering in Brittany and France of King Henry VII, when Earl of Richmond, was due the first recorded journey of a French troupe across the channel. During his prolonged sojourn in Paris in 1483, the coming king had ample opportunity, in the full flush of his young manhood, to revel in the pungent *soties* and farces of the Clercs de la Basoche and the Enfants sans Souci. It may be, indeed, that it was one or other of these famed organisations that pioneered the way for the French player in England. What more likely than that desire on the part of the play-loving Tudor to renew some of the delights of his Parisian experience led to negotiations for the bringing over of one or both companies? On that point, however, records are silent. It is impossible to determine the identity of these first French visitants, or what they acted. But of their coming to the English court we are fully assured through the following important entries in the two extant account books showing Henry the Seventh's daily expenses from 1492 to 1509:

8 Henry VII, January 6. — — To the Frenche Pleyers for a rewarde. — — — £ 1. 0. 0.
9 Henry VII, January 4. To the Frenche Pleyers in rewarde — — — £ 2 0. 0.[1]

One must confess one's inability to believe that a troupe of French players remained for a whole year at the English court, if even the nature of the entries did not tend to disprove any such supposition. It may be taken with safety that these payments indicate two successive visits, and possibly of two separate companies, in the years 1494 and 1495. It is distinctly unfortunate that the early account books of the court have not come down to us, as there is some reason to believe that a body of French players visited England in 1489. The following citation from the Scottish

---

[1] Collier, *Hist. Eng. Dram. Poetry*, i. 49. No suspicion can be entertained as to the genuineness of the entries. Malone had known of them previously, and cites one under a wrong date.

Exchequer Rolls, proving a performance before King James IV at Dundee in 1490, is apposite :

Item, on Fryda the xxiij Julij in Dunde to the king to gif the Franschemen that playt . . . . xx unicornis xviij li. [1]

Although positive evidence as to the pieces performed at the English court in 1494 and 1495 is wholly lacking, grounds exist for sensible conjecture. Apart altogether from its perennial popularity, there is reason to believe that the epoch-marking farce of *Maistre Pierre Patelin* figured among the selections from the French repertory acted before the King. Attention has already been drawn to the fact that it was not through Rabelais the play began its influence on English literature. [2] The story of "hym that payde his dette with crienge bea" had appeared in an English collection of *Merry Tales* at least as early as 1535, and possibly in 1525. Holbrook hazards the conjecture that "one or more of the many editions of *Maistre Pierre Patelin* printed in France had crossed the Channel before 1500". It may be, however, that England made its first acquaintance with the immortal farce in acted form, at the hands of the French comedians. An important side issue attaches itself to this surmise. The construction of *Maistre Pierre Patelin* demanded a setting of the multiple order—what is known in France as a *décor simultané*. To show that it had been acted before Henry VII at this perod would be to afford the investigator a *terminus a quo* from which to date that peculiar system of court dramaturgy which flourished in the time of Lyly and was not without its ultimate influence upon the popular drama. [3]

---

[1] Dibdin, *Annals of the Edinburgh Stage*, p. 15.

[2] Richard Holbrook, *The Farce of Master Pierre Patelin* (Boston, 1905), p. 109.

[3] I am not unmindful of the great service rendered by Chambers in showing (what Collier and others have so long obscured) that the primitive English miracle play was stationary, with a multiple setting, and that the processional play was a later variant. (Cf. *The Mediæval Stage*, ii. 134). But assuming that the remoter court dramatists derived the the principle of the simultaneous scene from the miracle-play, what is the earliest court play in which the principle was followed ? Could it have preceded the first visit of the French comedians ? My earliest trace of a secular play with multiple setting is Lyndsay's *Satyre of the Three Estaitis*, performed in the open at Cupar in 1535 and at Edinburgh in 1540. It is significant that this play was derived from a French source.

Unless an entry in a later account book can be very liberally interpreted, no further visits of the French players can be traced for over one hundred and thirty years. In "The Kyngs boke of paymentis, begynnyng primo die Octi A° 21 Regis Henrici VII^mi" occurs the following entry:

23 Henry VII Oct. 4. To 6 Mynstrells of Fraunce that played affore the kings grace at Habyndon . . . . . £ 2. 0. 0.[1]

"Five straunge Mynstrells" had also "played afore the King" a little better than two years previously, but viewing the interpretation put on the word "minstrell" in the legislative enactments of the period,[2] one is not disposed to believe that either troupe performed plays. On the other hand, it seems highly improbable that no further visit of the French comedians took place before 1629. Apart from Henry the Eighth's predilection for foreign artists and musicians there is reason to infer the occasional presence of French players at his court. Visits of the sort would account for the inspiration undoubtedly derived by John Heywood from Gallic *sotie* and farce.[3] The *Dyalogue du fol et du Sage* and the farces *D'un pardonner, d'un triacleur, et d'une taverniere* and of *Pernet qui va au vin*—all pressed more or less into English service by Heywood—might have pleased the burly King so well in their original form as to create a desire on his part to have them ready to hand in the native repertory. And in this connection one must remember that John Heywood, as player of the virginals, was a servant of the King's household.

Strive as we may to fill up this mysterious and perplexing gap, conjecture can only be taken for what it is worth. The fact remains that no further visit of the French comedians is recorded until 1629, when the arrival of a luckless and utterly unfriended troupe was marked by two distinct

---

[1] Collier, i. 47–8.

[2] Ibid, i. 60 note.

[3] Cf. K. Young, "The Influence of French Farce upon the Plays of John Heywood", in *Modern Philology*, June, 1904.—The *Enfants Sans Souci* were in disgrace in 1516, and acted for a time in the provinces. They might possibly have revisited England at this period. See also Sir Sidney Lee's *The French Renaissance in England*, pp. 372–4.

innovations. So far as we know, the newcomers were the first of their kind to bring with them women players, and the first to make appeal to the ordinary playgoer. Expelled from their native country for reasons not apparent, they were frowned upon by the court and left to the tender mercies of the British philistine.

It is a moot point whether this unhappy visit marks the first appearance of an actress in the English theatre. Although one feels assured that no very serious attempt had previously been made to break in upon the time-honoured custom of allotting female parts to boys, the fact cannot be overlooked that Coryat, in discussing the characteristics of the Venetian theatre, says, " Here I observed certaine things that I never saw before, for I saw women act, a thing that I never saw before, though I have heard that it hath been some times used in London; and they performed it with as good a grace, action, gesture and whatsoever convenient for a player, as ever I saw any masculine actor".[1] Possibly Coryat's allusion may have been to the appearance of ladies in masques at court; at any rate, no record of the employment of women players in the English theatres of his time has come down to us. [2]

The precise period of the arrival of this ill-treated French company is determined by an entry in the Office Book of Sir Henry Herbert, Master of the Revels :

For the Allowinge of a French Company to play a farse at Black-fryers, this 4 of November, 1629, ... £ 2. 0. 0.

Prynne's evidence as to the reception accorded to the foreign players is very contradictory. It might readily mislead us as it misled Malone, had we not other and sounder data to go upon. In discussing the question of women on the stage, Prynne first says, "they had such Frenchwomen actors in a play, not long since personated in Blackfriars playhouse, to which there was great resort." [3] This savours

---

[1] *Coryat's Crudities* (1611), p. 247.
[2] Cf. Thomas Jordan's lines headed " A Prologue to introduce the first woman that came to act on the stage, in the tragedy called The Moor of Venice ", first printed in *A Royal Arbour of Loyal Poesie*, c. 1662.
[3] *Histriomastix* (1633), p. 215.

of approval of the innovation on the part of the public,
but a couple of hundred pages farther on one comes
across a marginal note to the effect that "some Frenchwomen, or monsters rather, in Michaelmas term 1629,
attempted to act a French play at the playhouse in Blackfriars, an impudent, shameful, unwomanish, gracelesse, yf
not more than whorishe attempt."¹ This "attempted to
act" seriously qualifies the earlier statement "to which there
was great resort". The new complexion thus put upon the
matter gains confirmation from a passage in a private letter
sent by one Thomas Brande to some person unknown, and
bearing date (apparently without year) "the 8th Nov.":²

> Furthermore you should know, that laste daye certaine vagrant
> French players, who had been expelled from their owne contrey,
> and those women, did attempt, thereby giving just offence to all
> vertuous and well-disposed persons in this town, to act a certain
> lascivious and unchaste comedye, in the French tonge at the
> Blackfryers. Glad I am to saye they were hissed, hooted, and pippin-
> pelted from the stage, so as I do not thinke they will soone be ready
> to trie the same againe.—Whether they had license for so doing I
> know not, but I do know that if they had license, it were fit that
> the Master³ be called to account for the same.

Apparently no one in authority thought fit to challenge
Sir Henry Herbert for the course he had taken in the
matter. A little over a fortnight later he permitted the unfortunate exiles to give another performance, this time at a
public theatre. The entry in his own handwriting recording
this omits mention of the fee, but £2 is understood :

> For allowinge the Frenche att the Red Bull for a daye, 22 Nov.
> 1629.

Another three weeks elapse, and then we learn of the
wretched foreigners at a third house, again for a single day
only, and with very ill success :

¹ Ibid, p. 414.
² Discovered by Collier in the Archives of the Archbishop of Canterbury at
Lambeth, and printed by him in *Annals*, ii. 23. He conjectures that the letter was sent
to Laud when Bishop of London. As no axe is ground with the details one has no
reason to suspect forgery.
³ "Of the Revels" interpolated by Collier within brackets.

For allowinge of a Frenche companie att the Fortune to play one afternoone, this 14 of Dec. 1629 . . . . £ 1. 0. 0.

Appended is the note—showing that for all his rapacity Herbert was not without generous impulses : " I should have had another peece, but in respect of their ill fortune, I was content to bestow a peece back."

Basing evidently on Prynne, who was a prejudiced witness (not only because of his whole attitude towards the stage but from his especial abhorrence of women players), Collier thinks the ill-reception of the French was due to the presence of actresses in the company.[1] He makes no allowances for their possible raggedness nor for the bias created by their unprotected state. Jealousy on the part of the native players might easily have aroused a certain amount of organised opposition. Brande's communication has the air of having been inspired from some such source, and his charge of obscenity was clearly a subterfuge, calculated to stir into action some powerful ecclesiastic. One has no belief in an early seventeenth-century audience expressing vigorous disapprobation solely as censor of morals. Indecency, thick and slab, had been indulged in with complacency by the Elizabethan dramatists.

Collier's conclusions on this point, allied with an imperfect knowledge of the contemporary French stage, led to his hazarding of an absurd conjecture in connection with the more important French visit of 1635. Overlooking the fact that the later company was of a superior order and enjoyed the protection of the Queen, he takes leave to think they met with little opposition because they had the good sense to profit by the experience of their predecessors, and leave their actresses behind them. This contention is easily refuted. The French players of the time were not habituated like the English to the casting of female parts to boys.[2] Not only that, but the pieces presented by the later company called for careful acting on the spindle side.

---

[1] *Annals*, ii. 66. This view has been adopted by Prof. A. W. Ward, in *English Dramatic Literature*, i. 418.

[2] This refers only to youthful characters. Elderly women were mostly represented by men. For fuller details see Eugène Rigal, *Le Théâtre Français avant la Période Classique*, pp. 172–81.

Whether or not the newcomers were brought over directly at the instance of the Queen, they signalised their arrival by performing before her in private on February 15, 1634-5. A favourable impression was created, and her Majesty at once induced the King to take the company under his patronage. Two days later the French players appeared before the court at the Cockpit in Whitehall, giving a performance of *La Melise, ou les Princes Reconnus*, a comic pastoral of Durocher, "with good approbation".[1] The King was so gratified that he not only gave the company a reward of ten pounds, but immediately granted them a remarkable concession. On February 20th following, Herbert records :

> This day being friday, and the 20 of the same monthe, the kinge tould mee his pleasure, and commanded mee to give order that this Frenche company should playe the too sermon daies in the weeke, during their time of playing in Lent, and in the house of Drury-lane, where the queenes players usually playe.

> The king's pleasure I signified to Mr. Beeston, the same day, who obeyd readily.

> The house-keepers are to give them by promise the benefit of their interest for the too days of the first weeke."[2]

Collier points out that this unexampled concession was in nowise injurious to Beeston's Cockpit company as the Wednesdays and Fridays in Lent, on which the French were permitted to play, were tabooed to the English. The Cockpit in Drury Lane (not to be confounded with the Cockpit in Whitehall) was a private theatre with a select audience, one eminently well disposed to take its cue from the royal lead. That it did so in this instance is shown by Herbert's statement to the effect that the French players

---

[1] Cf. *The Athenaeum*, No. 3326, where a wrong date for the performance is given. Mr. Swinburne here expresses the opinion that the piece might have been the *Mélite, ou Les Fausses Lettres* of Pierre Corneille, first acted in 1629, but printed four years earlier. There is really, however, no valid reason to dispute Herbert's statement. Durocher's was the newer piece, having been produced in 1633.

[2] Malone's *Shakespeare by Boswell* (1821), iii. 121. The French players were to have the entire profits of the first two performances, but subsequently were to fall in line with English theatrical custom and share the receipts with the house-keepers.

while there "got two hundred pounds at least, besides many rich clothes were given them".[1] To Herbert as Master of the Revels the visitors made proffer of a fee of £10, but so high was their standing at court that he thought it politic to refuse, jotting down as his reason that " he wished to render the Queen, his mistress, an acceptable service". Having momentarily conquered his greed, he did not stop there but made it his business to obtain permission from the King for the French to continue performing at the Cockpit during Passion week, a concession which must have occasioned much jealousy and heart-burning. [2] No English company had ever been allowed to give representations during that solemn period.

With the arrival of Easter, Beeston's players resumed full control of the private house in Drury Lane. On Easter Monday, April 4, the French company appeared before the court at Whitehall in *Le Trompeur Puni, ou Histoire Septentrionale*. Unless one misinterprets Herbert's somewhat ambiguous entry,[3] Scudéri's tragi-comedy was better liked than the earlier pastoral. It had then been about four years on the acting list. A still newer tragi-comedy, the *Alcimedon* of Duryer, was given at Whitehall " with good approbation" on the 16th of the month.

Dilatory as Charles I. was in paying his English players, he lost no great time in rewarding the French for their three performances at court. On May 10th following, a warrant was issued directing £30 to be paid " unto Mons. Josias Floridor, for himself and the rest of the French players, for three plays acted by them at the Cockpit". [4]

These details indirectly reveal that the French sojourners were no important company direct from Paris but merely a troupe of strollers. Josias de Soulas,[5] who, under his stage name of Floridor, was to become a favourite at the Théâtre

---

[1] Vide op. cit.   [2] Ibid.   [3] Ibid.
[4] i. e. at Whitehall. Cf. Chalmers, *Apology.* p. 508.
[5] After due consideration I adopt the routine opinion, as expressed by Hawkins, *Annals of the French Stage from its Origin to the Death of Racine*, i. 148. But there is some reason to believe from an entry in Sir Henry Herbert's Office Book (vide infra), that Floridor's real name was Josias d'Aunay.

du Marais, as " orator " in 1643, and to proceed thence to
the Hôtel de Bourgogne, had not yet made his début in
Paris. The well-nurtured son of a German father and a
French mother, he began life in the army but speedily
turned stroller, and was manager of his own troupe before
thirty. Although London saw him in the first flush of his
career, he had already added to his natural powers and graces
considerable artistic judgment, so that his success at Whitehall is not to be marvelled at. Stage history cherishes his
memory as the first French tragedian who departed from
convention, and spoke, instead of chanting.

One favour followed another at the hands of the King
until the lucky visitors were finally allowed to set up a
theatre of their own. The authority for this is again Sir
Henry Herbert :

A warrant granted to Josias d'Aunay, Hurfries de Lau, and
others, for to act playes at a new house in Drury-lane, during
pleasure, ye 5 may 1635.

The king was pleased to commande my Lord Chamberlain to
direct his warrant to Monsieur Le Fevure, to give him a power
to contract with the Frenchmen for to builde a playhouse in the
manage house, which was done accordinglye by my advise and
allowance. [1]

Herbert adds in a marginal note, " These Frenchmen
were commended unto mee by the queene, and have passed
through my handes, *gratis* ". Later on, however, they gave
Blagrave, Herbert's deputy, "three pounds for his pains ".
Acting at the new playhouse probably began early in May.
On April 18, the Lord Chamberlain had recorded in his
Memorandum Book that the King had commanded him
"to signify his royal pleasure that the French comedians
(having agreed with Mons. le Fabure), may erect a stage,
scaffolds and seats, and all other accommodations, which
shall be convenient, and act and present interludes and
stage plays, at his house during his Majesty's pleasure
without any disturbance, hindrance or interruption." [2]

[1] *Shakespeare by Boswell* (1821), iii. 121 ff.
[2] Chalmers, *Apology*, p. 506.

No evidence exists to show whether or not the foreign players made any employment of scenery during their visit, but on divers counts it hardly seems probable their performances were given on a bare, or merely tapestried, stage. The poorest of provincial French companies at this period were habituated to the use of a modest pictorial background, and generally carried a scene-painter in their train. Moreover the court at Whitehall had now grown accustomed to look for luxurious mounting of the masques owing to the brilliant catering of Inigo Jones, and it is doubtful whether the King would have tolerated a theatrical representation given with the Spartan simplicity of Elizabethan times. Assuming, however, that the French players used scenery, the next difficulty that arises is to determine what kind. On the one hand we know that in the court masques Inigo Jones had long adopted the principle of successive backgrounds, employing scenery that changed rapidly, in full sight of the audience; on the other, it is equally certain that French strollers were still following the quaint old system of the *décor simultané*. In Paris, the public theatres were only just abandoning the multiple setting, and it may be taken (although the fact has never been demonstrated) that the production of *Le Prince Déguisé* of Scudéri marks the regular introduction to the French stage of successive scenery.

No clue presents itself as to the repertory of Floridor's company at the new house in Drury Lane. Little more can be gleaned about their doings, save that they seem to have acted there, on and off, until the close of the year. Malone cites an entry from the Office Book of the Lord Chamberlain, showing that in 1636 a warrant was issued for £10, payable to "Josias Floridor, for himself and the rest of the French players, for a tragedy by them acted before his Majesty in December last."[2]

---

[2] *Shakespeare by Boswell*, iii. 122. On December 23, 1635, a troupe of Spanish players under John Novarro performed before the King and were granted £10 in reward. There had been several earlier visits by Italian players, but no previous Spanish company is recorded, and none probably was seen again for a couple of centuries.

French acting was now so much in the air at Whitehall that' the Maids of Honour must needs indulge in it. Herbert's memorandum of the event is written, appropriately enough, in French :

Le Pastorale de Florimene fust representé devant le Roy et la Royne, le Prince Charles, et le Prince Palatin, le 21 Decem. jour de St. Thomas, par les filles Françoise de la Royne, et firent tres bien, dans la grande sale de Whitehall, aux depens de la Royne.[1]

It is difficult to determine whether the pastoral of *Florimene* was some old piece, already performed in France, or whether it had been specially written by some courtier for the occasion. No play so called can be traced on the French stage of the early seventeenth century. *Florimene* was presented at Whitehall with scenery by Inigo Jones,[2] and, according to a synopsis of the entertainment printed at the time in English, was arranged in five acts, with *intermezzi* of the Four Seasons. Seeing that the antimasques at court were invariably performed by professional players,[3] it is not improbable that the grotesque characters in the interludes were sustained by members of Floridor's company. That the dancing between the acts took place, not on the raised stage where the pastoral was represented, but on the floor of the hall, can readily be seen by examination of Inigo Jones's ground-plot for the stage and its attendant auditorium. The characters in the interludes came on at first within strictly scenic regions, descending to the floor of the hall by stairs placed at the two ends of the proscenium front.

The native player folk would have been considerably more than human and very uncharacteristic of their class

[1] Not the first time, apparently, that a French play had been acted by the ladies of the Court. In *Cal. State Papers, Dom. Ser.* xii. (1625-6), 4, one finds a letter of Sir Benjamin Rudyerd to Sir Francis Nethersole informing him that the Christmas of 1625 was to be spent at Hampton Court, with plays. "The demoiselles mean to present a French pastoral wherein the Queen is a principal actress." But on December 31 he writes again from Hampton Court to say "the Court removes on Tuesday next and keeps the end of Christmas at Whitehall. The Queen intends to act her pastoral at Denmark House."

[2] The original ground-plot for the scenery, &c., is preserved in the Lansdowne MSS. in the British Museum, and the design for the special proscenium in the Duke of Devonshire's collection of Inigo Jones's drawings at Chatsworth.

[3] Cf. Dekker, Epistle Dedicatorie to Endymion Porter in *Dekker his Dreame* (1620) : " Besides, I herein imitate the most courtly Revellings ; for if Lords be in the Grand Masque, in the Antimasque are players."

had they not experienced some heart-pangs over the favour shown to their foreign rivals in high quarters. If envy existed it was all the more excruciating from having to be cloaked. There could be no stirring up of popular prejudices against those whom the Queen had taken under her protection, and for once the pippin-pelters were impotent. All the native players could do was to take a poor revenge by mimicking the fervid delivery and profuse gesticulation of the strangers within the gate. Precisely at what juncture this mild retaliation was attempted one cannot say, probably at the close of 1635. All that is known for certain is that somewhere about that period the Cockpit company brought out a comedy by Henry Glapthorne called *The Ladies' Priviledge* [1] in which the whole point of a scene in the second act depended upon the skill with which the actor of Adorni burlesqued the characteristics of the French players. Possibly there was no venom in the caricature: one notes on the imprint of the comedy that it had been twice performed before the King at Whitehall. But, as will be remarked on reading the following citation of the salient portion of the scene, the mimicry in question was a matter of sheer improvisation, and its nature and intensity may have varied with the place of performance :

> *La(ctantio).*   But Adorni,
> What thinke you of the French ?
> *Ad(orni).* Very ayry people, who participate
> More free than earth; yet generally good
> And nobly disposition'd, something inclining
>
> > *Ent. Corim(ba).*
>
> To overweening fancy—This Lady
> Tells my remembrance of a Comick scene,
> I once saw in their Theatre.
> *Bon(ivet).*   Add it to
> Your former courtesies, and expresse it.
> *Ador.*   Your entreaty
> Is a command, if this grave Lady please,
> To act the Lady I must court.

---

[1] First printed in 1640.

Cor. Why doe you thinke I cannot play the woman ? I
have plaid a womans part about twenty, twenty years agoe in
a Court Masque, and tho' I say't as well as some o' them, and
have bin courted too. But it is truth, I have a foolish quality,
as many more women are guilty of besides myselfe, I always
love them best, which slight me most, and scorne those that
doe court mee : look you Signior, if 't be a lovers part you are
to act :
Take a black spot or two, I can furnish you.
'Twill make your face more amorous, and appeare
More gracious in your Mistris eyes.
   Ador.   Stande faire Lady,
   Cor. Tis your part to stande faire sir; doubt not my car-
      riage—
O most rare man : sincerely, I shall love the French
The better while I live for this.

               Ador. Acts furiously.

Nay pray sir, gentlemen entreat the man
To pacifie his wrath, tell him Ile love him,
Rather than see him rage thus.
   Bon. He would have just reason to be mad indeed then,
      but now
The Mood is alter'd.

               Ador. acts ut antea.

   Cor. Excellently ravishing : this of force
To make the hardest hearted Lady love him :
Can I intreat him but to teach my Cosen
Some of his French, he will for ever be engallanted.

         Enter Eurione and Frangipan.

   Bon.   Beautious Cosen,
Y' ave mist the quaintest sport; honest Adorni
You would endeare this Lady to you, would you
Please to react it.
   Ador. Nay, if you make me common once, farewell ;
I am not for your company.

As Adorni presently undertakes to teach Frangipan
French, we may conclude that in his "acting" he babbles
French, or something supposed to represent it.

Viewed from our present standpoint, the exile of Charles II proved much more far-reaching in its ultimate results than the exile of the Earl of Richmond (afterwards Henry VII). In literature and the arts French exemplars were servilely followed throughout the easy-going Stuart's reign. One traces their domination in the new heroic drama, in the recurrence of the theatrical couplet, in Restoration music, and in the florid accessories of the new scenically adorned stage. The King brought back with him a Gallic hedonism that debased the moral currency. French parasites of all sorts and conditions swarmed at Whitehall, and French (or French-Italian) comedians were seldom long absent from England. The King had hardly settled himself on his throne before the first French troupe came over. It occupied for a time the old Cockpit in Drury Lane, the scene of Floridor's early triumphs. Pepys, who seldom missed any sight that was going, from an Italian puppet show to a bearded woman, took his long-suffering wife to see the French players on August 30, 1661. But the impression gained was far from favourable, constraining him to jot down in his diary, "to the French comedy, which was so ill-done, and the scenes and company and everything else so nasty and out of order and poor, that I was sick all the while in my mind to be there." A rare pamphlet in the Malone collection in the Bodleian library apparently reveals to us full details of the play seen by Pepys on this occasion. It consists of eighteen pages in English and French, and the imprint runs :

The | Description | of the | Great Machines | Of the Descent of Orpheus | Into Hell. | Presented by the French Commedians at the Cockpit in Drury Lane. | The Argument | Taken out of the Tenth and Eleavnth Books of Ovid's Metamorphosis. | London | Printed for Robert Crofts at the Crown in Chancery Lane, | 1661.

The piece in question was probably *Le Mariage d'Orphée et d'Eurydice* of Chapoton, the scene of the fourth act in which is laid in the infernal regions. It dates from 1648, but, curiously enough, was revived in Paris in 1662. One

can only account for Pepys' depreciation of the performance by the supposition that the small stage of the Cockpit
was ill-adapted for the elaborate scenic effects required.
That the company was not altogether so despicable as the
diarist indicates is shown by the fact that it made frequent
appearances before the King at Whitehall. Evelyn records
the performance of a French comedy at court on December
16, 1661 ; and exactly six days earlier a warrant had been
issued " to pay to John Chemnoveau 300 l. as the King's
bounty to be distributed to the French comedians ".[1]

It is noteworthy that once the foreign players became
assured of the Merry Monarch's countenance, they made
careful preparation for their visits, bringing with them all
the necessary accessories. We have no evidence of any
such course being followed in earlier Stuart times. Among
the State Papers preserved in the Record Office is a copy
of a Permit dated August 25, 1663, authorising "the French
comedians to bring over their scenes, stage decorations,"
&c. Some historical value attaches itself to this document
inasmuch as we have no other record of the visit implied.
But the coming of the French players to England was now
of sufficient frequency to justify Sir William D'Avenant
in the mild fun he poked at them. This was heard in his
composite piece, *A Playhouse to be Let*, produced at the
Duke's theatre in Lincoln's Inn Fields in the Long Vacation of 1663.[2] In the first act, which in earlier days would
have been called an induction, a whimsical picture is drawn
of the dire straits of the native players in their off season.
As the theatre is to be let, there are several applicants for
temporary lesseeship, and the remaining four acts show
the performances (or rehearsals) given under their auspices.
One of the aspirants is a Frenchman who has crossed the
Channel with a troupe, and who is anxious to perform a
farce in broken English. This affords the *raison d'être* for

---

[1] Jusserand, *Shakespeare in France*, p. 131. In *Cal. of State Papers, Dom. Series,
Charles II*, the name is given as "Channoveau".

[2] Dr. Edward Browne includes the play in the list of pieces seen by him at that
house in 1662-3 (cf. Mem. Book in Sloane MS., 1900) ; and the epilogue to the piece
makes allusion to the fact that the sterner critics were out of town.

the version given in the second act of Molière's *Sganarelle*, *ou le Cocu Imaginaire*, a comedy which, it will be remembered, had originally been produced at the Petit Bourbon in May, 1660.

D'Avenant in his proem makes no bones about pandering to the blunt prejudices of an English audience. Says the Player to the French manager:

> Your farces are a kind of mongrel plays,
> But sir, I believe all French farces are
> Prohibited commodities and will
> Not pass current in England.

And then the Tirewoman is made the mouthpiece of British sentiment.

> I like not that these French *pardonney moys*
> Should make bold with old England.

Doubtless it would be idle to infer that the ridicule of D'Avenant had any serious influence, but the fact remains that at this juncture there is a considerable break in our records. Beyond Pepys' reference to the magnificent singing of a French eunuch in *The Faithful Shepherdess* at the Theatre Royal, in October, 1668, we have no further note of the French in London for a period of nine years. Meanwhile, however, there had been some exchange of compliments, artistically speaking, between the two countries. The facetious Joe Haines had been sent over to amuse the French court, and abundantly fulfilled his mission. Perwich writes from Paris to Sir Joseph Williamson on October 25, 1679:

I think I told you something of Jo. Haines; now I can add that he behaved himselfe there[1] to everybody's wonder, and diverted the King by severall English dances, to his great satisfaction and that of all the court. I believe he will have a present made him. If you should think it convenient, it would do him a great kindnesse in England to mention him in the *Gazette* among the King's divertisements at Chambort, where, whilst the Balets were preparing, he hunted the wild bore and pheasants. By the enclosed you see

[1] Evidently St. Germain in Laye from the context.

the severall entries and manner of the Balet ; between every one Haines had order to dance by himselfe, and notwithstanding the confronting of the best dancers, carried it off to admiration, and was ordred to dance some things twice over.[1]

Of the visit paid to London by some French players early in 1672 little is known save what can be gathered from an allusion in one of Dryden's prologues. It would appear, however, that they performed at one of the regular playhouses—possibly in that old haunt, the Cockpit in Drury Lane—and were responsible for two striking theatrical innovations. There was no such thing as numbered seats or advance booking in those days, and playgoers, irrespective of rank, had to make early resort to the theatre to secure good places. The visitors introduced the French custom of sending footmen to purchase and occupy seats until claimed by their actual owners, a custom that eventually gave rise to much disturbance in the house, but remained in vogue for over a century.[2] The other novelty lay in the employment of coloured daybills to allure audiences, a device that had never struck the tradition-ridden English manager.

On January 25, 1671-2, or about the period of the arrival of the innovators, The Theatre Royal in Bridges Street was burnt down. During the process of rebuilding, the King's players had to content themselves with the small, ill-equipped theatre in Lincoln's Inn Fields. Stripped bare by misfortune, they were unduly sensitive to the lash of competition. Dryden makes bitter reference to their state in the prologue to *Arviragus and Philicia*, first spoken in the following March or April :

> A brisk French troop is grown your dear delight;
> Who with broad bloody bills[3] call you each day
> To laugh and break your buttons at the play ;

---

[1] *Dispatches of William Perwich* (Camden Society, 1905), p. 116.—Haines was evidently associated with the first performance of *Le Bourgeois Gentilhomme* at Chambord on October 14, 1670.

[2] Cf. Robert W. Lowe, *Thomas Betterton*, p. 18. For the trouble which ensued and the duration of the custom, see John Fyvie, *Comedy Queens of the Georgian Era*, p. 14.

[3] In Paris at this period each theatre used differently coloured daybills. Red bills were the prerogative of the Hôtel de Bourgogne. See V. Fournel, *Curiosités Théatrales* (1878), p. 126.

Or see some serious piece which we presume
Is fallen from some incomparable plume ;
. . . .
We dare not on your privilege entrench
Or ask you why you like 'em ? They are French.
Therefore some go with courtesy exceeding,
Neither to hear nor see, but show their breeding.
Each lady striving to outlaugh the rest ;
To make it seem they understand the jest.
Their countrymen come in, and nothing pay,
To teach us English where to clap the play.

A trifle over a year later another French company came
to London for a spell. Their visit is referred to in the epilogue written by Dryden for delivery at Oxford by the King's
players in the Long Vacation of 1673 :

Heaven for our sins this summer has thought fit
To visit us with all the plagues of wit.
A French troop first swept all things in its way,
But these hot Monsieurs were too quick to stay ;
Yet to our cost in that short time we find,
They left their itch of novelty behind.
The Italian Merry-Andrews took their place,
And quite debauched the stage with lewd grimace.

The Italian comedians from Paris, under Tiberio Fiorelli
(better known as Scaramuccio, from his favourite character),
came to England in May, 1673, and acted at Whitehall till
the second week in September. On the 22nd August, James
Vernon wrote a gossiping letter from court to Sir Joseph
Williamson, telling him incidentally that

Senior Scaramouchio and his band have begged his Majesty's
leave to returne, their affaires requiring their presence att home. It
seemes Baptiste hath a grant of the Palais Royal to play the operas
in it, and these gentlemen are to remoove to Sourdiacs Theatre
in the Faunbourg St. Germains; and now I am among players I
ought not to omitt to acquaint your Excellency that the Duke's
house are preparing an Opera and great machines. They will have
dansers out of France, and St. André comes over with them, who

is to have a pension of the King, and a patent of master of the compositions for ballets, etc.[1]

The opera here referred to as in preparation was undoubtedly Shadwell's version of *Psyche*, which I take to have been brought out at the Duke's (notwithstanding old Downes' somewhat later dating[2]) about Christmas, 1673. One cannot well see to what other production Evelyn's record of January 5, 1673-4, could have applied. " I saw an Italian opera in music ", he writes in his Diary, " the first that had been in England of this kind." That *Psyche*, after being " long expected ", as Downes tells us, was eventually brought out about this period is indicated by the following allusion in Dryden's prologue for the opening of the New Theatre Royal, as spoken there on March 26, 1673-4 :

> Whilst scenes, machines, and empty operas reign,
> And for the pencil you the pen disdain,
> While troops of famished Frenchmen hither drive,
> And laugh at those upon whose alms they thrive.

The particular sort of rivalry which the King's players had now to combat was soon to be experienced within the walls of their new house, where the newly-constituted Academy of Music had arranged to produce, for the first time in England, genuine French Opera. The approximate period of the operatic season at the Theatre Royal can be arrived at by two entries in the Lord Chamberlain's Accounts :

1674, March 27. Warrant to deliver to Monsieur Grabu, or to such as he shall appoynt, such of the scenes remayning in the theatre at Whitehall, as shall be useful for the French Opera at the theatre in Bridges street[3] and the said Monsieur Grabu to return them again safely after 14 days' tyme to the theatre at Whitehall.

1674, April 27. Warrant to deliver to Sir Christopher Wren, His Majesty's surveyor generall of the works, the scenes belonging to

---

[1] *Letters to Sir Joseph Williamson at Cologne* (Camden Society), i. 179. André certainly came over subsequently ; there are abounding references to him in contemporary squibs. See Dryden's epilogue to Lee's *Mithridates, King of Pontus* (1678).

[2] See his *Roscius Anglicanus*, where the date given is February, 1673-4. *Psyche* was published before February 15, 1674-5 (when it is announced in the *Term Catalogue*) and Shadwell in his preface speaks of it as having been written sixteen months previously, or c. September, 1673.

[3] Such was the usual contemporary description of the new theatre, which, however, is generally referred to by historians as the second Theatre Royal, Drury Lane.

His Majesty's Theatre at Whitehall, which were formerly delivered to Mr. Grabu for the use of the French Opera in Bridges Street.[1]

Although possibly others were produced, only one piece is on record as having been brought out at the Theatre Royal during the French operatic season. This was a musically re-composed version of Perrin's opera, *Ariane, ou le Mariage de Bacchus*, as originally performed in Paris (after many delays) in 1669. Cambert, the original composer, is said to have superintended the English production. He had certainly left France for England in the August or September previous,[2] but the statement otherwise admits of no confirmation, and runs counter to the definite details on the title-page of the book.[3] Tradition also maintains that sometime before his mysterious death in March, 1677, Cambert's opera, *Pomone*, originally produced in Paris in 1671, was performed at the English court. Of this one finds no trace, but it may be that *Pomone* formed one of the productions of the French operatic season at the Theatre Royal. If the season lasted a fortnight or three weeks, as the entries in the Lord Chamberlain's Accounts indicate, more than one opera must have been performed.

In all probability the visits of the French players to Whitehall would have been much more frequent had it not been for the fact that the easy-going King was very dilatory in his payments. It was seemingly by way of compensation for undischarged liabilities that he permitted Scaramouch and his fellows to establish, on their return to England in 1675,

---

[1] H. C. de Lafontaine, *The King's Musick*, pp. 269–70.

[2] Cf. Nuitter et Thoinan, *Les Origines de L'Opéra Français* (1886), pp. 303 ff. These authorities err in stating that *Ariane* was sung at the Theatre Royal in English. In July, 1674, Cambert was superintending the King's Music at Windsor. (Cf. H. C. de Lafontaine, op. cit. pp. 273 and 280).

[3] Two books of the Opera, one in French and one in English, were published simultaneously at the period of production. Both versions have an engraved frontispiece giving a view of London with the Thames in the background, the scene of the specially localised prelude. In the English copy the imprint reads: "Ariadne, or the Marriage of Bacchus, an Opera, or a Vocal Representation; first compos'd by Monsieur P. P. Now put into Musick by Monsieur Grabut, Master of his Majesties Musick. And acted by the Royal Academy of Musick at the Theatre Royal in Covent Garden . . ." It should be noted that the new house in Bridges Street was sometimes spoken of as "the Theatre Royal in Covent Garden", thus taking its description from the parish in which it was situated. No Covent Garden Theatre, in the latter-day sense of the term, then existed. Nuitter and Thoinan blunder sadly over this (op. cit.) p. 304.

what was virtually a public theatre in Inigo Jones's great
Banquetting House. There was much whispering about
town over this reprehensible concession. Andrew Marvell,
writing to his friend William Ramsden on July 24, 1675,
says *inter alia*, "Scaramuccio acting daily in the hall of
Whitehall, and all sorts of people flocking thither and paying their money as at a common playhouse ; nay even a
twelve penny gallery is builded for the convenience of his
Majesty's poor subjects." Two months later Evelyn went
to see the Italians, and was shocked to find entrance money
being charged, "which was very scandalous and never so
before at court diversions ".[1]

It would appear that the King, indisposed to remain for
long without exotic entertainment and unable to recompense
the foreign players with the necessary promptitude, had determined upon making the public pay at first hand for his
pleasures. Both the French and the Italians would be more
disposed to return to Whitehall when they knew they had
the right to charge for admission. One consequence of this
was that the English players grew to look upon the court
theatre as a serious opposition. The doings there, so far from
being sacro-sanct, were viewed as fair game by the native
dramatist. One finds some French company which happened
to be acting at Whitehall early in 1677 held up to ridicule at
Dorset Gardens in the epilogue to *The French Conjuror*.[2] The
speaker, in the character of a Frenchman, is made to say :

> All my French blood be in a rage,
> Damn'd English Acteur, English Teatre,
> Dere's no such thing as Wit nor Acting dere.
> De Wit, de Sense, de Fame, and de Renown
> Be in the French troop at toder end o' Town.[3]
> Dere Player be brisk aery spark, here Dog
> Of Actor, more like heavie English Log.

[1] These details upset the contention of Wheatley, who maintains in his recension
of Pepys that admission to court performances was obtainable by payment from the
dawn of the Restoration.

[2] A precise date for Porter's comedy cannot be determined, but the play was
licensed for publication on August 2, 1677, and was probably brought out a month or
two earlier.

[3] Undoubtedly a reference to Whitehall.

Writing to a relative on May 31, 1677, John Verney says:

On Wednesday, his Majesty's birth night, was some gallantry at Whitehall, where was acted a French opera, but most pitifully done, so ill that the king was aweary on't, and some say it was not well contrived to entertain the English gentry, who came that night in honour to their King, with a lamentable ill-acted French play, when our English actors so much surpass; however the dances and voices were pretty well performed.[1]

Unless some postponement of the performance took place Verney must have written "Wednesday" in mistake. The King's birthday (May 29) fell this year on a Tuesday. As to the despised French opera presented on the occasion, we have a clue to its identity in the entry in the Lord Chamberlain's Accounts made under date May 22, 1677:

Order to Mr. Staggins, Master of his Majesty's Musick, and in his absence to Mr. Lock who officiates for him :—That all His Majesty's musitians doe attend to practise in the theatre at White-hall at such tymes as Madam Le Roch and Mr. Paisible shall appoint for the practising of such musick as is to be in the French comedy to be acted before His Majesty on the 29 May instant.[2]

The opera in question was an entirely new production, in a prologue and three acts, written in the French court style by one Madame La Roche-Guilhen, and composed by James Paisible. When published a few months afterwards it bore the following title :

Rare en Tout. Comedie Meslée di Musique Et de Balets Représentée devant Sa Majesté Sur le Theatre Royal de Whitehall. A Londres. Chez Jacques Magnes, & Richard Bentley, à la Poste de Russel-street, au Covent Garden, 1677.[3]

At least two French troupes visited London in 1677. Care must be taken not to confound the troupe referred to in Porter's epilogue (which may possibly have taken part in the representation of *Rare en Tout*) with the troupe performing at Whitehall at the close of the year. Of the

---

[1] *Verney Papers*, Hist. MSS. Comm., Appendix to 7th Report, p. 469.
[2] *The King's Musick*, p. 318.
[3] Cf. *The Musical Antiquary* for Oct., 1910, p. 57.

latter we glean some curious details in a letter from Henry Saville to Lord Rochester. Writing from Whitehall on December 17, 1677, the coming Vice-Chamberlain conveys the intelligence that Mrs. Barry the actress had just borne the libertine lord a daughter. This prelude strikes the keynote of the communication :

I had allmost forgott for another argument to bring you to towne (continues Saville) that a French troop of Comaedians bound for Nimeguen were by adverse winds cast into this hospitable port, and doe act at Whitehall soe very well that is a thousand pittyes they should not stay, especially a young wench of fifteen who has more beauty and sweetnesse than ever was seen upon the stage since a friend of ours left it. In good earnest you would bee delighted above all things with her, and it were a shame to the nation shee should carry away a maydenhead shee pretends to have brought, and that noe body heer has either witt or addresse or money enough to goe the price of. The King sighes and despaires and sais noebody but Sir George Downing or my Lord Ranelagh can possibly purchase her. [1]

One would say from the tenor of this quaint epistle that the troupe which had been accidentally cast into the port of London had not more than a month arrived. It may be deemed a happy circumstance that the identity of the charming young actress whose virtue proved so unassailable at the hands of Comus and his rabble rout can be readily determined. She was none other than Mlle. Pitel, better know to theatrical fame as Mlle. Raisin. Long before the publication of Saville's letter, records had been unearthed in France showing that at about this period Henri Pitel, Sieur de Longchamp, a not undistinguished theatrical manager, came to England, bringing with him his daughter Françoise (the future Mlle Raisin), his wife, and her eldest daughter Anne, the last of whom was married to a member of the troupe called Durieu. [2] Pitel's company is said to

---

[1] Hist. MSS. Comm., *Calendar of MSS. of the Marquis of Bath at Longleat, Wiltshire*, ii, 160.
[2] Charton, *La Troupe du Roman Comique* (1876), p. 98. Durieu was a nephew of Mlle. Beauval. He was received, together with his wife, at the Comédie Française in 1685.

have remained at the English court some fifteen or eighteen months, but this is probably an exaggeration.

In the spring of 1683, Charles II entered into negotiations through his envoy, Lord Preston, for the return of the Franco-Italian comedians to England, but Fiorelli proved impossible to persuade. And little wonder : the King was still in arrears to him over his last visit. Baffled in his hopes in this direction, "Old Rowley ", in the following August, dispatched Betterton the tragedian to Paris to make arrangements for the performance of French opera at Whitehall. On September 22, 1683, we find Lord Preston writing from Paris to the Duke of York :

> I should not have presumed to give your Highness the trouble of this if something of charity had not induced me to it. I do it at the instance of a poor servant of his Majesty's, who some time since was obliged by a misfortune to leave England. It is Mr. Grahme, Sir, whom perhaps your Highness may remember. Mr. Betterton coming hither some weeks since by his Majesty's command, to endeavour to carry over the Opera, and finding that impracticable, did treat with Monsr. Grahme to go over with him to endeavour to represent something at least like an Opera in England for his Majesty's diversion. He hath also assured him of a pension from the House, and finds him very willing and ready to go over. He only desireth his Majesty's protection when he is there, and what encouragement his Majesty shall be pleased to give him if he finds that he deserves it, etc. [1]

In the above extract, given exactly as cited in the Historical MSS. Commission Report, it seems to me that the name "Grahme" is a pardonable misreading[2] of "Grabut" or "Grabue" (as the name of the mediocre French composer was often phonetically rendered). It is necessary here to recall that Louis Grabut, after having been master of the King's Music from 1667, was cashiered late in 1674 in favour of Nicholas Staggins. His salary at that period was seriously in arrears, but, though he suffered much from want,

---

[1] Hist. MSS. Comm., 7th Report, Part 1, p. 290.

[2] Doubly pardonable for the reason that there were several Grahmes at this period at the English Court. Cf. *The Secret Service Papers of Charles II* (Camden Society), wherein payments are recorded in 1686 to James and Richard Grahme. In *The Ellis Correspondence* mention is made of "Rene Grahme and other officers."

it was not until three years later that, after many importunings, he received payment of the large sum (over £600) due to him. Being a Catholic and timorous, he fled from London towards the close of 1678, and settled miserably in Paris, where Betterton apparently found him in 1683.[1] Lord Preston's application to the Duke of York evidently led at once to the extension of Charles II's protection to his old servant. Within three or four months Grabut must have returned to London. Did he not supply the music for the songs in Southerne's comedy of *The Disappointment, or the Mother in Fashion,* as produced at the Theatre Royal, c. February, 1684? About the same period he entered into collaboration with Dryden in the composition of an opera intended for performance at Whitehall. The death of the King on the verge of its production upset all their arrangements ; but, under the title of *Albion and Albanius,* the opera was eventually brought out at Dorset Gardens on June 3, 1685.

Beyond the return of Louis Grabut, and certain improvements in the working of English stage mechanism, Betterton's visit to Paris had no immediate outcome. Not to be baulked in his desire for some sort of exotic entertainment, Charles II bethought himself to ask William, Prince of Orange, for the loan of his French court players. The sequel to the request, is indicated in a letter written from London on June 10, 1684, by B. Grenville to W. Leveson Gower :

. . . . . . The Dutch letters bring that Sir Thomas Armstrong was seized and secured at Leyden in Holland by the King's minister, Mr. Chudley, and was immediately put on board one of his Majesty's yaughts that was attending the transportation of the Prince's French players, expected with the prisoner this night.[2]

The Prince of Orange's players under the directorship of one Francis Duperier, remained in England for close on five months, and performed before the King both in town and

---

[1] These details concerning Grabut are largely based on the records published in *The King's Musick.*

[2] Hist. MSS. Comm., 5th Report, Part 1 (1876), p. 186.

country. On October 29th a payment of £45 bounty was ordered "to Francis Duperier for the charge of ye French players attending his Majestie at Windsor and Winchester and returning to London".[1]

King Charles's predilections for exotic amusements were shared to the full by his ill-fated brother. French opera was given at James the Second's court in the spring of 1686. Writing to the Duchess of Rutland on January 23, 1685-6, Peregrine Bertie says, "next week begins the French Opera". But a postponement took place, and on the 28th following he writes again to Her Grace conveying the news that "last night was acted *The Chances* at Whitehall" and that "the French opera will begin the weeke after the next". On February 11th he hastened to inform her, "to-day was the French opera. The King and Queen were there, the musicke was indeed very fine, but all the dresses the most wretched I ever saw; 'twas acted by none but French. A Saturday the court goes to another play, to take their leaves of those vanitys till after Lent".[2] It seems not unlikely that Jacques Rousseau, formerly operatic scene-painter in Paris, provided the mounting for these court performances. We know that he came to England on the revocation of the edict of Nantes, and remained there till his death in 1693.

Between a period of two and three years later occurs the last recorded direct visit of a troupe of French players to the English court. Among the secret service accounts of James II passed for payment in October, 1688, one finds an entry of £200 "to John de Sureis for himself and the rest of the French players, being 12 in number, bounty".[3]

The waning of the century saw a temporary disappearance of all prejudice against foreigners in the English theatre. Thanks largely to the initiative of Betterton, at his wits' end to know how to draw audiences, French dancing came to be looked upon as a boon and a blessing. But the

---

[1] *Secret Service Accounts of Charles II and James II* (Camden Society, 1851), p. 93.

[2] Hist. MSS. Comm., *Rutland Papers*, II. (1889), pp. 102 et seq. For an allusion to the French Opera, see the prologue to Jevons' play, *The Devil of a Wife, or a Comical Transformation*, spoken at Dorset Gardens on March 4, 1685–6.

[3] *Secret Service Papers*, p. 209.

tastes catered for were rather those of the classes than of the masses. Downes, writing in 1708, says :

In the space of Ten years past, Mr. Betterton to gratify the Desires and Fancies of the Nobility and Gentry; procur'd from Abroad the best dancers and Singers, as Monsieur L'Abbe, Madam Sublini, Monsieur Balon, Margarita Delpine, Maria Gallia, and divers others; who being Exhorbitantly Expensive, produc'd small Profit to him and his company, but vast Gain to themselves.

Nine years earlier, Wright in his *Historia Histrionica* had made his puppet Trueman say with a sigh for the good old days that formerly the players

could support themselves merely from their own merit, the weight of the matter and goodness of the action, without scenes and machines; whereas the present plays with all that show can hardly draw an audience, unless there by the additional invitation of a Signor Fideli, a Monsieur l'Abbe, or some such foreign regale express'd in the bottom of the bill.

Three years later, or in 1702, Gildon, in his *Comparison of the Two Stages*, leads his interlocutors to discuss this matter :

Rambler : At six I'll meet you at Lincoln's Inn Playhouse.

Sullen : I wonder what Play is it?

Ramb. : The *Way of the World*, with the new dancer, Madam d'Subligny.

Critic : There's another toy now, God ! There's not a year but some surprising monster lands ; I wonder they don't first show her at Fleet Bridge with an old drum and a cracked trumpet.—"Walk in and take your places; just going to show."

Ramb. : Let's meet there ; methinks I long to be ogling madam's feet.

Sull.: . . . No, I'm not for meeting there; *The Generous Conqueror* is acted at the other house, [1] and lest it should never be acted again, let's go see it to-night.

Sull. : . . . It was otherwise lately with Balon ; [2] the town ran mad to him, and the prices were raised to an extravagant degree to bear the extravagant rate they allowed him.

[1] Drury Lane. The foreign singers and dancers were mostly engaged at Lincoln's Inn Fields.

[2] Cf. *The Post Man* of April 6, 1699 : "On Easter Monday at the New Theatre in Little Lincoln's Inn Fields will be an entertainment of Dancing, performed by Monsieur Balon, newly arrived from Paris."

Gildon, we take it, was a typical British playgoer, and in the voice that speaks for his puppets we hear the first faint mutterings of the storm which was to burst forty years later, and to recur again and again. For full arousal of these bitter passions it only needed the upspringing of grave foreign complications and the resultant fostering of a spirit of Gallophobia. The whirligig of Time brought all these revenges. Not so soon, however, as the summer of 1718, when a French company, exiled from Paris by the suppression of the Théâtres de la Foire, came to Lincoln's Inn Fields and played *Tartuffe*, *Le Foire de Saint Germains* and *Les Deux Arlequins* unmolested. Nor can it be traced that any splenetic feeling was evinced towards the visitors styling themselves " the French Comedians of his Grace the Duke of Montague ", who opened the New Theatre in the Haymarket on December 29, 1720, with *La Fille à la Mode, ou la Badaud de Paris*, and remained there until early in the following May.[1] If they suffered, it was from the apathy of the *beau monde*, which took so mild an interest in their enterprise that the weekly nights of acting had to be reduced from four to two and the prices of admission lowered. Only one member of the company, Mlle. de Livri, Voltaire's erstwhile mistress, had any reason to look back upon the visit with satisfaction. On the closing of the theatre she took a situation in a French café off the Strand, and there so infatuated one of its frequenters, the Marquis de Gouvernet, as to receive from him an offer of marriage. Overawed by his station, she gave her suitor a point-blank refusal. But the Marquis was no believer in a woman's "No", and by a clever device, eventually induced her to change her mind. Having first presented her with a lottery ticket, he made her believe later on that she had won a large prize. He had loved her when she was poor, would she not marry him now she was rich? The charming young actress swallowed the bait and returned to Paris Madame la Marquise.[2]

[1] Cf. H. Barton Baker's *The London Stage* (1889), i. 173-4. The opening piece was a prose comedy in three acts by M. Barbier, an advocate of Lyons, where it had originally been produced in 1707.

[2] Frederick Hawkins, *The French Stage in the Eighteenth Century*, i. 174-6.

In 1738 the storm-cloud burst, racial antipathies having been excited by a curious concatenation of circumstances. In October, shortly after the Haymarket had been closed under the terms of Walpole's new Licensing Act, it was announced that the theatre, whence the English players had been banished, was to be re-opened, "by authority," by a company of French players. Aroused by the sense of injustice John Bull rose to the occasion. There was an organised opposition, and the opening night proved the closing one. Here is the account of the riot, written by an eye-witness :

People went early to the Theatre, as a crouded house was certain. I was there in the centre of the Pit ; where I soon perceived that we were visited by two WESTMINSTER Justices, DEVEIL and MANNING. The Leaders, that had the Conduct of the Opposition, were known to be there ; one of whom called aloud for the song in Praise of English Roast Beef, which was accordingly sung in the Gallery by a Person prepared for that Purpose; and the whole House, beside Joining in the Chorus, saluted the Close with three Huzzas ! This, Justice DEVEIL was pleased to say, was a Riot ; upon which Disputes commenced directly, which were carried on with some degree of Decency on both Sides. The Justice at first informed us, "that he was come there as a Magistrate to maintain the KING's Authority ; that Colonel PULTENEY, with a full Company of the Guards, were without, to support him in the execution of his office; that it was the KING's COMMAND the Play should be acted ; and that the obstructing it was opposing the KING's AUTHORITY ; and if that was done he must read the Proclamation ; after which all Offenders would be secured directly by the Guards in waiting." To all these most arbitrary Threatnings, this abuse of his MAJESTY's Name, the Reply was to the following Effect:—"That the Audience had a legal Right to shew their Dislike to any Play or Actor; that the common Laws of the Land were nothing but common Custom, and the antient Usage of the People ; that the Judicature of the Pit had been acknowledged and acquiesced to, Time immemorial; and as the present Set of Actors were to take their fate from the Public, they were free to receive them as they pleased."

By this time the hour of six drew near; and the *French* and *Spanish* Embassadors, with their Ladies; the late Lord and Lady Gage; and Sir T[homas] R[obinson], a Commissioner of the

Excise, all appeared in the Stage Box together ! At that instant the Curtain drew up, and discovered the actors standing between two Files of Grenadiers, with their bayonets fixed, and resting on their Firelocks. There was a sight! enough to animate the coldest *Briton*. At this the whole Pit rose, and unanimously turned to the Justices, who sat in the Middle of it, to demand the Reason of such arbitrary Proceedings? The Justices either knew nothing of the Soldiers being placed there, or thought it safest to declare so. At that Declaration, they demanded of Justice Deveil (who had owned himself the commanding officer in the affair) to order them off the Stage. He did so immediately, and they disappeared. Then began the Serenade ; not only Catcalls, but all the various portable Instruments, that could make a disagreeable Noise, were brought on this occasion, which were continually tuning in all parts of the House; and as an attempt to speaking was ridiculous, the Actors retired, and they opened with a grand dance of twelve Men and twelve Women; but even that was prepared for, and they were directly saluted with a Bushel or two of Peas, which made their Capering very unsafe. After this they attempted to open the Comedy ; but had the Actor the Voice of Thunder, it would have been lost in the confused Sounds from a thousand various Instruments. Here, at the waving Deveil's Hand, all was silent, and (standing up on his seat) he made a Proposal to the House to this effect :—"That if they persisted in the opposition, he must read the Proclamation; that if they would permit the play to go on, and to be acted through that Night, he would promise (on his Honour) to lay their Dislikes, and Resentment to the Actors, before the King, and he doubted not but a Speedy End would be put to their acting." The Answer to this Proposal was very short, and very expressive. "No Treaties, No Treaties !" At this the Justice called for Candles to read the Proclamation, and ordered the Guards to be in Readiness; but a gentleman, seizing Mr. Deveil's Hand, stretched out for the Candle, begged of him to consider what he was going to do, for his own Sake, for ours, for the King's ! that he saw the unanimous Resolution of the House ; and that the appearance of soldiers in the Pit would throw us all into a Tumult, which must end with the Lives of many. This earnest Remonstrance made the Justice turn pale and passive. At this Pause the Actors made a second Attempt to go on, and the Uproar revived; which continuing some Time, the Embassadors and their Ladies left their Box, which occasioned a universal Huzza from the whole House ! and after calling out some Time for the Falling of the

Curtain, *down it fell*. I will venture to say, that at no Battle gained over the *French* by the *immortal* MARLBOROUGH, the Shoutings could be more Joyous than on this Occasion. What greatly added to my pleasure was, to see the two Justices join in this grand Huzza, by waving their Hats over their Heads, and at the same Time wore faces more like the conquered than Conquerors. [1]

There was a series of disturbances of a similar order at the same theatre in November, 1749, when Jean Monnet brought his company over and got quite innocently embroiled in the rivalries of a fierce electioneering contest through gaining the ardent patronage of my Lord Trentham, one of the candidates. From the violent prejudices with which the town now became obsessed it took it a whole century to recover. The very suspicion of a French dancer in the theatre sufficed to cause its destruction. Drury Lane was wrecked on this score in 1755, although Garrick's sole offence had been the bringing over of Noverre and a number of Swiss executants to dance in *The Chinese Festival*.

[1] Benjamin Victor's *History of the Theatres of London and Dublin* (1761), i. pp. 53 ff. According to an epigram in *The London Magazine* for Oct. 1738, (p. 514), the comedy intended to be acted on the opening night was *L'Embarras des Richesses*.

Proscenium Doors: an Elizabethan Heritage

Proscenium Doors: An Elizabethan Heritage

Although the terms "platform stage" and "picture stage",[1] as applied to the non-scenic and the scenic theatre, are very convenient and come ready to the pen, they prove on examination to be arbitrary, unscientific and, worst of all, misleading. The popular idea of an abrupt transition from the platform stage to the picture stage at the period of the Restoration is wholly astray. Then, and for two hundred years after, the two principles overlapped. The picture stage, as we now know it, i.e., with the picture entirely within the frame, only dates back a matter of half a century.

When acting was first renewed after the blank period of the Civil War and the Commonwealth, it was strictly on Elizabethan principles. Three of the old dismantled theatres, Salisbury Court, the Cockpit and the Red Bull, were hastily restored in 1660 to their original condition, or a sound approximation thereto. Not only that but the first wholly new theatre of the Restoratian era, the house erected in a tennis court in Vere Street in the same year, was based on the old formula. There was an immediate revival of Elizabethan conventionalism, which, despite the altered conditions of a lustrum later, permeated and informed the technique of the Restoration and the Post-Restoration dramatist.

In England the picture stage in its crudity began with the opening of the new Duke's Theatre in Lincoln's Inn Fields in June, 1661, with D'Avenant's opera, *The Siege of Rhodes*. Even then the pristine platform stage was not wholly abandoned, for the King's players remained at Vere Street until the opening of their scenically-equipped house, the Theatre Royal in Bridges Street, on May 7, 1663. The influence of

---

[1] Due, I think, to the inventive resource of Mr. A. B. Walkley. See his anonymous theatrical article in *The Edinburgh Review* for July, 1902.

continental models on our first two theatres of the picture stage order was much slighter than has been popularly supposed. From first to last the English theatre has preserved a certain individuality. We may concede that the prime characteristics of the picture stage, viz., the proscenium arch and the front curtain, together with movable scenery and its attendant mechanism had been derived from the French or Italian theatres, although as a matter of fact all had been seen years before in the Carolan court masques. But here at best all resemblance ends, and there were many differentiating factors. French models could have had little influence, for the French theatre of the latter half of the seventeenth century preserved the standing pit. In the Restoration scenic theatres, the auditorium was, *sui generis*, based on the latest development of the Elizabethan private theatre. The benches of the pit rose in gradually ascending tiers until checked by the front partition of the boxes. Where the one ended and the other began the difference in elevation between the two was inconsiderable, probably only three or four feet. [1]

In adopting the Italian principle of a changing pictorial background, the Restoration players apparently had their doubts concerning the efficiency of the new medium as a satisfactory substitute for the old physical conditions, especially in its application to the old plays which still formed the major portion of their repertory. The result was that they decided to combine the prime characteristics of the obsolescent platform stage with the essentials of the new picture stage. How to do this was the puzzle, seeing that the various features of the tiring-house front could no longer be preserved at the back of the stage. Finally, they resolved to bring them forward and place them in or about the proscenium. The result was that the two main entering doors with the superincumbent balconies were embedded in either side of the proscenium arch, and the music-room placed above it. As the arch was to serve many of the purposes of the old tiring-house façade, it was vital that some

---

[1] Cf. R. W. Lowe, *Thomas Betterton*, p. 34.

considerable stage room should be left in front of it. Hence the origin, so far as the English stage is concerned, of the longevous principle of "the apron."[1] Inartistic as we should now reckon it, the result proved wholly grateful. Since the proscenium doors formed the normal mode of entry and exit, action mostly took place on the apron, thus making for the better hearing and (at a time of indifferent lighting) sight of the spectator.

Since I have argued that the distinctive arrangement of the Restoration proscenium was based on the conventions of the Elizabethan stage, it may be as well, before proceeding to a lengthened consideration of the usages and literary influence of the doors and balconies, to prove the analogy by demonstrating the hitherto unsuspected position of the early picture stage music-rooms. We know that in practically all the Elizabethan theatres the musicians occupied an elevated position at the back,[2] and we have solid reasons for believing that, despite some attempts to place the musicians in front of the stage, a similarly elevated position was allotted to them in the Restoration houses of the new order.

Let us first look at the evidence for the Duke's Theatre in Lincoln's Inn Fields, the earliest of our picture stage theatres. On November 7, 1667, when Pepys repaired thither to see *The Tempest*, he found the house crowded owing to the lateness of his arrival, and had perforce "to sit in the side balcony over against the musique-room." From this it would appear that the music-room at the Duke's was situate above the proscenium. It might be argued, of course, on the strength of French analogy[3] that the musicians were placed beyond stage regions, somewhere in the auditorium

---

[1] The apron already existed in some of the larger Italian opera-houses, where it had originated through the necessity to throw the voice of the singer well forward. (Cf. Count Algarotti's *Essay on the Opera*, 1767, pp. 96-7). On the other hand, proscenium entering doors were utterly unknown on the continent; so we are safe in assuming that the English apron was not derivative.

[2] Vide ante pp. 90-2

[3] Cf. Chappuzeau, *Le Théâtre François*, p. 240, where reference is made to the fact that the French musicians then occupied a box at the back of the auditorium, and were so little in touch with the traffic of the scene that people had to cry out to them to play when music was necessary.

proper. But a little reflection shows this to have been impossible. The old Elizabethan necessity for the musicians to occupy a position allowing of ready access to the stage still held good. Many scenes in the works of contemporary dramatists called for their presence on the boards. [1]

With the opening of the new Theatre Royal in Bridges Street in 1663 an attempt was made to introduce the Italian principle of the orchestra as practised to-day. Pepys went there on the second day of acting (May 8), and records "the musique being below, and most of it sounding under the very stage, there is no hearing of the basses at all, nor very well of the trebles, which sure must be mended." It would appear that, because of these defects, the musicians were transferred later on to an elevated position, probably, as in the Duke's, to a room over the proscenium arch. In a curious old ballad [2] relating the destruction by fire of the Theatre Royal on January 25, 1671-2, we read:

> But on a sudden a Fierce Fire 'gan rage,
> In several scenes, and overspread the stage
> The " Horrors " waiting on the dismal sight
> Soon taught th' players to th' life to act a Fright.
> The Boxes where splendors us 'd to surprise
> From constellations of bright ladies' eyes,
> A different blazing lustre now is found
> And th' music-room with whistle flames doth sound.
> Then catching hold o' th' roof it does display,
> Consuming fiery trophies every way.

From the progressive nature of this description, beginning at the stage and gradually working upwards, it is plain to be seen that the music-room in the King's playhouse was situated not very far from the roof. One notes also that, when the house was rebuilt, no orchestra, in our latter-day sense of the term, was provided. The view of the stage given in the frontispiece to the opera of *Ariane, ou le Mariage de Bacchus* (as performed at the new Theatre Royal in April, 1674)

---

[1] Cf. Dryden's *An Evening's Love* (1671), Act ii; also his *Troilus and Cressida* (1679), iii. 2.
[2] Percy Fitzgerald's *New History of the English Stage*, i. 137.

shows a projecting semi-oval front with an ornamented base, and no enclosure.

For the second Duke's Theatre, as built in Dorset Gardens and opened on November 9, 1671, we have both pictorial and textual evidence, the two being apparently in conflict. It is possible, however, to reconcile these contradictions. In Settle's tragedy, *The Empress of Morocco*, as acted at this house and published in October, 1673, several illustrations of the scenes are given, each with an elaborate (but not wholly complete) view of the proscenium and its immediate surroundings. [1] In examining these one notes that the top of the proscenium arch projects over the apron by way of soffit, or sounding-board,[2] and that it bears upon it a large room with three curtained openings, one in front and two at the sides. As no spectator could have seen the inner stage and scenery from this position, and as the whole arrangement was too elaborate to be merely ornamental, one takes it that this was the position normally occupied by the musicians, that is to say at periods when their duties almost wholly consisted of the playing of preludes and act-tunes. [3] It would appear, however, that on special operatic occasions, when the violins were increased from twelve to twenty-four, the musicians generally sat at the front of the stage. This would explain the apparent contradiction presented by the initial instruction in Shadwell's anonymously published opera of *The Tempest* : [4]

The front of the stage is open'd and the Band of 24 Violins with the Harpsicals and Theorbos, which accompany the voices, are plac'd between the Pit and the Stage. While the Overture is playing the Curtain rises and discovers a new Frontispiece Joyn'd to the great Pylasters, on each side of the Stage.

[1] One of these is badly reproduced in Mr. Albright's *The Shakesperian Stage*, p. 46 ; for another and better example, see *The Pall Mall Magazine* for Sept. 1894, p. 89 (Mr. E. Manson's article on "Nell Gwyn").

[2] Thus bearing a superficial resemblance to "the heavens" of the Elizabethan theatres.

[3] Those who feel inclined to dub this line of argument preposterous should bear in mind that once or twice within living memory the musicians have been placed over the proscenium in a box similarly arranged. See the illustration of the Madison Square Theatre, New York, in *The Scientific American* for April 5, 1884 (Vol L. No. 14).

[4] Quarto, 1674, as acted at Dorset Gardens in April or May of that year.

It is plain to be seen that this was a special arrangement; had it been otherwise the description would have been superfluous. With the increasing popularity of opera (or what passed as such in Post-Restoration times), the orchestra, as we now know it, was more and more resorted to, until, finally by the end of the century, it had become the normal position of the musicians. Some relics, however, of the old elevated music-room still lingered. Dunton, the itinerant bookseller, who visited Ireland in 1698, writes, in *The Dublin Scuffle*, of a visit paid to the Smock Alley Theatre at that period. He found

> the Dublin playhouse to be a place very contrary to its owners; for they on their outsides make the best show; but this is very ordinary in its outward appearance, but looks much better inside with its stage, pit, two galleries, lattices [1] and music loft, &c.

Before proceeding to an exhaustive consideration of the history and usages of the proscenium doors and balconies, it will be necessary to prove that—whatever other doors or ways of entrance might have been used, as occasion required, in the scene—there were only two permanent, conventional doors, and that these formed the regular, but not sole, method of entrance and exit. It is imperative this should be thrashed out first, seeing that Lowe, in his careful study of the period, has made out a plausible case for four permanent doors, situated in or near the proscenium.[2] Had he exercised his sound sense of the theatre, instead of speaking strictly from his brief, it would have dawned upon him that two such doors on both sides of the proscenium would have been in excess of all requirements.

Lowe's first item of evidence is derived from Etherege's *She Would If She Could*, ii. 1., as performed at the Duke's Theatre in Lincoln's Inn Fields in 1668. The scene is the Mulberry Garden, whither come Ariana and Gatty, in masks, to meet their gallants. They pass briskly over the

---

[1] i. e. side boxes in the middle gallery. The term was apparently peculiar to Dublin and lingered there until the last century.

[2] *Thomas Betterton*, pp. 49–52.

stage, and Freeman and Courtal, having espied them, go off in ardent pursuit. Then the scene proceeds as follows :

> *Enter Women again, and cross the Stage.*
>
> *Ariana.* Now if these should prove two Men of War, That are Cruising here, to watch for Prizes.
>
> *Gatty.* Wou'd they had Courage enough to set upon us. I long to be engag'd.
>
> *Ariana.* Look, look yonder, I protest they chase us.
>
> *Gat.* Let us bear away then : if they be truly Valiant they'll quickly make more sail and board us.
>
> [*The Women go out, and go about behind the Scenes to the other Door.*
>
> *Enter* Courtal *and* Freeman.
>
> *Free.* 'Sdeath, how fleet they are ! whatsoever Faults they have, they cannot be broken-winded.
>
> *Court.* Sure, by that little mincing step they shou'd be Country Fillies that have been breath'd a Course at Park, and Barly-break : we shall never reach 'em.
>
> *Free.* I'll follow directly, do thou turn the cross walk and meet 'em.
>
> *Enter the Women, and after 'em* Courtal *at the lower door, and* Freeman *at the upper on the contrary side.*

It is these references to upper and lower doors that induced Lowe to believe there were four permanent entering doors in or about the proscenium. But it is clear that the upper door spoken of must have been a door (or entrance-way) in the actual scene itself, the scene of the Mulberry Garden. Otherwise there would be no sense in the previous direction, where reference is made to "the other [permanent] door". What confirmed Lowe in the belief that there were ordinarily four entering doors was the finding of a passage in Colley Cibber's *Apology* referring to the "lower doors". In dealing with the alterations made in Drury Lane Theatre[1] by Christopher Rich c. 1696, with the view of enlarging the pit, Cibber writes in his twelfth chapter :

It must be observ'd then that the Area or Platform of the old Stage projected about four Foot forwarder, in a Semi-oval figure,

---

[1] Originally opened, as we have seen, in March, 1674.

parallel to the Benches of the Pit ; and that the former lower
Doors of Entrance for the Actors were brought down between the
two foremost (and then only) Pilasters, in the place of which Doors
now the two Stage Boxes are fixt. That where the Doors of Entrance now are, there formerly stood two additional Side Wings,
in front to a full Set of Scenes, which had then almost a double
Effect in their Loftiness and Magnificence.

By this Original form the usual Station of the Actors, in almost
every Scene, was advanc'd at least ten Foot nearer to the Audience
than they now can be, because, not only from the Stage's being
shorten'd in front, but likewise from the additional Interposition of
those Stage Boxes, the Actors (in respect to the Spectators that
filled them) are kept so much more backward from the main audience than they us'd to be; but when the Actors were in possession
of that forwarder Space to advance upon, the Voice was then more
in the Centre of the House, so that the most distant Ear had scarce
the least Doubt or Difficulty in hearing what fell from the weakest
Utterance; All Objects were thus drawn nearer to the Sense; every
painted Scene was stronger, every grand Scene and Dance more
extended; every rich or fine-coloured Habit had a more lively
Lustre; nor was the minutest Motion of a Feature (properly
changing with the Passion or Humour it suited) ever lost, as they
frequently must be in the Obscurity of too great a Distance : and
how valuable an advantage the facility of hearing distinctly is to
every well-acted scene, every common spectator is a Judge.

Basing on these two items of evidence Lowe argues that
our early picture stage theatres had four permanent entering doors, that, up to the year 1700, the whole four were in
front of the curtain, and that subsequently two were in front
of, and two behind, the proscenium. But in assuming that
because Cibber speaks of " the former lower doors of entrance" he infers the presence of upper doors, Lowe is clearly
wrong. Cibber merely uses the word "lower" the better to
indicate to the ordinary reader the precise locality of the
doors. The truth is, if we are to base wholly on evidence
of this sort, there is no reason why we should stop at four
entering doors. Why not six ? In Lacy's comedy, *The Old
Troop*, Act ii, as acted at the Theatre Royal c. 1665, we have
the direction " Enter Twelve Troopers at six doors : two at
a door." If we reckon upon two permanent proscenium

doors this would imply the presence of four doors (or entrance-ways) in the actual scene. Curiously enough, Flecknoe in his unacted comedy, *Damoiselles à la Mode* (1667), writes of his piece, "the scaenes and cloaths being the least considerable in it; any *Italian* scaenes with four doors serving for the one, and for the other any French cloaths à la mode." The "chambre à quatre portes" was a common feature at this period of the French stage, where it was utilised as the sole setting of a play to preserve (fallaciously, or at the expense of all illusion) the Unity of Place. Such was the nature of the setting employed for the revival of *Le Cid* in 1673.[1] Apart from all this, we must bear in mind that not in all cases where the Restoration dramatist mentions doors does he mean doors. It is easy to show that the word was often used in a loose sense. In Dryden's *An Evening's Love*, Act v. Bellamy says, "Maskall, open the door." Maskall goes to the side scene which draws and shows a tableau of seven figures. Later on the scene shuts when Maskall is told to close the door. Again in Crowne's *Sir Courtly Nice*, Act i, on Leonora calling for the door to be opened, the scene draws and reveals her aunt and a company of friends at breakfast.[2]

Opposite Lowe's misleading items of evidence for four doors can be placed scores of stage directions proving that all our picture stage theatres of the seventeenth century had but two permanent doors of entrance. A few examples may be cited :

DUKE'S THEATRE, LINCOLN'S INN FIELDS (1662-74).

Orrery's tragedy, *Mustapha the Son of Solyman the Magnificent* (4to 1669. Acted in April, 1665), v. "Exeunt Queen and Haly. Enter Zarma at the other door."

Orrery's comedy, *Guzman* (4to 1693. Seen by Pepys on April 16, 1669), iii. 4. " They go out hastily at one Door, and Ovie. and Pirac pass out at the other."

THE THEATRE ROYAL IN BRIDGES STREET (1663-72).

Dryden's *The Wild Gallant* (4to 1669 as acted in 1667), v. 3. " Enter at one door, Trice drunk with the Watch : Bibber and

---

[1] Cf. M. Eugène Rigal, *Le Théâtre Français avant la Période Classique*, 291 note 1.
[2] See the final scene of the play for another example; also *Love for Love*, iv. 1.

Frances following; at the other, Nonsuch and Servants, and Failer."

DUKE'S THEATRE, DORSET GARDENS (1671-1709).

Otway's *Friendship in Fashion* (1678), iv. 1. Night Garden. "Enter Goodvile at one Door, Mrs. Goodville and Lettice following her at the other."

Dryden's *Troilus and Cressida* (1679), v. 2. "Clattering of swords at both Doors; he runs each way and meets the noise."

Dryden's *King Arthur* (1691), iii. ("A Deep Wood.") "Exeunt Arthur and Merlin at one door. Enter Osmond at the other door."

SECOND THEATRE ROYAL IN BRIDGES STREET (1674-1789).

Dryden's *All for Love; or The World Well Lost* (acted 1677), iii. 1. "At one Door enter Cleopatra, Charmion, Iras, and Alexas, a train of Ægyptians; at the other Antony and Romans. The entrance on both sides is prepar'd by musick."

Dryden's *Don Sebastian King of Portugal* (1689) iii. "She runs off, he follows her to the door; then comes back again and goes out at the other."

THEATRE IN LITTLE LINCOLN'S INN FIELDS
(OPENED APRIL 30, 1695).

Lord Lansdowne's comedy, *The She Gallants* (1695), v. "Enter Angelica in Women's apparel, and masked at one door; and Bellamour at the other." [1]

When we come to look for evidence as to the precise number and disposition of the doors and balconies in contemporary illustrations of the seventeenth-century picture stage theatres the result is unsatisfactory. Only three views of the kind are known, the plates in Settle's *Empress of Morocco* showing the Dorset Gardens' stage, the frontispiece to *Ariane* (1674) dealing with the second Theatre Royal in Bridges Street (afterwards known as Drury Lane), and a later view of the same house showing Joe Haines speaking an epilogue riding on an ass (1697).[2] In Settle's plates

---

[1] Many of the directions of the Post-Restoration period read "one door . . . . another door." These evidently imply two doors only, otherwise they would render the more precise directions unmeaning.

[2] The only exemplar I know of the Haines' print is preserved in the British Museum in Smith's Compiled History of the Stage (press-mark "11826 r") Vôl. iv. (unpaged). It is inscribed in writing, "Joe Haines, mounted upon an Ass, speaking the Epilogue to *Unhappy Kindness*" (a play by Thos. Scott, acted at Drury Lane in 1697.)

DRURY LANE THEATRE, 1697:

Joe Haines, mounted on an ass, speaking an epilogue.

[*To face p.* 169.

we get only a partial view of the immediate front of the proscenium, and although entrance-ways, surmounted by balconies, are clearly indicated, the entrances appear to be large, open arches rather than actual doors. In the frontispiece to *Ariane* no indication of doors or balconies occurs, but we see the projecting semi-circular stage. As the apron in the Haines' prints shows the right-hand corner of a rectilinear apron, the print evidently deals with Drury Lane after the alterations made by Christopher Rich. In it a door is depicted, not set obliquely, as we should anticipate from a knowledge of later theatres, but built into a brick wall and running parallel to the front of the stage. No overhanging balcony is indicated. These details require to be recorded, but the truth is old theatrical prints are seldom scrupulously accurate, and no dependence can be placed on their evidence. If the original proscenium entrances were based, as I maintain, on Elizabethan conventions they must have been, as Restoration stage directions imply, solid wooden doors, and not mere apertures. Had our first picture stage theatres employed open archways it is hardly likely that doors would have been substituted in the eighteenth century, a period in which we have abundant evidence of their employment.[1]

There is no room to doubt that the proscenium doors of our first picture stage theatres were suggested by the tiring-house entering doors of the old platform stage and, subject to some modifications due to the employment of scenery, carried on their conventional usages. In the Elizabethan playhouses the doors were provided with knockers [2] and with locks and keys,[3] so as to assist the illusion of the scene as occasion demanded. We have no direct evidence of a similar provision in connection with the first proscenium

---

[1] It should be noted, however, that in Vander Gucht's emblematic frontispiece to the third edition of *Harlequin Horace, or the Art of Modern Poetry* (1735), the proscenium entrances bear a marked resemblance to the arch-ways indicated in the illustrations to *The Empress of Morocco*. Over them are balconies occupied (as customary at that period) by spectators. From 1735 onwards, for close on a century, all genuine English theatre views depict unmistakable doors.

[2] In Middleton's comedy *The Phoenix* (c. 1605), the use of a ring knocker is indicated.

[3] Cf. Massinger's *The Renegado*, ii. 5 ; Webster's *Devil's Law Case*, v. 4.

doors, but it seems not unlikely that in scenes where the knocking and locking and breaking open of doors took place on the early picture stages, it was these doors that were utilised. If it can be assumed that the later disposition of the doors and balconies was largely traditional, and I think it can, then it is important for us to note that the proscenium doors of the early nineteenth century were all provided with knockers.[1]

On the early picture stages entrance and exit by the proscenium doors were not imperative, but, as action took place mostly on the apron, the doors were used in the generality of cases. Characters could be discovered by the rising of the curtain or the drawing of a scene and they could be closed in by the running on of a pair of flats. But at first little use was made of the new medium, and in many early Restoration plays the characters enter with the opening of the scene.[2] In dramatic construction and stage arrangements there was a curious persistence of Elizabethan conventions. Tableaux endings of acts were slow in arriving. Down to the close of the century the termination of the act was marked by a clear stage. Lest it should be argued that "exeunt" simply meant " curtain ", cases may be cited where this would not apply. In *An Evening's Love*, end of act iv, we have " Exeunt, the Men leading the Women." Sometimes the characters depart one after the other, leaving a clear stage, as in Otway's *Don Carlos, Prince of Spain*, acts iii and iv.[3] This system was apparently an unnecessary perpetuation of the Elizabethan convention. The conclusion would be that, as in the contemporary French theatre, the curtain did not fall in the inter-acts, and, as a matter of fact, it has yet to be proved that it did so fall. All we know for certain is that the curtain rose at the beginning and fell at the close. The usual direction at the opening of intermediate acts in the Restoration

---

[1] See Cruikshank's illustrations to Boz's *Memoirs of Joseph Grimaldi*. Some also had street bells—a latter-day addition.

[2] e.g. Etherege's *The Comical Revenge* (1664). A decennium later, Dryden made frequent use of discoveries.

[3] In *The Careless Husband* of Colley Cibber (1704), one notes two rapid separate exits at the close of Act iv.

and Post-Restoration drama is either "the scene opens" or "the scene draws."[1] The difficulty is to know whether these directions have a literal meaning or merely imply the rising of the curtain. If they mean what they say, then we can only assume that the scene with which the previous act terminated remained in full view of the audience while the inter-act music was being played, and that the drawing of the scene marked the beginning of the succeeding act. In that case the few definite examples we possess of the curtain falling between the acts would be the exceptions proving the rule.[2] The point is a very puzzling one to determine, but from the tenor of the following extract from Cibber's prologue to *She Wou'd and She Wou'd Not* (1703), referring to the attempt to preserve the Unity of Place, I am inclined to believe that from the Restoration to at least the reign of Queen Anne the curtain usually remained up until the close of the play :

> His action's in the Time of Acting done,
> No more than from the Curtain.up and down.
> While the first Musick plays he moves his Scene,
> A little space, but never shifts again.

Returning to our consideration of the usages of the proscenium doors, it is noteworthy that one particular mode of separate entrance at the back of the scene, so far from running counter to Elizabethan tradition, clearly perpetuated it. On the platform stage eavesdroppers never entered through either of the two doors but invariably came on through the inner stage to peep through the traverses in front. "Enter behind" was the conventional instruction in these cases, and where one comes across that direction one may be always prepared for a scene of eavesdropping.[3]

---

[1] Cf. Howard and Dryden's *The Indian Queen* (1664), Acts iv and v; Lee's *The Massacre of Paris* (1690), iv; Settle's *Empress of Morocco* (1672), ii; Motteux's *The Island Princess* (1699), iv.

[2] The curtain drew up on Act iv of Orrery's *Henry V* at the Duke's in 1664; and in the same author's tragedy of *The Black Prince* (1667), the curtain fell on Act i and was drawn up again before Act ii.

[3] Cf. *The Phoenix*, v. 1; *The Roaring Girl*, iv. 1; *Hyde Park*, iii. 1. Sometimes the direction reads "enter privately", as in *The Prophetess*, iv. 6, and *The Little French Lawyer*, iii. 1. But the variant seems peculiar to Beaumont and Fletcher.

In the drama of the early picture stage era the same thing applies. Listeners always came on at the back.[1] Where characters were not closed in by the running on of a front scene, exits were generally made by the proscenium doors. Now and again, however, the stage arrangements called for departure at the back, as in *The Plain Dealer*, iii. 1, where Manly leaves Fidelia, and goes out "at the end of the stage."

For long the technique of dramatic construction was not materially altered by the introduction of scenery. The Restoration dramatist wrote as if he still had the old platform stage in his mind's eye, and, regardless of the worries of stage mechanists and managers, continued to shift his scene with almost breathless rapidity. The consequence was that, to admit of ready handling, the scenery had to be of the lightest framework. With a rapidly changing stage elaborate built-up backgrounds were wholly out of the question. Under these conditions the presence of the proscenium doors and their attendant balconies proved extremely grateful. They admitted of the realising of many situations and incidents that otherwise could not have been dealt with. All the action that usually took place "above" on the platform stage was transferred to the proscenium balconies. Hence the persistence of the old stage direction.[2] One great advantage of the two sets of doors and balconies was that they could be used either singly or in combination. To the variety of situation thus admitted of was largely due the vogue at the Restoration period of the comedy of intrigue, and drama of the cape and sword order. Serenade scenes abounded, and plays seem almost to have been written to exploit the possibilities of the doors and balconies. Once more the physical conditions of the theatre were exercising a potent influence upon dramaturgy.

Of the simple, as contrasted with the complex, use of the balconies we have a good illustration in *The Comical Revenge*,

---

[1] Cf. *The Wild Gallant*, iv. 1, "Enter Loveby behind"; *The Country Wit*, ii. 1; *All for Love*, iv. 1. Occasionally characters not eavesdropping entered at the back, as in Mrs. Behn's *The Rover*, Part 1, i. 2.

[2] Cf. St. Serfe's *Tarugo's Wiles; or The Coffee House* (1668), v. 1, "enter Liviana above"; *All for Love*, iv. 1; *Œdipus*, v, at close; and *An Evening's Love*, Act ii.

iii. 2 (as in 1664 at the Duke's), where the chambermaid and her mistress come successively to "the window" and speak down. To avoid confusion it is necessary here to point out that there was no separate permanent window on the picture-stages of the seventeenth century, and that the terms "window", "balcony" and "above" were all interchangeable. It is difficult from the stage directions to arrive at the exact disposition of the early balconies but, in keeping with their recognition as windows, it is significant that in the early nineteenth century they were invariably provided with lace curtains. In George Digby, Earl of Bristol's comedy *Elvira, or the Worst Not always True*, ii. 7-8 (as probably acted at the Duke's in 1666), we read of a balcony door capable of being locked. At first one is inclined to think this was merely the entering door below until one is given pause by the following stage directions in Orrery's *Guzman*, as acted at the same theatre three years later: "A balcony opens, in which Antonio appears drest in Pink Colour, &c. . . . . . . Pastr. and Anto. shut the balcony and retire." In Mrs. Behn's *The Amorous Prince, or the Curious Husband*, iv. 4 (as played at the same house in 1671), an interesting situation occurs. Lorenzo descends from the balcony by means of sheets, taken from a bed by Isabella and knotted together. A variant of this "business" is to be found in the second part of *The Rover*, by the same author, as acted at Dorset Gardens in 1675. In Act iv. 5, we read: "Scene the Street, a Sheet ty'd to the Balcony, and Feth. sitting across to slide down." Fetherfoot subsequently "goes half down and stops. . . . . . The Door opens, Beau. goes up to it; Will. puts him by, and offers to go in, he pulls him back." A quarrel ensues; "strikes him, they fight, and blows light on Fetherfoot who hangs down." The indication in these two plays of the distance to be traversed between balcony and stage shows that when the King in *Œdipus* (1679) throws himself from the window, it is a dummy figure that falls, as evidenced by the fact that to mask the deception "the Thebans gather about his body." No dramatist of the time had a better sense of the theatre than

Mrs. Behn and none made more adroit employment of the balconies. In proof of this take *The Rover*, Part 1, Act ii. 1, as performed at Dorset Gardens in 1677. The scene is the exterior of the house of Angellica the courtesan. "Enter two Bravos, and hang up a great picture of Angellica's against the Balcony, and two little ones at each side of the Door." Blunt and his companions comment on the portraits and speak of the rapacity of the fair original. Then "enter Angellica and Moretta in the Balcony, and draw a silk Curtain." They listen to what is going on below, and talk. "Enter at one Door Don Pedro, Stephano; Don Antonio and Diego at the other Door," &c. Later on "Angellica throws open the curtains, and bows to Antonio, who pulls off his vizard and bows, and blows up kisses."

The complex use of the doors and balconies admitted of many situations of considerable ingenuity and uncommon illusion. Probably the best example is that capital scene in the fifth act of *Sir Martin Mar-All* (as given in 1668 at the Duke's), where the thick-witted Knight makes pretence of serenading his lady-love, and exposes his own trick by continuing to finger on the lute and to make mouths as if singing, long after his concealed substitute has ceased. The stage directions run: "Enter Mrs. Millisent, and Rose, with a Candle by 'em above. . . . Sir Martin appears at the adverse Window, a tune play'd." In the Second Part of *The Rover*, Act ii, spectators come on at both balconies to view the tricks of the mountebank on his temporary stage. In Crowne's *The Country Wit*, as acted in 1675 at Dorset Gardens, Act ii occurs in "The Street" and Lady Faddle and Bridget appear at the opening on the balcony. Considerably after they have retired, "Lord Drybone, Betty Frisque and Cis, come to the Window " and talk while Ramble and Merry below listen. Here the window was doubtless the adverse balcony.

While it seems to have been unusual on the early picture stages for the curtain to be let down between the acts, [1]

---

[1] In Mrs. Behn's tragi-comedy *The Young King, or The Mistake* (as at Dorset Gardens in 1679), we read at the opening of Act iii : "The Curtain is let down—being drawn up, discovers Orsames seated on a Throne asleep . . . Above is discovered the

instances occur, curiously enough, where it was lowered in the middle of an act, and that, too, without serious break in the action. About the earliest example of this occurs in the last act of Orrery's *Henry V*, as given at Lincoln's Inn Fields in 1664. The curtain having been let down, two Heralds appear "opposite to each other in the balconies near the stage." A proclamation is made and the curtain again rises. A similar expedient was resorted to at the same house two years later when Caryl's play, *The English Princess, or the Death of Richard III* was produced there. This was probably due to the many changes of scene in Act iv, the act in which it was employed. Scene viii begins with the premature announcement "The Scene is changed to the King's Lodging," premature because the scene really represents the ante-chamber to the King's Lodging, which forms scene ix. Then comes the following sequence of directions : "[The Curtain is let down.] . . . Enter Catesby and Ratcliffe at one of the Doors before the Curtain." . . . Some dialogue ensues revealing that the two are in the King's ante-chamber. . . . "Enter Lovel at the other Door before the Curtain . . . Sc. ix. The Curtain is opened". Here we have evidence of the presence and employment of the apron in the first English scenic theatre. I have already said that scene viii was probably played before the curtain because of the great amount of scene-shifting that had preceded. That explanation, however, would not apply to a much later representation of an ante-room, where a similar arrangement was followed. This was in Southerne's comedy, *The Wives' Excuse*, as produced at Drury Lane in 1692, a year or two before Rich reduced the dimensions of the apron. The opening scene of the piece was played in front before the rising of the curtain. It represented "the Outward Room to the Musick-meeting" and showed a number of servants in attendance, exchanging confidences ; after which "the curtain drawn up shews the company at the Musick-meeting."

Queen Olympia, and Women." This would surely indicate that it was not then usual to drop the curtain at the end of an act.

Scenes of this peculiar order were of no great frequency but one finds them persisting for over a century in rehearsal plays.[1] In that famous exemplar, *The Rehearsal*, as originally produced at the Theatre Royal in December, 1671, portions of the piece were certainly played on the apron with the curtain down, but exactly how many it would now be difficult to say. At the end of the fourth act, Bayes, after clearing the stage, says "let down the curtain" and goes off with the others. The fifth act opens on the apron to which Bayes and the two gentlemen enter through one of the proscenium doors. Evidently this is the position they occupy during the ensuing rehearsal, which begins with the direction " the curtain is drawn up, the two usurping Kings appear in state, with the four Cardinals," &c., &c. The precedent thus established was followed for long in most pieces of a similar order. Curtain scenes were employed by Fielding in no fewer than three of his Haymarket travesties, *The Author's Farce* (1729), *Tumble Down Dick; or Phaeton in the Suds* (1736), and *The Historical Register for 1736* (1737). If it can be taken that Hogarth's "Pasquin" plate represents the Haymarket stage (on which Fielding's *Pasquin* was first produced in 1736), then it is worthy of note that the plate shows a deep apron, flanked by proscenium doors and balconies. Foote adopted the Duke of Buckingham's old device in writing his *Occasional Epilogue* for the opening of the Haymarket in 1767.[2] The first part of this represented the street, the second the stage of the theatre, and the rising of the curtain in the middle indicated the change of locality. From an incidental remark one notes that the Haymarket proscenium at this period was adorned with statues typifying Ancient and Modern Comedy.[3] Finally, Sheridan, in writing *The Critic* for production at

[1] See also Dennis's comedy *Plot and No Plot*, as acted at Drury Lane in 1697 and revived at Covent Garden in April, 1746. The second act is laid in "The Playhouse before the Curtain," and the characters speak from the stage, the stage box and the side boxes. Genest thinks Foote derived his device in *The Orators* (1762) from this arrangement.

[2] For which, see *The Monthly Mirror* of January 1804.

[3] Similar statues adorned most of the early eighteenth century London theatres. For Drury Lane at an earlier period see Hogarth's print, *A Just View of the British Stage*.

VIVITUR
INGENIO

Vander Gucht Inv.^r & Sculp.

Shakespear, Rowe, Johnson, now are quite undone
These are thy Tryumphs, thy Exploits O Lun.!

FRONTISPIECE TO *HARLEQUIN HORACE*, 3RD EDITION (1735).
Proscenium entrances and balconies.

[*To face p.* 177.

Drury Lane in 1779, followed the lead of Buckingham and Fielding, in staging portions of the second and third acts on the apron with the curtain down.

At what exact period spectators were first allowed to sit in the proscenium balconies it would be difficult to say. Writing of earlier times in the *Memoirs of his Own Life* (1790), Tate Wilkinson says :

> Whenever a Don Choleric in *The Fop's Fortune*, or Sir Amorous Vainwit in *A Woman's a Riddle*, or Charles in *The Busybody*, tried to find out secrets, or plot an escape from a balcony, they always bowed and thrust themselves into the boxes over the stage door, amidst the company, who were greatly disturbed, and obliged to give up their seats.

Some reason exists to believe that the custom of spectators sitting in the proscenium balconies originated almost at the very outset. In D'Avenant's ballad epilogue to *The Man's the Master*, as acted at the Duke's in March, 1668, we read :

> Nay, often, you swear, when places are shewn ye
> That your hearing is thick
> And so by a love-trick,
> You pass through our scenes up to the balcony.

Lowe[1] assumes that the balcony here referred to was simply the boxes in the auditorium, but the whole passage, and especially the allusion to assumed deafness, seems to indicate that the proscenium balcony was in the writer's mind. The problem could be readily solved if one could determine the position of " the side balcone over against the musique room " to which Pepys made unwilling resort at the same house on November 7, 1667. That the custom of spectators sitting in the proscenium balconies was practised throughout the greater part of the eighteenth century old theatrical prints clearly show.[2] At one theatre at least the

---

[1] op. cit. p. 21–2.
[2] See the frontispiece to the third edition (only) of *Harlequin Horace* (1735) already referred to ; also the broadside "Fitzgiggo", showing a view of Covent Garden stage in 1763 (reproduced in Mr. Henry Saxe Wyndham's *Annals of Covent Garden Theatre*, i. 154).

price of admission there was duly advertised. At Goodman's Fields in 1734 the cost was five shillings, or a shilling more than to the boxes.

Acting at this period still remained a rhetorical art. Notwithstanding the long habituation to pictorial backgrounds little progress had been made towards scenic illusion or stage realism. Not only were spectators allowed to sit in stage boxes and proscenium balconies, but they also occupied benches running on the sides of the stage from the orchestra halfway to the back scene, and railed in with heavy balustrades, or draped enclosures.[1] Owing to the frequency of disturbances behind the the scenes it was decreed in 1721 that a guard of soldiers should be sent nightly to the principal theatres, and from this period onwards for half a century two grenadiers kept watch and ward at each performance beside the proscenium doors. We find a reference to their presence in the first number of *The Centinel*, a weekly Journal, published in London on January 6, 1757 :

> The *Centinel* has likewise engaged in his service those tall gentlemen of the cloth, who at our theatres appear upon the stage in clean spatter-dashes, nodding-caps and burnished arms, seeming to support the wooden ornaments of the Proscenium, and adding a terrific grandeur to the drama. They are instructed to superintend the representation with a critical eye; to make a faithful report of the excellencies and demerits of each performer; &c., &c.

In Dublin, where the proscenium doors had been a regular stage feature from late in the seventeenth century,[2] the custom of having a military guard in front was soon followed. In connection with her engagement at the Smock Alley Theatre in 1746-7, Mrs. Bellamy writes :

> Mr. Sheridan, in consequence of the insult I had received from Mr. St. Leger, as before related, and on account of the inconveniences arising from the custom, had given a general order at the

---

[1] See the reproduction of Hogarth's painting of "The Beggar's Opera" in *The Magazine of Art* for August, 1895, p. 386 (article on "Stage Scenery in the Eighteenth Century").

[2] In Charles Shadwell's *The Hasty Wedding*, ii. 4, as acted at Smock Alley c. 1718 and first printed in Shadwell's collected works in 1720, we have the direction, "Exit. Enter, at the other door, Herriot."

doors of the theatre, and notice in all the public papers, that no gentleman was, on any account, to be admitted behind the scenes. It happened one night, just as I was so far recovered as to venture to the house, but not to perform; that an officer who had more wine in his head than humanity in his heart, insisted on passing the centry placed at the [proscenium] stage-door. The poor fellow persisting in his refusal of admittance, the officer drew his sword and stabbed him in the thigh, with so much violence that the weapon broke, and left a piece in the most dangerous part. Hearing a riot on the stage, I ran from the box in which I sat, and flew in my fright to the next centinel for protection. This happening to be the man who had been wounded, I found myself in a moment encompassed by numbers, and was obliged to be a witness to the broken steel being taken out.[1]

Ireland by no means formed the western limit of the travels of the proscenium doors and balconies. By 1767 the conventional disposition had been adopted in New York, to remain in vogue in all the leading American theatres for half a century.[2]

After the abolition of the custom of spectators sitting on the stage managers sought to make up for their consequent loss of revenue by increasing the number of stage boxes. Eventually the tendency in this direction operated against the preservation of the proscenium doors. In a rare engraving of the Screen scene in *The School for Scandal*, issued in October, 1778, showing the stage front of Drury Lane, one notes no fewer than twelve stage boxes on the two sides in four vertical rows. Probably only eight of these were for actual use, as the uppermost pair on either side are shown empty, and were doubtless added to be in harmony with the general architectural scheme of the auditorium. Beyond the stage boxes were the two entering doors with their small balconies, and finally, in the distance, the proscenium arch.[3]

[1] *An Apology for the Life of George Anne Bellamy* (Dublin, 1785), i. 94.
[2] A quaint old view of the primitive John Street Theatre, New York, c. 1767, shows the doors and balconies but gives no indication of the apron. For the doors at Philadelphia in 1811, see Dunlap's *Memoirs of Geo. Fredk. Cooke*, ii. 286.
[3] For an exemplar of the engraving (the only one I know of), see the Grangerised copy of George Daniel's *Garrick in the Green Room* (1829), in the British Museum (pressmark "₁871 b").

As acting still took place well to the front, the players were flanked on both sides by tiers of spectators. Liberal as this supply of stage boxes at old Drury now appears, it apparently did not suffice to meet the demands ; in September, 1780, the entering doors were taken away and extra boxes put in their place. [1] We know that these doors were subsequently restored, in deference probably to the wishes of the tradition-ridden players, but the exact period of restoration is difficult to determine. The only definite evidence that can be unearthed points to the year 1794, but two items of no great cogency suggest a much earlier date. Boaden in writing, *longo intervallo*, of Mrs. Siddons's acting as Jane Shore at Drury Lane in 1782, apparently from personal recollections, says :

> There was in my early days such a permanent property as a stage-door in our theatres, and the proscenium beyond it ; so that when Shore was pushed from the door, she was turned round and staggered till supported by the firm projection behind her. Here was a terrific picture full in the eye of the pit, and this most picturesqe of women knew the amazing value of it. [2]

It may be, of course, that in writing a quarter of a century after the event, Boaden fell a victim to a confused memory. On the other hand there is some slender evidence to hand which tends to prove the accuracy of his statement. In a collection of Drury Lane ana preserved in an old scrapbook in the British Museum is a cutting [3] dated "1785", without mention of the source, which runs :

> We wish to point out to the managers of old Drury a little circumstance to which we hope they will pay immediate and strict attention. We mean the eternal jar of the stage-doors. The ladies of this Theatre are most of them, we must confess, very pretty women, and well frized, well feathered, well-rouged, and well-dressed ; we never see them without pleasure. We should be happy therefore to be spared the mortification of such unseasonable peeps

---

[1] See the account of the opening of Drury Lane for the season in *Walker's Hibernian Magazine* for October, 1780.
[2] *Memoirs of Mrs. Siddons* (1827), Chap. x.
[3] Copied by me some years ago. Unfortunately I omitted to note the press-mark of the volume.

at the dear creatures in their dishabille, with their unpowdered locks about their ears, or tucked under a black bonnet, and their sweet persons disguised in long cloaks, and loose-bodied coats.[1]

Whether or not the doors at old Drury were soon restored, one notes that in September, 1782, Covent Garden made a faint attempt to follow the lead given. Extra boxes were placed on the stage and the entering doors removed behind the curtain.[2] Boaden explains why the alteration created general discontent among the players :

I well remember the effect of its additional boxes in the situation of the old stage doors, and that these essential things in the new structure were behind the curtain. The actors seemed to feel embarrassed by the more extended area of the stage. There was no springing off with the established glance at the pit and projected right arm. The actor was obliged to edge away in his retreat towards the far distant wings with somewhat of the tedium, but not all the awkwardness, which is observed in the exits at the Italian Opera.[3]

The result was that, when Covent Garden was reconstructed in 1792, the stage was provided with a deeper apron, the extra boxes were removed, and the doors brought back to their old position. That is to say, they were ensconced between the Corinthian pilasters and columns of the proscenium, and adorned attractively with white and gold. Boaden's contemptuous reference to the Italian Opera is amusing, seeing that the absence of proscenium doors and cumbersome stage boxes at the King's Theatre in the Haymarket had led there to a forestalment of the latter-day triumphs of scenic illusion. In a notice[4] of the *Don Giovanni* of Mozart at that house in 1817, we read :

We have never seen upon any stage so perfect an exhibition of moonlight as that at the King's Theatre in the new opera of Don

---

[1] It was customary for players and others in those days to linger (and sometimes sit) behind the proscenium doors. See an anecdote of Tom King in Dublin in 1794 in Michael Kelly's *Reminiscences* (1826, second edition), ii. 49.

[2] *Walker's Hibernian Magazine* (October, 1782), p. 508.

[3] op. cit. Chap. viii.

[4] Quoted from some London paper, unspecified, in *The Freeman's Journal* of Dublin for April 23, 1817. The King's Theatre was built in 1790 from designs by Novosielski.

Juan; it is produced also by the simplest means. The blue trans-
parent veil through which the light falls on the statue is a perfect
imitation of nature; and we see in this instance how preferable for
dramatic effect is the form of stage in the front of which there is
no projection, either by side wings, doors, pillars, or picture frames.
Here the scene and the hall (i. e. the part allotted to spectators) run
into one another, without a break or interruption—and the spectators actually sit in the moonlight, so perfect is the illusion.

For some considerable time before this the Italian opera-
houses had been enabled to give a series of object-lessons in
scenic realism to the London theatres owing to their freedom
from the conventional doors. Foreign singers, accustomed
to enter by the wing, set their faces resolutely against all
attempts to introduce the English principle. A view of the
Pantheon, published in 1815 by Robert Wilkinson, shows
the opera house as it was after its reconstruction four years
previously on the model of the great theatre at Milan. The
position within the proscenium arch on either side, normally
occupied at the patent theatres by the entering doors and
balconies, was filled up from the boards to the proscenium
border with boxes, eight in all, in vertical sets of four.
Although a capacious apron, flanked by other rows of boxes,
was provided the singers were prevented from coming out
beyond the proscenium by a series of formidable footlights
ranged in line with the front pilasters.

If the entering doors were restored to their old position
at Drury Lane about 1781, it is curious to find, when the
house was rebuilt in 1793, that the extra stage boxes still
held their pride of place and that no entering doors were
to be seen. One would be inclined to think from this that
they had never been replaced. At best the whole story of the
choppings and changings at this house reveal woeful inde-
cision on the part of its proprietors. In September, 1797,
the doors were once more restored to their old position.
Concerning the alteration we read in *The Monthly Mirror:*

There is a stage door on each side, forming a segment of a circle,
and over these doors are two tiers of boxes. The effect of this addition is a contraction of the width of the stage, and an additional

space behind the scenes, which gives more facility to the move-
ment of the scenery.[1]

The difficulty experienced from this onward in insti-
tuting a wholesale reform was due to the fact that the
London stage of the early nineteenth century was mostly
recruited from the ranks of country players, and that in the
country the convention of the proscenium doors died exceedingly hard. Players, as a rule, are more concerned for
the effect of their own individual acting than for the general
artistic result, and they fight stubbornly for anything that
panders to their own selfish instincts. It is this attitude that
still preserves the footlights in spite of the century-long
clamouring of the reformers.

Owing to the prolonged employment of the proscenium
doors England had failed to keep step with other nations
in the steady march towards scenic realism. This point was
soundly driven home by an acute observer in 1807 :

In England there is hardly ever a central door contrived in the
flat which closes the scene. Whatever be the performance, and
whosoever be the personages, they either all walk in and out at the
permanent doors, which form part of the proscenium, or they slide
in and out between the intervals of the wings, which are generally
intended to represent a solid cohering wall ; so that, were the laws
of perspective so sufficiently attended to in the painting of the
scenes, and they were made, as they should be made, to look like
an uninterrupted mass of masonry, the entrance and exit of each
personage through the solid wall would every time appear to be
effected by downright witchcraft.[2]

In France at this period, the writer goes on to say, things
were differently ordered. If a room were represented it
bore the normal aspect of a room and had appropriate fold-
ing doors. Or, if the business of the scene required that the
room should lead into several others, then two or three

---

[1] In a view of Drury Lane in May, 1800, preserved in Smith's Compiled History
of the English Stage, Vol. xvii (in the British Museum), showing George III standing in
the left hand stage box after being shot at by Hatfield, a proscenium door on that side
of the modest apron is clearly indicated. For interior views of Drury Lane, Covent
Garden and the Haymarket in 1808, see Thomas Gilliland's *The Dramatic Mirror*,
Vol. i. All three show the doors.
[2] Cited by Dutton Cook in *On the Stage*, i. 190, without mention of the source.

doors were provided. Illusion by this means was heightened, and the story of the play made more comprehensible, "not to speak of the infinitely more striking effect which is produced by a performer of commanding mien, invested with a dignified character, entering the scene in the centre, and, from his very first appearance, presenting himself in front to the spectators, instead of being obliged to slide edgeways on and off the boards through an interstice in the side scenes."

Reform in this direction was snail-paced; it was not until the period of the Bancroft management at the Prince of Wales' Theatre sixty years later that anything material was effected.[1] But in 1812 Drury Lane again essayed to pioneer the way. When the house was rebuilt after the disastrous fire, several improvements, suggested by Samuel Whitbread, the brewer, one of the managing committee, were carried out. Once more the permanent doors were taken away. For the old-fashioned proscenium arch was substituted a gilded picture frame, remote from the footlights, over which the actors were forbidden to step.[2] Grumblings both loud and deep were heard among the players over their various deprivations, and finally old Dowton, pluckier than the rest, broke into open rebellion. "Don't tell me of frames and pictures!" he exclaimed, with choler, "if I can't be heard by the audience in the frame, I'll walk out of it." And out of it he came. The absurdity, of course, was in preserving a useless apron before the frame. To the removal of the proscenium doors mordant allusion was made in one of "The Rejected Addresses", wherein the ghost of Dr. Johnson, after rising through a trap, indulges in a disquisition from which the following is extracted:

Permanent stage doors we have none. That which is permanent cannot be removed; for, if removed, it soon ceases to be perma-

---

[1] Cf. Mr. William Archer's *The Theatrical World of* 1897, pp. 180-1, article on "The Drama of the Reign."

[2] When a similar device was adopted at the Queen's Theatre, Manchester, in March, 1846, a local journal characterised the innovation "an outrage upon the best principles of theatrical usage." The proscenium picture frame, with hidden footlights, was finally established by the Bancrofts at the Haymarket in 1879.

DE. BURSON'S NEW STAGE FRONT OF THE THEATRE ROYAL, COVENT GARDEN.

COVENT GARDEN THEATRE, 1821   [*To face p.* 184.
(Model for a Toy Theatre.)

nent. What stationary absurdity can vie with that ligneous barri-
cade which, decorated with frappant and tintinnabulant appendages,
now serves as the entrance of the lowly cottage, and now as the
exit of a lady's chamber: at one time insinuating plastic harlequin
into a butcher's shop, and at another yawning as a floodgate, to
precipitate the Cyprians of St. Giles's into the embraces of Macbeth.
To elude this glaring absurdity, to give to each respective mansion
the door which the carpenter would doubtless have given, we vary
our portal with the varying scene, passing from deal to mahogany,
and from mahogany to oak, as the opposite claims of cottage, palace,
or castle may appear to require.

Amid the general hum of gratulation which flatters us in front,
it is fit that some regard should be paid to the murmurs of despon-
dence that assail us in the rear. They, as I have elsewhere expressed
it, "who live to please," should not have their own pleasures entirely
overlooked. The children of Thespis are general in their censures
of the architect in having placed the locality of exit at such a distance
from the oily radiators which now dazzle the eyes of him who addresses
you. I am, cries the Queen of Terrors, robbed of my fair proportions. When the King-killing thane hints to the breathless auditory
the murders he means to perpetrate in the castle of Macduff " ere
my purpose cool," so vast is the interval he has to travel before he
can escape from the stage, that his purpose has even time to freeze.
Your condition cries the Muse of Smiles, is hard, but it is cygnet's
down in comparison with mine. The peerless peer of capers and
congees has laid it down as a rule, that the best good thing uttered
by the morning visitor should conduct him rapidly to the doorway,
last impression vying in durability with first. But when on this
boarded elongation it falls to my lot to say a good thing, to ejacu-
late, "keep moving," or to chaunt, "hic hoc horum genitivo,"
many are the moments that must elapse ere I can hide myself from
public vision in the recesses of O.P. or P.S.

Irritated beyond endurance by the complaints of the
players, the Drury Lane management restored the doors
for the last time in the course of a year or two. As if to
prove they still had their utility, they were pressed effectively into service in an amusing epilogue about an epilogue
spoken after the new comedy of *Lost Life,* on November 13,
1821. No sooner had the curtain fallen than Mrs. Edwin
and the prompter came on through the P.S. door to wrangle

over the lines that should be delivered. In her distress, after the departure of the prompter, the actress goes to the door and rings up the curtain. Then the players are discovered on the stage in confusion. Willing as they are to help, they finally decree that no epilogue shall be spoken—and, in so expressing themselves in rhyme, speak it![1] This, however, was but an expiring flicker ; within a year the doors were banished from Drury Lane for ever. When the house re-opened for the season on October 16, 1822, Terry spoke an address by George Colman in which incidental reference was made to the change :

> Thus, then :— our Manager, who scouts the fears
> Of pulling on old house about his ears,
> Has spared of our late edifice's pride,
> The outward walls, and little else beside :
>
> . . . .
>
> Look round and judge ; his efforts are all waste
> Unless you stamp them as a work of taste ;
> Nor blame him for transporting from the floors
> Those old offenders here—the two stage doors ;
> Doors which have oft with burnish'd pannels stood
> And golden knockers glittering in a wood,
> Which on their posts, through every change remain'd
> Fast as Bray's Vicar, whosoever reign'd ;
> That served for palace, cottage, street or hall,
> Used for each place, and out of place in all ;
> Station'd, like watchmen who in lamplight sit,
> For all their business of the night unfit.[2]

Exactly a year later Covent Garden fell in line. A report of the re-opening of that house in October, 1823, tells us "the stage doors have been removed, and superb boxes put in their places."[3] But as yet only half the battle had been won. Neither in town nor country was the example of the two great patent theatres immediately followed.[4] In 1828-30, when the French players occupied the Lyceum

---

[1] Given *in extenso* in *The Drama ; or Theatrical Pocket Magazine* (1821), i. 354.
[2] *The Drama ; or Theatrical Pocket Magazine*, iii. 228.
[3] *The Drama*, v. 128.
[4] For a view of the Olympic in 1826, showing the doors, see *The Era Almanack* (1891), p. 21. A reform took place there in 1831.

theatre, the doors were still *in situ* but were hidden during their tenancy by draperies.[1] It was probably owing to the contempt with which they were treated by the visitors that they were removed within the next year or two. Most of the outlying theatres, however, continued to cling stubbornly to the outworn convention. In 1853 the doors were actually restored at the Royal Standard Theatre after a long banishment.[2] In 1865 they were still in existence at the Surrey at the period of the fire there.[3] When the house was rebuilt the apron was again to be seen, but the doors were not replaced. So far as the metropolis was concerned, the old doors lingered longest at Sadlers Wells, where they survived the theatrical glories of Islington, remaining *in situ*, as silent testimonies to a creed outworn, until about the year 1879. Writing of his juvenile experiences at that historic house in the early fifties, Clement Scott says :

Two things were impressed on my young mind in the arrangement of the theatre soon after Grimaldi had quitted the stage of life for ever. One was the orthodoxy of the proscenium, as may be seen from the pictures by George Cruikshank, . . . and the second was the solemn custom of never playing tragedy at any theatre save on a green baize carpet. The proscenium was to all intents a little house, and it was fascinating to a child to see on either side of the stage proper a little green door with brass knockers and handles, and over each door a window with lace curtains and a balcony with flower pots on it. These proscenium doors were never used, except occasionally in pantomime for the purposes of the play ; but no one dreamed of taking a call or of coming on to make a managerial speech except through these little doors, a survival, no doubt, of the Theatre of the Greeks, as you will see in Donaldson's remarkable book.[4]

[1] Cf. Austin Brereton's *The Lyceum and Henry Irving* (1903), p. 53, for a view of the Lyceum at this period. Above the draperies are to be seen the proscenium boxes shown above the doors in the cut of the Lyceum in 1817, given at p. 42.

[2] Cf. *The Theatrical Journal*, xiv. No. 712, p. 238.

[3] See the view of the theatre on fire in Vol. 1 of W. C. Streatfeild's *Theatrical Notices from Newspapers*, in the British Museum (press-mark "314 b").

[4] *English Illustrated Magazine* (Christmas, 1898), p. 271, article on "The King of Clownland". For the reference to Donaldson, see *The Theatre of the Greeks* (eighth edition, 1875), p. 262 et seq. But the suggested origin (as applied to the Elizabethan doors) would be difficult to prove.

One may be pardoned here for going off at a tangent to discuss an interesting point suggested by the above extract, a point too trivial to admit of separate consideration. It would appear that the custom of covering the stage with a green cloth when a tragedy was to be performed was of some little antiquity. (Tragedy and it, by the way, died together fifty years ago). In Garrick's epilogue to Home's tragedy, *Alfred*, as spoken at Covent Garden by Mrs. Barry in 1778, we read:

> If this green cloth could speak, would it not tell,
> Upon its well-worn nap how oft I fell?
> To death in various forms deliver'd up
> Steel kills me one night, and the next the cup.

Some slight evidence exists to show that even when these lines were spoken the custom was old. In a slipshod translation of Sorbières' "Relation d'un voyage en Angleterre où sont touchées plusieurs choses qui regardent l'estat des sciences et de la religion et autres matières curieuses",[1] issued in London in 1709, under title *A Voyage to England*, we find, at p. 69, the following passage:

> The Playhouse is much more Diverting and Commodious: the best places are in the Pit, where Men and Women promiscuously sit, every Body with their Company. The Stage is very handsome, being covered with green cloth, and the Scenes often change, and you are regaled with new Perspectives.

In this last sentence are both an omission and a mistranslation. Insert the one and you prove the other. What Sorbières wrote[2] was: "Le Théâtre est fort beau, couvert d'un Tapis verd, et en scene y est toute libre, avec beaucoup de changemens, et des perspectives." The word "théâtre" here refers to the auditorium, not to the stage, which was free (not encumbered, as in Paris, with spectators); and it was the benches of the pit that were "couvert d'un Tapis verd." But the fact that the translator made a palpable misreading proves that the custom of placing a green cloth on the stage for tragedies was known early in the reign of

[1] Paris, 1664.   [2] p. 166.

THE LAST OF THE PROSCENIUM DOORS.

Adelphi Theatre, Liverpool (1832–1905).

Queen Anne. What Sorbières meant to convey is indicated in the following passage from the *Journal des Voyages de Monsieur de Monconys*[1] describing a visit paid to the Theatre Royal in Bridges Street on May 22, 1663:

> L' apres-dinée nous fusmes chez le Milord de S. Alban, et de la à la Comedie dans la loge du Roy. Le Théâtre est le plus propre et le plus beau que j'aye Jamais veu, tout tapissé par le bas de bayette verte; aussi bien que toutes les loges qui en sont tapissées avec des bandes de cuir dore. Tous le bancs du parterre où toutes les personnes de condition se mettent aussi, sont rangez en amphitheatre, les uns plus hauts que les autres.

It needs to be said that this demonstration of the translator's mistake is made "without prejudice". The custom of placing a green cloth on the stage for tragedies may have existed in Restoration days. We have no record of it earlier.

Returning to our main theme one may say, in concluding, that the "last scene of all" ending our "strange, eventful history" is laid in what is quaintly known in theatrical argot as "the provinces." Driven from London, the convention of the proscenium entering doors made its last stand in the country playhouses, and was "an unconscionable long time a-dying." Here and there in the backwaters of life some memorials of its former rule remain. No need, however, to depart from the main stream in seeking for examples. Down to the period when it ceased to be used for dramatic purposes, or about six years ago, the old Adelphi in Liverpool continued to preserve its time-honoured proscenium doors, with their over-hanging balconies traditionally arrayed in white lace curtains. The theatre is now used for cinematograph exhibitions, but the stage is untouched and the doors still remain.

[3] Lyon, 1666, Part II, p. 25.

DID THOMAS SHADWELL WRITE AN OPERA ON "THE TEMPEST"?

Did Thomas Shadwell write an Opera on "The Tempest"?

The sole authority for the ascription of an opera on *The Tempest* to Thomas Shadwell is the *Roscius Anglicanus* of John Downes, a rambling stage record published in 1708, when the quondam prompter who penned it was in the decline of his years and his intellect. Having little or no documentary evidence to rely upon, and fully conscious of the defectiveness of his memory, Downes takes shelter behind the hope that " he is not very erroneous in his relation." In the face of this warning, and owing to the difficulty of obtaining testing data, later historians have taken his statements largely on trust, and thereby perpetuated many a falsity. It cannot be too strongly emphasised that through slovenliness of arrangement the *Roscius Anglicanus* is positively honeycombed with error. It is the perspective of the thing that is wholly wrong. In other words, the events related mostly took place, but seldom in the sequence indicated. It is the old story of a senile memory with nothing to check its vagaries. One takes it that Downes is least likely to have erred in dealing with matters which came directly under his own notice, when he was prompter at the old Duke's theatre in Dorset Gardens. In accordance with that view, the present inquiry has been undertaken with the hope of demonstrating the accuracy of his statement concerning Shadwell's provision of an operatic version of *The Tempest* for that house, and of arriving at some approximation to the date of its production. The discussion is not profitless, for one cannot solve the problem without clearing up on the way one or two minor mysteries of Post-Restoration stage history.

When we come at the outset to look for explicit corroboration of Downes' statement all historical resources fail. No version of *The Tempest*, bearing Shadwell's name on the title-page, was ever printed. Winstanley, in dealing with his friend's career in his *Lives of the Famous English Poets* (1687), is careful to mention his *Psyche*, although it was little better than a bald translation, but is silent regarding *The Tempest*. A few years later Langbaine and Gildon, in similar works, are equally ill-informed. One says ill-informed advisedly, because the silence of all three on the point indicates, not the possible blundering of Downes, but that the secret of Shadwell's association with the opera had, for some reason, been carefully preserved.

Let us now minutely consider what Downes says on the subject. Treating of what appears to have been the original production of Aphra Behn's maiden effort, *The Forced Marriage ; or The Jealous Bridegroom*, he implies that the play was brought out at Dorset Gardens in 1672. We are directly informed that it held its place in the bills for six nights, and that in it Otway, as the King, made his first and last appearance on the stage, his failure being so pronounced that he abandoned all hope of following acting as a profession. Continuing, Downes writes :

> The year after, in 1673, *The Tempest, or the Inchanted Island*, made into an opera by Mr. Shadwell, having all new in it ; as Scenes, Machines ; particularly one Scene painted with myriads of Ariel (sic) Spirits ; [1] and another flying away, with a Table Furnisht out with Fruits, Sweetmeats and all sorts of Viands ; just when Duke Trinculo and his companions were going to Dinner ; all was things perform'd in it so admirably well, that not any succeeding opera got more money.

Now, to begin with, unless Downes is referring to a revival of Mrs. Behn's tragi-comedy, which is extremely unlikely, his implied date for *The Forced Marriage* is wrong. Not only that, but he has assigned the production to a wrong

---

[1] At this period, and for half a century later, it was customary, in scenes of a silent multitude, to paint the figures on the canvas, and not to bring on a host of supernumeraries. This was the cheaper, but hardly the more illusive method. For a later example, see Chetwood's *General History of the Stage* (London, 1749), p. 154. The custom had been introduced by D'Avenant in his Commonwealth operas and was doubtless derived from the French stage. Cf. *La Mort de Cyrus*, tragi-comedy of M. Rozidor (1659). Also Eugène Rigal, *Le Théâtre Français avant la Période Classique*, p. 255 (reference to the tragedy of *La Pucelle d'Orléans* c. 1642).

theatre. It is necessary to recall that the Duke's Theatre in Dorset Gardens, as first opened on November 9, 1671, succeeded to the title of an earlier theatre in Lincoln's Inn Fields. It was certainly at the latter house that *The Forced Marriage* was produced, and the period must have been about the close of the year 1670, for the play was printed in January or February, 1671, "as acted at the Duke's Theatre".[1] In the cast of characters prefixed, the name of Westwood is placed opposite the King. If Otway the poet made his début as an actor in the original production of the play and never appeared afterwards, then Westwood cannot be taken as his *nom de guerre*, for Westwood's name crops up again in the cast of Crowne's *Juliana*, a tragi-comedy acted at Lincoln's Inn Fields in the summer of 1671. From what Downes says it seems probable that Otway broke down during the first performance of *The Forced Marriage*, and in that case he may have been at once succeeded by Westwood in the part of the King.[2]

Here one must cry a halt to discuss the earlier stage history of *The Tempest*. By a curious regulation, made in December, 1660, D'Avenant's company—the company which afterwards occupied the two Duke's theatres in succession—were given the monopoly of nine of Shakespeare's plays, *The Tempest* among the number.[3] The result was most injurious to the poet. After long delay, a brutally augmented version of *The Tempest*, the work of Dryden and D'Avenant, was brought out, as a comedy, at the Duke's in Lincoln's Inn Fields on November 7, 1667. In this painful, long-lived sophistication Miranda was provided with a sister, Dorinda, and, by way of balancing the sexual equilibrium, a youth, Hypolito, was introduced, who had never seen a woman. It is generally, perhaps justly, considered

---

[1] It is announced in the *Term Catalogue* issued on Feb. 13, 1671.

[2] Most authorities render confusion worse confounded in dealing with this matter. The *Dict. Nat. Biog.*, *sub nomine* "Otway", bases on Downes and manipulates the facts accordingly. Cf. Mr. Edmund Gosse's *Seventeenth Century Studies*, p. 273, where we are told, after some discussion of Downes' blunder, that Otway went to Christ Church in 1669, appeared at Lincoln's Inn Fields in the Long Vacation of 1671, and returned to Oxford, where he remained till 1674.

[3] Cf. R. W. Lowe's *Thomas Betterton*, p. 75.

that the discredit of these additions must mainly fall upon Sir William D'Avenant. Be that as it may, the play, after his death, remained the property of his widow, who, in conjunction with her son, at once assumed control of the Duke's Theatre. As first printed in quarto (Quarto 1) by Henry Herringman early in 1670, this maltreatment of *The Tempest* had a signed preface by Dryden, written in 1669. Now comes the important point. In 1674 the same publisher issued a piece entitled " *The Tempest, or The Enchanted Island*, a Comedy, as it is now acted at his Highness the Duke of York's Theatre " (Quarto 2).[1] It will be remarked that nothing is here said as to the authorship, but seeing that the quarto not only includes Dryden's earlier preface but the prologue and epilogue of 1667 as well, the unwary student is apt to jump to the conclusion that the whole is merely a reprint, or corrected impression, of the Dryden-D'Avenant play. Into the trap thus laid by a stupid publisher all the editors of Dryden and of D'Avenant carelessly fell.[2] It never dawned upon them (what remains to be demonstrated) that in Quarto 2 they had the book of Shadwell's opera. It is far from easy to divine why Herringman should have reprinted the old preface and rhymed addresses where they had absolutely no relevancy. The senselessness of this course is all the more remarkable from the fact that the opera, as will shortly be seen, had a special prologue and epilogue of its own. It may be, however, there was method (of a kind) in Herringman's madness, for he had previously been guilty of at least one act of similar stupidity. When he reprinted *The Siege of Rhodes* in 1659, immediately after its revival at the Cockpit theatre, he reproduced D'Avenant's original

---

[1] Announced in the *Term Catalogue* of Nov. 25, 1674.

[2] Scott, in editing Dryden's Dramatic Works in 1808, gave the text of Quarto 2 as that of the Dryden-D'Avenant comedy. Cf. Furness, *Variorum Shakespeare*, ix, pp. 389 ff., where the error is repeated. Credit is due to Prof. Saintsbury for having been the first to draw attention to the discrepancies between the two quartos. (See his recension of Scott's *Dryden*, 1883, iii. 104). Unfortunately, instead of recognising that they represent two different versions of the altered play, the one a comedy and the other an opera, he assumes Quarto 2 to be a mere corrected copy of Quarto 1, and takes great pains to indicate the variations in his footnotes. In connection with Dryden this is labour wholly mis-spent.

preface of 1656, with all its inapposite references to the restricted space of "the room " in Rutland House, where the opera had been first performed.

Next to the reprinting in Quarto 2 of the Dryden preface, prologue and epilogue of Quarto 1, the one thing that has long obscured the truth concerning Quarto 2 is the description, "a Comedy ", on the title-page. This, too, helped to lead up to the erroneous conclusion arrived at by the various editors of Dryden and D'Avenant. But as evidence it really is of no value. Downes refers to the D'Avenant *Macbeth* and to *Circe* as operas, although in the quartos of both they are styled tragedies. It may be that the mis-description of *The Tempest* was Downes's and that Shadwell's version was not actually announced as an opera. The piece does not come fully within the meaning of the term as interpreted by Dryden. "An *opera*," he writes, "is a Poetical Tale, or Fiction, represented by Vocal and Instrumental Musick, adorned with Scenes, Machines, and Dancing." Elsewhere, in the same essay, he points out that the story in an opera must be wholly sung, and shows that he looked upon the Shadwell *Tempest* as a comedy "mixed with *opera*, or a *Drama* written in Blank verse, adorned with Scenes, Machines, Songs, and Dances." [1] Downes, who was not given to nice distinctions, calls the Shadwell *Tempest* an opera because it had pronounced operatic features. New instrumental music had been provided by Matthew Lock, particularly the First, Second and Third Music (the third distinctively known as the "Curtain Tune"), which, after the Restoration custom, preceded the rising of the curtain, no matter what the nature of the performance. [2] Some of the vocal music to the genuine Shakespearean songs was old, written, it would appear, by Banister and Pelham Humphreys for the Dryden-D'Avenant comedy of 1667; but some new vocal music

---

[1] Preface to *Albion and Albanius* (1685). North, in his *Memoirs of Music*, calls the ornate musical productions of the period "semi-operas".

[2] A selection of Lock's *Tempest* music was published in 1675, together with his music for *Psyche*. Cf. *Quart. Mag. of the International Society of Music*, Year v, Part iv. 1904, p. 552, article by Mr. W. Barclay Squire on "Purcell's Dramatic Music", wherein the matter is fully discussed.

was also provided by Pietro Reggio and J. Hart. Apart, however, from these extrinsic items of evidence, the operatic nature of the piece is indicated by the preliminary description in Quarto 2 :

> The front of the stage is opened and the Band of 24 violins with the Harpsicals and Theorbos, which accompany the voices, are placed between the Pit and the Stage.[1] While the Overture[2] is playing the Curtain rises, and discovers a new Frontispiece, joyn'd to the great Pylasters, on each side of the Stage. This frontispiece is a noble Arch, supported by large wreathed columns of the Corinthian Order ; the wreathings of the columns are beautifi'd with Roses round them, and several Cupids flying about them. On the Cornice, just over the Capitals, sits on either side a Figure, with a Trumpet in one hand, and a Palm in the other, representing Fame. A little farther on the same Cornice, on each side of a Compass-pediment, lie a Lion and a Unicorn, on each side of a Royal Arms of England. In the middle of the Arch are several Angels holding the King's Arms, as if they were placing them in the midst of that Compass-pediment. Behind this is the Scene, which represents a thick, Cloudy sky, and very Rocky Coast, and a Tempestuous Sea in perpetual agitation.

Here, at the outset, we have proof, partly in the increased orchestra and partly in the provision of a special frontispiece, or secondary proscenium, of the operatic nature of the production. All the operas of the latter half of the seventeenth century, from *The Siege of Rhodes* to *Albion and Albanius* were adorned with these individual proscenia. As an interesting side issue, it may be noted that the main characteristics of the frontispiece to *The Tempest* suggest that Shadwell's version was prepared by command of Charles II and enjoyed his patronage. Confirmation of this is lent by the

---

[1] Malone, Collier and Karl Elze have all gravely confused the issue by attributing this description to Quarto 1, in which, of course, it has no place. Their conclusion that it affords positive proof that the musicians had begun to occupy what we now consider their normal position, c. 1667, must fall to the ground. Note we have here mention of 24 violins ; the ordinary theatre band of the period had only twelve.

[2] For the music of Lock's "Curtain Tune for *The Tempest*", see Stafford Smith's *Musica Antiqua*, i. 68, where also a *Lilk* from the same piece is given. Cf. *The Oxford History of Music*, iii. 288, where the term "curtain tune" is misinterpreted. It was never applied to inter-act music.

fact (shortly to be demonstrated) that the men and boys of the Chapel Royal were allowed to sing in the production.

Based on the Dryden-D'Avenant comedy of 1667, and comprising all its features, Shadwell's opera has several distinguishing characteristics. As these have been fully noted by Prof. Saintsbury, [1] one finds no need to discuss them in detail now. It will suffice to say that the main differentiation of the operatic version lies in the terminal Masque of *Neptune and Amphitrite*. But it is vital for us to note that in Act ii. 4 of Quarto 2 occurs a new song, "Arise ye subterranean winds," the music for which was published in 1680, in Part ii. of Pietro Reggio's Songs, under title "A Song in the Tempest. The Words by Mr. Shadwell." Here we have ample corroboration of Downes' statement regarding the authorship, as well as proof that Quarto 2 represents the book of Shadwell's opera. Other proof is afforded by the book itself. Downes' reference to the "scene painted with myriads of Ariel spirits" tallies with the description at the end of the fifth act, where the "Scene changes to the Rising Sun, and a number of Aerial Spirits in the air, Ariel flying from the sun advances towards the pit." Downes' other reference to the "flying away, with a Table Furnisht with Fruits, Sweetmeats and all sorts of Viands," deals with the incidents in Act iii. 3 : "Dance of fantastick Spirits, after the dance, a Table furnish'd with Meat and Fruits is brought in by two Spirits. . . . . Two Spirits descend and flie away with the Table."

Our next task is to determine the period when the opera was produced. An important clue is afforded by an unpublished "Prologue and Epilogue to the Tempest" preserved in the Egerton MSS. in the British Museum. [2] These two addresses, now reproduced, were undoubtedly written by Shadwell for his own opera. They are marked by that "shambling doggerel," to quote Prof. Saintsbury, for which the nascent poet laureate was noted :

[1] Vide *supra* p. 196 note 2.   [2] No. 2,623.

PROLOGUE

Wee, as the ffathers of the stage have said,
To treat you here, a vast expense have made;
What they have gott from you in chests is laid,
Or is for purchas'd Lands, or houses paid.
You, in this house, all our estate may find,
Wch for your pleasures wholly are design'd.
'Twas foolish, for we might, we must confesse,
Value ourselves much more, and you much lesse;
And like those reverend men, we might have spar'd
And never for our Benefactors car'd: 10
Still made your Treatment, as they do, more Coarse,
As if you did, as fast as they, grow worse:
But we young men, are apt to slight advice,
One day, we may decrepid grow and wise:
Then, hoping not to time to get much more,
We'll Save our money, and cry out wee'r poore.
Wee're young, and look yet many yeares to live,
And by your future Bounty hope to thrive;
Then let us laugh, for now no cost wee'l spare
And never think we're poor, while we your favours share, 20
Without the good old Playes we did advance,
And all ye stages ornament enhance;
To splendid things they follow in, but late:
They ne're invent, but they can imitate:
Had we not, for yr. pleasure found new wayes
You still had rusty arras had, and thred-bare playes;
Nor scenes nor Woomen, had they had their will,
But some some with grizl'd Beards had acted Woomen still.[1]
Some restive horses, spight of Switch and spurre,
Till others strain against 'em, will not stir.   30
Envying our Splendid house, and prosp'rous playes,
They scoff at us, and Libell the high wayes.
Tis fitt we, for our faults, rebukes shou'd meet.
The Citty ought to mend those of ye street.
With the best poets' heads our house we grac'd
Wch we in honour to ye Poets plac'd.[2]

---

[1] Equal to claiming that Sir William D'Avenant had first introduced actresses and scenery on the English Stage.

[2] Cf. Tom D'Urfey's *Collin's Walk Through London* (1690), Canto iv, where the peripatetic, on visiting Dorset Gardens,

Too much of the old witt They have, tis true:
But they must look for little of ye new.

Epilogue

When feeble Lovers' appetites decay
They, to provoke, and keep themselves in play,
Must, to their Cost, make ye gay Damsells shine;
If Beauty can't provoke, they'l do't by being fine;
That pow'rfull charme, wch cannot be withstood,
Puts offe bad faces, and adornes ye good.
Oft an embroider'd Damsel have we seen ⎫
Ugly as Bawd, and finer than a Queen,   ⎬
Who by that splendor has victorious been. ⎭
She, whose weake Eyes had nere one Victory gott   10
May conquer with a flaming petticoat;
Witt is a Mistresse you have long enjoy'd,
Her beauty's not impair'd but you are cloy'd!
And Since 'tis not Witt's fault that you decay,
You, for yo^e want of appetite must pay.
You to provoke yo^e Selves must keep her fine,
And she must now at double charges shine. [1]
Old Sinners thus ———
When they feel Age and Impotence approach,
Double the charge of furniture and Coach;   20
When you of witt and sence were weary growne,
Romantick, riming, fustian Playes were showne,
We then to flying Witches did advance, [2]
And for your pleasures traffic'd into ffrance.
From thence new acts to please you, we have sought ⎫
We have machines to some perfection brought,   ⎬
And above 30 Warbling voyces gott. [3]   ⎭

> " . . . saw each box with beauty crown'd
> And pictures deck the structure round,
> *Ben, Shakespear*, and the learned rout,
> With noses some and some without."

These portraits remained *in situ* until the demolition of the theatre in 1709.

[1] Prices of admission were advanced during the run of new operas, owing to the expense of mounting. Duffet girds at the practice in the prologue to his *Psyche Debauch'd* (1678).

[2] Referring to a revival of the D'Avenant *Macbeth* at Dorset Gardens early in 1673.

[3] Mostly the boys and men of the Chapel Royal. Vide *postea* p. 203.

Many a God and Goddesse you will heare ⎞
And we have Singing, Dancing, Devils here ⎬
Such Devils, and such gods, are very Deare.[1] ⎠   30
We, in all ornaments, are lavish growne,
And like Improvident Damsells of ye Towne,
For present bravery, all your wealth lay downe,
As if our keepers ever wou'd be kind,   ⎞
The Thought of future wants we never mind, ⎬
No pittance is for your Old age design'd.   ⎠
Alone, we on yo*e* Constancy depend,
And hope yo*e* Love to th' stage will never end.
To please you, we no Art, or cost will spare
To make yr. Mrs. look still young, still faire.   40

Shadwell's prologue practically dates itself. It is nothing more than a lumbering rejoinder to Dryden's prologue and epilogue for the opening of the new Theatre Royal on March 26, 1674. It will be readily recalled that the King's company suffered severe loss by the fire which destroyed their first house in January, 1672, and that during the period of rebuilding they removed temporarily to the old Duke's in Lincoln's Inn Fields. The first twenty lines of the MS. prologue make sneering reply to Dryden's modest appeal for the King's players :

They, who are by your favours wealthy made,
With mighty sums may carry on the trade;
We, broken banquiers, half destroyed by fire,
With our small stock to humble roofs retire;
Pity our loss, while we no longer strive;
We yield in both, and only beg to live;

Lines 32-4 form a lame rejoinder to the sting administered in Dryden's epilogue for the opening of the new Theatre Royal :

Our house relieves the ladies from the frights
Of ill-paved streets, and long dark winter nights;
The Flanders horses from a cold bleak road
Where bears in furs dare scarcely look abroad.

---

[1] For the "dancing devils" see *The Tempest* (Quarto 2), ii. 4, and for "the gods" the terminal masque of *Neptune and Amphitrite*.

Similarly, lines 35-8 deal impotently with Dryden's neat point in the same address :

> Though in their house the poets' heads appear,
> We hope we may presume their wits are here.

While discussing these matters it will not be inopportune to recall that Dryden has an allusion—which has been sadly misinterpreted[1]—to Dorset Gardens in his prologue for the opening of the new house. His concluding couplet gives humorous expression to the mock fear—

> That, as a fire the former house o'erthrew,
> Machines and tempests will destroy the new.

The allusion here is not, as has been inferred, to the opera of *The Tempest* (which, like the British Fleet in *The Critic*, was not yet in sight), but to the superfluity of thunder and lightning and flying effects in D'Avenant's *Macbeth*.[2]

But enough of these addresses. Since, then, Shadwell's prologue is merely an ineffective reply to Dryden's prologue as spoken at the new King's Playhouse on March 26, 1674, it follows that, to have been by any means apposite, it must have been delivered at Dorset Gardens within a month or six weeks after. Prologues and epilogues in those days were frequently repeated and often printed and vended in the streets as broadsides. This would fix the date of production of the Shadwell *Tempest* at circa April 30, 1674, probably a sound approximation. That the opera was in the first flush of its success a fortnight later is clearly shown by the following entry in the Lord Chamberlain's Accounts :

1674, *May* 16. It is his Majesty's pleasure that Mr. Turner and Mr. Hart,[3] or any other men or boys belonging to his Majesty's Chappell Royall that sing in ye *Tempest* at his Royall Highnesse Theatre, doe remaine in towne all the week (dureing his Majesty's

---

[1] Genest, I think, was the original offender, but others have since fallen in line.

[2] Cf. the epilogue to Ravenscroft's *The Careless Lovers* (1673) :

> "Gallants tis fear'd, after our last loud play.
> You will be deaf to all Low Wit can say.
> Lightning, Machine and Noise your favourites are
> These Murdering Playes, the stage's Men of War," &c.

[3] Query, the J. Hart, who wrote the music for Dorinda's Song, " Adieu to the pleasures" in Shadwell's opera?

absence from Whitehall) to perform that service, onely Saturdayes to repaire to Windsor, and to returne to London on Mundayes if there be occasion for them.

And that they also performe ye like service in ye opera in ye said Theatre or any other thing in ye like nature where their helpe may be desired upon notice given them thereof. [1]

It was doubtless in the following winter that Duffet's gross travesty of Shadwell's opera, entitled *The Mock Tempest, or The Enchanted Castle* was produced at the King's Theatre. The announcement of its publication occurs in the *Term Catalogue* of February 15, 1675. Baker relates that "although it met with some little success at first, it presently fell to the ground ; and when it came to be presented in Dublin, several ladies and persons of the first quality testified their dislike of such low and indecent stuff by quitting the house before the performance was half over." [2]

And now something requires to be said about the subsequent history of Shadwell's opera, both from a theatrical and a bibliographical standpoint. The two considerations really go hand-in-hand, for, in the Post-Restoration period, reprints of old plays invariably indicate recent revivals, and may be taken as evidence of revival when no other evidence exists. After Quarto 2 all succeeding issues of *The Tempest* published by Herringman (save the quarto of 1691 which I have not seen) reproduce the text of the Shadwell opera, but the misleading Dryden preface and prologue and epilogue continue to appear. Owing to this fatuous iteration an idea became current towards the close of the century that Dryden himself had written the opera, and before long this crystallised into a tradition. It cannot be too strongly emphasised that Dryden was nothing more than Shadwell's involuntary collaborator in the matter. He has enough of his own sins to answer for.

Not content with misleading future generations by the senseless repetition just referred to, Herringman must needs crown his career by setting the unborn bibliographer the

---

[1] H. C. de Lafontaine, *The King's Musick*, p. 271.
[2] *Biog. Dram.* (1782), ii. 239. No. 204.

deepest of riddles. In 1676 he issued two quartos of *The Tempest*, both textually identical, but set up in different founts of type, and the one with typographical errors not in the other.[1]

It is noteworthy that from 1674 onwards the Shadwell opera completely superseded (possibly because it comprised) the Dryden-D'Avenant comedy. As for the genuine play of Shakespeare, it lay perdu from the outbreak of the Civil War, until near the middle of the eighteenth century, and even then very rarely got an innings. On the other hand revivals of Shadwell's opera were fairly frequent. One notes that it was one of the three ornate spectacular productions seen by the Morocco Ambassador at Dorset Gardens early in 1682.[2] Its anonymous book was re-issued by Herringman in June, 1690 "as now acted at their Majesty's Theatre; and again in October, 1691[3] "as it is now acted at their Majesties Theatre in Dorset Gardens." Somewhere about the period of 1690-5, Shadwell's version, with additions, was wholly re-set by Henry Purcell. No clue to the exact date presents itself. All we know for certain is that about the close of 1695 Dorinda's additional song, "Dear Pretty Youth" (not to be traced in any of the extant seventeenth-century quartos), was published in Book iii of *Deliciae Musicae* as "A New Song in *The Tempest*, sung by Miss *Cross* to her Lover who is supposed Dead. Set by Mr. Henry Purcell."

Half a century later, a malignant fate still pursued the genuine play of Shakespeare. By an irony of circumstance,

---

[1] Both were "printed by J. Macock for Henry Herringman". Exemplars are to be seen in the Dyce collection at South Kensington. No announcement of re-issue occurs in the *Term Catalogues* for 1676.

[2] Cf. *The Antiquary*, VI. 4 (April, 1910), p. 133. Mr. W. C. Bolland, in quoting here a contemporary reference to the Ambassador being "extreamly pleased" at the performance of *The Tempest*, wonders what pleased him, seeing that he was wholly ignorant of the language, and that the period (in Mr. Bolland's opinion) was not remarkable for its spectacular brilliancy! I commend to him a careful study of *Psyche, Circe*, and the operas of Dryden.

[3] Vide *Term Catalogue*, Michaelmas, 1691. I have failed to unearth an exemplar of this edition. Should the text differ materially from Quarto 2 (or present Dorinda's song, "Dear Pretty Youth") it would serve as evidence to date Purcell's re-setting of the opera.

when it came at last to be revived at Drury Lane, with much
flourishing of trumpets, on January, 31, 1746, it was not
deemed strong enough to stand alone, and was bolstered by
Shadwell's old masque of *Neptune and Amphitrite* for which
Arne had written new music. At the same house on February 11, 1756, was seen Garrick's final sophistication of
the comedy, in which some of Shadwell's old lyrics were
sung to new music by John Christopher Smith. [1] Similarly
John Kemble's version of October, 1789, had, on its literary
side, equal parts of Shakespeare, Dryden, D'Avenant, and
Shadwell, and on its musical side disproportionate parts of
Purcell, Arne and Linley. It was not until the middle of
the nineteenth century that these musty textual accretions
were wholly exterminated.

[1] For proof, see Maidment and Logan, *Sir William D'Avenant's Dramatic Works,*
v. 402.

Who wrote the Famous "Macbeth" Music?

Who wrote the Famous "Macbeth" Music?

One of Life's little cynicisms is that while Error meets with ready acceptance, Truth has to fight its corner. Thus it is that in the sphere of antiquarianism the capacity to discover is of little value without the ability to demonstrate. One may stumble over the truth, call out loudly that it lies pinned beneath one, and yet only succeed in obscuring it from the light.

Here, in a nutshell, we have a clue to the mystery concerning the time-honoured masquerading of Matthew Lock's memory in the borrowed plumes of Henry Purcell. For over a century it has been known to experts, more by divination than by astute reasoning, that Purcell, not Lock, wrote the famous *Macbeth* music. Dr. Philip Hayes, of Oxford, Linley, the editor of *Shakespeare's Dramatic Songs*, Dr. Arnold, Joseph Warren, the musical antiquary, and Dr. Rimbault have all given expression to this truth, but none has possessed the cogency to drive it home. In our own day the claims of Purcell have had a strenuous and able advocate in Dr. W. H. Cummings, but even he has spoilt his case by wrong methods of attack and by irrational deductions. The result is that what should be recognised as a fact is still treated by the orthodox musical historian, somewhat contemptuously, as pure hypothesis.

From Dr. Cummings' attempt to prove that the *Macbeth* music was the work of Purcell's boyhood nothing but harm has ensued. His proposition has been reduced to absurdity in the new issue of *Grove's Dictionary*, wherein it is stated that " on the theory that the famous *Macbeth* music is by Purcell, we are driven to suppose it to have been written in Purcell's fourteenth year in 1672 ".[1] This is a delicious *non*

---

[1] An opinion evidently derived from Mr. J. Fuller Maitland's otherwise sound article on Purcell in the *Dict. Nat. Biog.*

sequitur : we are driven to suppose nothing of the kind.
Purcell's claims to the authorship of the *Macbeth* music do
not rest on Dr. Cummings' contention[1] that the score was
the product of his youth. As a matter of fact we shall have
to refute that argument before attempting to make some
approximation to the truth. One of the purposes of the
present paper is to show reason for believing that the music
was of later date than that usually assigned to it. New evidence will also be adduced to prove the existence in theatrical
circles of a tradition associating the score, considerably before
its publication, with Purcell's name. By this means it will
at last be made clear that Boyce, in giving it to the world in
readily accessible form, had no valid reason for crediting it
to Lock.

Among the stock plays of which the Duke's company
under Sir William D'Avenant (by mutual arrangement
with the King's Players) were allowed a monopoly at the
dawn of the Restoration, were nine of Shakespeare's, including *Macbeth*.[2] In the cartel drawn up on December 12,
1660, D'Avenant agreed "to reforme and make fitt for the
Company of Actors appointed under his direction and
command " all the old plays specifically allotted to them.
It was not, however, until three years later that any attempt
was made to revive *Macbeth*. This is shown by the fact that
in or about November, 1663, Sir Henry Herbert, as testified
by his books,[3] received a fee of £1 for licensing the tragedy
as "a revived play ".

Nothing could be wider of the mark than the widely
accepted statement that D'Avenant was the first to mingle
alloy with the pure gold of Shakespeare—unless perhaps
the accompanying fallacy that to him was due the interpolations in *Macbeth* from Middleton's comedy of *The Witch*.
That the tragedy had the misfortune to be altered by a
second hand during the period of Shakespeare's retirement,
or shortly after his death, is definitely indicated by the First

[1] Cf. *The Musical Times* (1882), Vol. xxiii, p. 471, art., "Purcell's Music to
Macbeth", a contribution to which I am under many obligations.
[2] Cf. Robert W. Lowe, *Thomas Betterton*, p. 75.
[3] Malone's *Shakespeare* (Dublin, 1794), ii. 224.

Folio, which is, unluckily, our sole authority for the text.[1]
The sophisticated copy of the play therein given clearly
proves the comparatively early introduction of a song and a
concerted piece from *The Witch*, viz., " Come Away " and
" Black Spirits and White ". When D'Avenant came to
revive the tragedy he made divers alterations and additions
but retained these two songs.[2] One has every reason to
believe, without having any positive data to go upon, that
they were sung then to the music originally composed for
them by Robert Johnson.[3] Although no performance of *The
Witch* can be traced in the latter half of the seventeenth
century, it is to be noted that between Johnson's somewhat
tenuous setting of " Come Away " and the *Macbeth* scores
of the Post-Restoration exists a certain similarity of phrasing, as if the earlier music had come to be looked upon as
a basis through active preservation in the theatre. Still, if
we concede the inclusion of Johnson's music in D'Avenant's
perversion of the tragedy, it cannot be taken as the only
music heard in the first years of the revival. Into a new scene
in the second act D'Avenant introduced a concerted piece,
" Speak, sister, speak ! is the deed done ? " and a song,
" Let's have a dance upon the Heath " ; and (as will shortly
be seen) one has every reason to believe that for these, as
well as for some of the dances, Matthew Lock composed
the music. No one disputes that Lock was associated with
D'Avenant in the early revivals of the tragedy ; what one

---

[1] See Mr. Henry Cuningham's introduction to *Macbeth* (Arden Shakespeare
series) for a full consideration of this point.

[2] No copy of the D'Avenant *Macbeth* was issued until 1673, early in the spring of
which year W. Cadman published his anonymous quarto (Quarto 1). A little better
than a year later, P. Chetwin printed another version, " with all the alterations, amendments, additions and new songs. As it is now acted at the Duke's theatre ". (Quarto 2).
Beyond some transpositions of the scenes and some alterations in the sequence of the
"business", Quarto 2 does not differ very materially from its immediate predecessor.
For the variations see Furness, *Variorum Shakespeare*, vii. (1873), introduction. In the
same volume will be found the text of Quarto 2. My impression is that the discrepancies between the two arose from the fact that Cadman, in his haste to take advantage
of the ornate revival at Dorset Gardens in 1673, derived his text from a copy of
D'Avenant's first version of the tragedy, and that Quarto 2 represents the maturer revisal.

[3] Of the original music for *The Witch* only the setting of "Come Away" has been
preserved. It was given by Stafford Smith in his *Musica Antiqua*, from a contemporary
manuscript, and reproduced by Rimbault in his *Ancient Vocal Music of England*. Robert
Johnson lives in memory as the original composer of the songs in *The Tempest*.

does dispute is that he wrote the famous and longevous score first published under his name by Boyce in 1750.

D'Avenant's stage monopoly of *Macbeth* passed after his death to his widow, and extended up to the period of the union of the two companies in 1682. Consequently all representations of the tragedy in the twenty years preceding took place either at the Duke's theatre in Lincoln's Inn Fields or (after 1671) at the fine new theatre bearing the same title, situated in Dorset Gardens.[1] Owing to the uniformly brilliant acting of Betterton and his wife in the two leading characters, *Macbeth* was a standing dish with D'Avenant's company. As presented by them the play had a perennial variety of appeal for Pepys, who, between 1664 and 1669, saw it no fewer than eight times. "A pretty good play, but admirably acted" is his verdict after having seen it, apparently for the first time, on November 5, 1664. His second visit, on December 28, 1666, elicited the opinion that it was "a most excellent play for variety". What he meant by "variety" can be inferred from two entries in his Diary concerning further experiences of the tragedy in 1667. On January 7th it stood well the test of familiarity, and though seen quite lately, "yet appears a most excellent play in all respects, but especially in divertisement, though it be deep tragedy; which is a strange perfection in a tragedy, it being most proper here, and suitable". He is more explicit on April 19th following, when *Macbeth* had been played in hot weather to a small house: "which, though I have seen it often, yet it is one of the best plays for a stage, and variety of dancing and musique, that I ever saw"

---

[1] One has only to grasp these facts to become convinced of the manifold absurdities of Maidment and Logan's bibliographical note on the D'Avenant *Macbeth* (*D'Avenant's Dramatic Works*, v, 294). They begin by giving circumstantial details of a quarto of 1673, issued by Henry Herringham (? Herringman), "as now acted at the Theatre Royal". They have no note of Quarto 2, but go on to speak of a quarto of 1687 as identical with Quarto 1. But their own text tallies with Quarto 2, as reproduced by Furness, and it is plain they cannot have examined Quarto 1, which was issued by Cadman as acted at the Duke's. No reprint of 1687 can be traced. The date is evidently a slip for 1689, in which year a quarto was issued by Henry Herringman "as it is now acted at the Theatre Royal" (Quarto 3). It was probably from this that Maidment and Logan derived their text, as well as the misleading details for the imprint of Quarto 1.

Still keeping to 1667, we note that on the 16th October, Pepys went to the Duke's and was mortified to find Young, a bad actor, playing Macbeth instead of Betterton, who was seriously ill. But the D'Avenant sophistication had other attractions for the diarist (nothing if not musical) besides the acting, and he and his wife went again to see it on the 6th of November, liking it immensely " though mighty short of the content we used to have when Betterton acted, who is still sick ". Later performances of the tragedy are recorded by Pepys on August 12th and December 21st, 1668, at the latter of which the King and Court were present, and finally on January 15, 1669.

One may note here, without desiring to make any deduction from the fact, that Pepys, from first to last, makes no mention of Lock's association with the revival, although he had long enjoyed the composer's acquaintance, and was accustomed to play his music on the flageolet. The omission is absolutely of no significance as we know full well that Lock had written music for D'Avenant's version of *Macbeth* either at the period of its first production or very shortly after. From published sources we can trace a Tune and a Dance as so written. The tune was given in *Musick's Delight on the Cithren* in 1666. It recurs as " The Dance in the Play of *Macbeth* " in *Apollo's Banquet for the Treble Violin* in 1669. One finds it again in *The Pleasant Companion ; or New Lessons and Instructions for the Flagelet* of Thomas Greeting in 1680, this time with the initials " M. L." attached. Two years later it was given in the key of C., in Playford's *Musick's Recreation on the Viol, Lyraway*, under the curt title of *Macbeth*.

In *Apollo's Banquet* (1669), occurs an air headed "Witches' Dance", undoubtedly another item of Lock's early *Macbeth* music. It has been satisfactorily identified by Dr. Cummings, who possesses an old MS., circa 1698, in which a variant of the tune is to be found, bearing title " Dance of Witches in *Macbeth*".[1] It is of paramount importance to note that none

---

[1] Vide *supra*, article in *The Musical Times*, wherein Lock's early *Macbeth* music is reproduced.

of these recur in the famous score, the so-called Lock's music published in 1750. This has, indeed, no trace of Lock's technique, and has been adjudged by a concensus of expert opinion immeasurably superior to the ruck of his compositions.

With Sir William D'Avenant's death in April, 1668, all his theatrical rights and privileges passed to his widow, for whom their son Charles acted. In November, 1671, the better to compete with their old rivals at Drury Lane, the Duke's Company removed to a splendid new theatre in Dorset Gardens, specially designed and equipped for imposing spectacular effects. About a year later a gaudy revival of *Macbeth* was indulged in, [1] chronicled and characterised by Downes in his *Roscius Anglicanus* thus :

> The Tragedy of Macbeth, altered by *Sir William Davenant ;* being dressed in all its finery, as new clothes, new scenes, machines, as flyings for the witches, with all the singing and dancing in it : the first composed by Mr. *Lock*, the other by Mr. Channell and Mr. Joseph Priest ; It being all excellently performed, being in the nature of an Opera, it recompensed double the expense : it proves still a lasting play.

Downes' irritating book is an edged tool that none but the most skilful of historical workmen can safely handle. What should have been one of the most important stage chronicles ever penned has been rendered nugatory by utter slovenliness of method. In narration of events—especially those which came under his own notice—Downes is seldom widely astray. Much truth lies embedded in his book if one only has the skill and patience to dig it up. His fatal weakness is lack of chronological sense. One could forgive his avoidance of dates if only the sequence of his events could be depended upon. But in the case of a book yielding valuable first-hand information, clumsiness of treatment

---

[1] It is impossible to fix an exact date for this revival. Downes, an indifferent chronologer, gives by implication the year 1672. Judging by the fact that the publication of Quarto 1, as "acted at the Duke's theatre" is recorded in the *Term Catalogue* of Easter, 1673 (issued on May 6th), one would be inclined to date the highly spectacular version from the end of 1672 or beginning of 1673. The allusion in Dryden's epilogue to *The Silent Woman*, as spoken at Oxford in the summer of 1673, shows that the production cannot have been earlier.

cannot be permitted to nullify its authority. Slips of memory as well as blunders in arrangement are to be found in the *Roscius Anglicanus*, but it cannot be too strongly emphasised that errors in narration occur with least frequency in Downes' account of the Dorset Gardens theatre, where he had officiated as prompter. But for him we should never have known—what I have already demonstrated—that Shadwell provided an operatic version of the Dryden-D'Avenant *Tempest* for the Duke's house in 1674. While looking Downes' shortcomings fairly and squarely in the face, I am not prepared to admit the presence of any flaw in his account of the spectacular revival of *Macbeth*.

The MS. score from which Dr. Boyce printed the *Macbeth* music in 1750, ascribing it by pure surmise to Lock, is now in the possession of Dr. Cummings. Upon it an eighteenth-century musician and musical antiquary of eminence, Dr. Philip Hayes, of Oxford, has written, "Purcell's score of ye music in *Macbeth*, also the score from whence it was printed under Mat. Lock's name". Even if it could be definitely established that the score was in Purcell's handwriting, the fact *per se* would prove nothing. Some Curious Impertinents have gone so far has to admit this moot point in order, as we shall see, the more completely to disallow Purcell's authorship. As a matter of fact, acceptance of the truth has been seriously delayed by a well-meaning endeavour to establish this contention. Dr. Cummings once submitted the cherished manuscript to the scrutiny of an expert graphologist, who saw in it rudimentary indications of Purcell's maturer hand. On this woefully insecure basis a tottering structure, all compact of plausibility and false reasoning, has been raised. Accepting the verdict of the graphologist, Dr. Cummings gave voice to his opinion as to the juvenility of the writing, thus leaving himself open to the powerful·rejoinder that young Purcell, in his admiration for his friend Lock's music, had copied it out for purposes of study.

Once having taken the plunge down this declivitous path, Dr. Cummings is unable to stop himself. "The MS. score of *Macbeth* music ", he avers, " is in Purcell's boyish hand; and certain passages are grammatically so erroneous that they could not have been the work of an experienced master of harmony like Lock, nor would they have been tolerated by Purcell when he came to years of discretion ".[1] Accordingly the music must have been written—this music which Hogarth rightly styles "a tremendous effort of genius "— in 1672, when Purcell was a boy of fourteen. In other words, it was composed for the spectacular revival of *Macbeth* at Dorset Gardens, and Downes must have blundered when he gave the name of Lock in that connection. Well, one might not be unwilling to admit that the old prompter's memory had deceived him on this point, if it had so happened that he had preserved silence as to the genesis of Purcell's theatrical labours. But this is precisely what he did not do. Treating of the production of Lee's *Theodosius* at Dorset Gardens in 1680, he says, "all the parts in't being perfectly perform'd, with several Entertainments of Singing, compos'd by the famous master, Mr. Henry Purcell, (being the first he ever compos'd for the stage) made it a living and gainful play to the Company". At worst, Downes is not very wide of the mark in his statement, as Purcell is not known definitely to have written for more than one earlier production, and that only a few months previously. This was D'Urfey's comedy of *The Virtuous Wife ; or Good Luck at Last,* which was printed, according to the *Term Catalogue,* about November, 1679, and probably produced a month or two earlier. But it may be that Downes is substantially correct in his statement, for while we know for cer-

---

[1] Little weight can be attached to,the traces of immaturity found by musical experts in certain of Purcell's compositions. In his excellent *History of Music in England* Dr. Ernest Walker speaks of a defectiveness in the overture to *Timon of Athens,* somewhat akin to the blemishes in the *Macbeth* score. But he dates the *Timon* music from 1678, forgetful of the fact that Grabut was the original composer for Shadwell's play. It was clearly for the revival of 1688 (in July of which year the play was reprinted) that Purcell wrote. Mr. Barclay Squire's date for Purcell's *Timon* music is 1694, much too belated. (Cf. *Quart. Mag. International Musical Society* Year v., 1904, Pt. 4, p. 556.) Dr. Walker impales himself on the horns of a dilemma by his several contentions, for he maintains that the period of 1689–92 was that of Purcell's richest maturity. How then to account for the deficiencies of 1688 ? Much, however, may be forgiven to a writer who accepts the *Macbeth* music as Purcell's without argument, merely speaking of it as "formerly attributed to Lock".

tain that both Farmer and Purcell composed for D'Urfey's piece, no evidence exists as to the precise period. Careful study of Purcell's theatrical career reveals the remarkable circumstance that the bulk of his music was written for revivals. Stage music in his day was apparently not long-lived. There was then, as now, a craze for new music rather than good music, and the theatrical managers were in a position to gratify it by reason of the cheapness of composition. No score enjoyed a fixity of tenure, and a play had only to be a few years in existence to have all its songs reset. This peculiarity of the Post-Restoration period must be borne carefully in mind in considering Purcell's claims to the authorship of the *Macbeth* music. Viewing the usages of the period, one feels assured that Purcell would have had no more compunction in superseding Lock and Johnson than he had in blotting out the music of Staggins and Smith, when he reset the songs in *Epsom Wells* in 1693.

Admitting, however, for the sake of argument, that Purcell wrote music for the original production of *The Virtuous Wife*, the earliest authentic record of his association with the stage would be in 1679. If then Purcell in 1672 was the youthful prodigy Dr. Cummings would have him to be, if at that period he burst upon the world with his great *Macbeth* score, how came it that in those intervening years he received no further commissions ? Of a surety that long blank pricks the bubble. Ordinarily speaking, twenty-one seems a more rational age for the beginning of a career of theatrical composership than fourteen, and one is safest in dating Purcell from 1679. [1]

Apply these deductions to the manuscript from which the *Macbeth* music of 1750 was printed, and what conclusion must be arrived at ? Either that the manuscript, with its grammatical deficiencies, represents the immature drafting of a score not perfected and performed until many years

---

[1] As against this comes the fact that on September 10, 1677, Purcell had been appointed " composer in ordinary with fee for the violin to his Majesty, in the place of Matthew Lock, deceased " (H. C. de Lafontaine, *The King's Musick*, p. 322). There must have been some demonstration of his creative ability before this, but it cannot be shown to have been made in the theatre.

later, or that it is not in the handwriting of Henry Purcell. Personally, I lean towards the latter.

Turn we now aside from the main issue for a while, to pursue our chronological review of *Macbeth* revivals during the Post-Restoration period. It was in many respects a memorable presentation of the tragedy, this Dorset Gardens revival of 1672, for in it (if Downes is to be believed), Nat. Lee, the mad poet, made an unsuccessful appearance on the boards as Duncan. The old prompter is as undoubtedly right in this as he is in other respects, for Lee's name is to be found opposite the character in the cast preserved in Quarto 2. That particular issue of the play is described in the *Term Catalogue* of Trinity, 1674, as containing " all the alterations, amendments and new songs, as it is now acted at the Duke's theatre". This statement testifies to the extended popularity of the spectacular revival, but affords little clue, save in the reference to the " new songs ", to the points of departure from D'Avenant's sophisticated version of an earlier date. One has grave doubts whether it differed very much either textually or musically from the tragedy which had such fascination for Pepys. In this connection too much stress must not be laid upon Downes' description "in the nature of an opera ", for throughout his book he makes woeful misuse of the term "opera", using it in an even laxer sense than his contemporaries. He speaks, for example, of the Shadwell *Tempest* of 1674 as an opera, although beyond a certain superiority in scenic auxiliaries and the appendage of a masque, it differed little from the Dryden-D'Avenant version of 1667, and was published as a comedy. [1]

While it is quite feasible that for the spectacular *Macbeth* of 1672 Lock may have embellished his old score, substituting, perhaps, some new lyrics in place of the old setting of Robert Johnson, there is no reason to believe that the success of the revival depended upon its music. On the

---

[1] In all the quartos of *Macbeth* issued during the seventeenth century the piece is described on the imprints as a tragedy, and yet these all deal with the D'Avenant sophistication.

contrary, its vogue was largely due to the inclusion of some of "those gilt-gauds men-children run to see ". Realistic flying effects, procured by stage machinery specially brought over from France, were shown in the play. Dorset Gardens was proud of its enterprise, boasted of it a year later in the epilogue to Shadwell's *Tempest* :

> When you of witt, and sence, were weary growne,
> Romantick, riming, fustian playes were showne.
> We then to flying witches did advance,
> And for your pleasures traffic'd into ffrance.
> From thence new arts to please you, we have sought,
> We have machines to some perfection brought,
> And about thirty warbling voyces gott. [1]

Duffet, who, with equal assiduity and scurrilousness, kept burlesquing the Dorset Gardens spectacles at Drury Lane, wrote (and printed in 1674) " an Epilogue spoken by witches, after the Mode of *Macbeth*. Perform'd with new and costly Machines, which were invented and managed by the most ingenious operator, Mr. Henry Wright, P.G.Q."[2] The whole of this imprint, down to the mystic initials, sounds like a jeer at some grandiloquent announcement made by the rival theatre.

No advocate who has held a brief in the interminable case of Purcell versus Lock seems to have been aware of the distinctive theatrical usages of the Post-Restoration era. Latterly all appear to think that Purcell's claim hinges solely upon the spectacular *Macbeth* of 1672, that if he cannot be identified as the composer for that revival, Lock must remain in peaceful possession of the honours. This is essentially the view of the new *Grove* based on Dr. Cummings' anxiety to prove that the famous score was the efflorescence of immaturity. But all who are conversant with the inner workings of the period from a theatrico-musical standpoint must concede that frank and full acceptance of Downes' statement concerning Lock's authorship of the score of 1672

---

[1] Vide *ante* p. 201.
[2] For an analysis of Duffet's burlesque, see Maidment and Logan, *D'Avenant's Dramatic Works*, v. 302.

does not negative Purcell's claim to the published score of
1750. Rather indeed does it strengthen it. One has only to
prove revivals of *Macbeth* at a period of about a decennium
later to bring Purcell into direct touch with the tragedy.
And that can be readily accomplished.

It may be assumed that Lock as theatrical composer was
left in undisputed possession of his *Macbeth* monopoly till
his death in August, 1677. True, that assumption flies
in the face of the theatrical usages of the period, but in
the absence of positive evidence to the contrary, no other
attitude can be taken. With the steady growth of Purcell's
popularity as a composer from 1679 onwards, it was
clearly open to him to reset the Witch scenes in *Macbeth*,
especially as the spectacular, sophisticated version of the
tragedy continued to prove attractive at Dorset Gardens.
Such, indeed, was Purcell's vogue, one feels assured that
even if the famous score had already been in existence, the
work, say of his dead friend Lock, not even the dread of
odious comparison would have checked him from trying his
hand. All through his career he was deliberately measuring
his strength with his predecessors, sturdily resetting what
they had set before, often blotting out their very memory.
It was thus with *Circe* in 1685, for which Bannister had
originally composed the music twelve years previously;
and thus with the Shadwell *Tempest* in 1690, for which
Pietro Reggio and Lock had provided the setting in 1674.
Why then should *Macbeth* have been taboo? Under the
circumstances, it was no more audacious for Purcell to
approach the task than it was for his immediate successor,
Eccles. By 1695 the famous *Macbeth* score must have been
in existence, whoever the composer, but Eccles in that year
summoned up his courage and drew upon his scholasticism
to reset the Witch scenes for Drury Lane.[1]

One other revival of *Macbeth* is recorded, of an earlier
date, before Purcell threw his gauntlet into the theatrical
arena. According to Langbaine, who states he was present

[1] For Eccles' *Macbeth* music see Add. MSS. No. 12, 219. It was probably written
for the revival indicated by Quarto 4, as issued in 1695.

on the occasion, the tragedy was in the bill at Dorset Gardens on August 28, 1675,[1] when the fatal quarrel took place in the pit between Scroope and Sir Thomas Armstrong. In view of the fact that *Macbeth* was a stock play and afforded Betterton one of his finest characters, the tragedy must have been frequently performed between 1675 and 1695 (the year of Purcell's untimely death). Owing, however, to the woeful incompleteness of Post-Restoration stage annals we know only of two revivals within those two decades. The first occurred at Dorset Gardens early in 1682, and was seen by the Morocco ambassador sometime between January and May in that year.[2] The second we only know of through Quarto 3, as issued by Herringman in 1689. It is clear from the statement made on the title-page, "as it is now acted at the Theatre Royal" that the tragedy had been recently revived at Drury Lane.[3] One takes leave to think that this date marks the latest period at which the famous score could possibly have been written. It is not to be conceived that Eccles reset the witch scenes on the very heels of Purcell's glorious effort, especially as the interests of the two companies still remained united in 1695. Apart from this, the year 1689, roughly indicates the period of Purcell's greatest activity, and it seems a not improbable date for the composition of the *Macbeth* music.

It only remains to see on what authority Dr. Boyce, in publishing the score in 1750, ascribed it to Lock. One looks naturally for some morsel of tangible evidence justifying such a course, but all search is fruitless. It cannot be too emphatically enforced that Boyce's attribution was mere guesswork. We shall see anon that so far from echoing theatrical tradition, he sets his face stubbornly against it

---

[1] For the date and other details see *The Hatton Correspondence* (Camden Society, 1878), i. 121.

[2] Cf. *Gentleman's Magazine* (1813), pp. 220, art. on Dorset Gardens Theatre ; also *Luttrell's Diary* (1857), i. 187.

[3] Beyond the substitution of "Theatre Royal" for "the Duke's theatre" the imprint is copied almost word for word from Quarto 2, and the same identity of phrasing is to be noted in the edition of 1710. Seeing that Quarto 3 presents no textual variations from its predecessor, no stress can be laid upon the iteration in the imprint "with all the alterations, amendments, additions and new songs ". I mention this to prevent future error.

Not the slightest hint was conveyed by the manuscript warranting the ascription. Nothing that Lock ever wrote bears any resemblance to the music or is of quite so fine a quality. No playhouse announcement of *Macbeth* can be traced in the newspapers before 1750, holding out as a lure the performance of Lock's music. That was a feature of the bills to come later and remain long, thanks to the blundering of Boyce. In stage (as opposed to musico-antiquarian) tradition, the memory of Lock had completely died out. Nothing is left to us but to agree with Dr. Cummings that Boyce had had the misfortune to fall across Downes' reference to Lock, in his account of the revival of 1672, and not conceiving the possibility of later scorings, had at once jumped to a conclusion.[1] In this absurd fashion was a fallacy set on foot which none since has been able to arrest.

One has considerable satisfaction in now putting forward for the first time four important items of evidence justifying the Purcellites of the faith that is them. They go to prove that, although no *Macbeth* music of Purcell's was published in his lifetime, a tradition long existed in theatrical circles associating his name with the great score. That tradition died hard, disappearing ultimately through unquestioning acceptance of Boyce's ascription.

In *Faulkner's Dublin Journal* of December 6, 1743,[2] is to be found an advertisement announcing the performance of *Macbeth* at the Smock Alley theatre on the 8th instant, with Thomas Sheridan for the first time in the great *rôle*. By way of extra attraction, "all the original songs and Musick by the celebrated Mr. Purcell" are promised. I hasten to anticipate the objection that misstatements were of common occurrence in the old playhouse announcements, and that in this case some error might have been committed.

---

[1] The circumstance that Boyce dedicated the music to David Garrick suggests an alternative solution. Garrick, as a theatrical bibilophile, is likely to have had some knowledge of Downes' chronicle, and the attribution might have been originally his. He had himself revived *Macbeth* at Drury Lane in 1744 (and again in 1748), discarding most of D'Avenant's interpolations, but retaining the witch music. Nothing, however, exists to show that he publicly attributed the score to Lock in either of the years mentioned.

[2] A file is in Marsh's Library, Dublin.

The drafter of the Smock Alley advertisements was not alone in his opinion, it was shared by Samuel Derrick, who, under his pen-name of "Thomas Wilkes," gave proof in his *General View of the Stage* of a wide acquaintanceship with stage history and theatrical tradition. Although his book came out nine years after the publication of the *Macbeth* score, Derrick, in speaking of it, ignores Boyce's attribution. "There is a grandeur in Purcel's music", he writes, " that is elevating, and will always please ; there is as much true genius in the Music which he composed for *Macbeth*, as in creating the Witches; and his song, *Britons strike home*, will immortalize him eternally, because in the mouth of every Englishman, and equally pleasing to the most refined taste, and the most vulgar capacity." [1]

The third and fourth items of evidence testifying to a long-lived tradition as to Purcell's authorship of the music consist of two Dublin advertisements issued at widely different periods. In an announcement of the performance of *Macbeth* at Smock Alley on January 12, 1767, when Mossop played the Thane of Cawdor, one finds appended in *Faulkner's Dublin Journal* the statement "with the original music of the famous Henry Purcel." When *Macbeth* was again presented at the same theatre on January 13, 1784, the same ascription, in almost identical terms, was made in the advertisement in *The Public Register, or Freeman's Journal*.

Viewed in association with these four items, the deductions of musical experts like Hayes and Arnold gain immeasurably in credence. No less skilled in technical knowledge, Dr. Cummings has still further grounds for his lifelong advocacy of Purcell's claims. In his collection are the following :

(1) MS. volume, written by Saville of Lichfield Cathedral, and formerly in the possession of Bartleman. This bears title, " Purcell's Theatre Music ", and contains (1) " Macbeth", (2) "The Indian Queen ", (3) "Œdipus", (4) "Bonduca",

---

[1] London, 1759, p. 77. Derrick was born in Dublin in 1724 and lived there till manhood.

(5) "Timon of Athens", (6) "The Libertine". (No one has ever disputed the genuineness of the last five items.)
(2) MS. volume, formerly belonging to the Musical Society of Oxford. Contains music for *The Tempest, King Arthur* and *Macbeth*, all attributed therein to Purcell.
(3) Word Book of the Academy of Music, published in 1768, containing " The Masque in Macbeth (Purcell)".

To sum up. Side by side with the fact that no *Macbeth* music attributed to Purcell was published in his lifetime, we see the existence of a healthy tradition giving him the honours due to the composer of the great score. Under the circumstances it would be absurd to imagine that this persistency of idea had any less stable basis than that of truth and actuality. Avoid confusion of the issue by separating hypothesis from ascertained fact, discard from the mind Dr. Cummings' untenable and misleading assumption as to the alleged juvenility of the work, and the mass of evidence is clearly in favour of Purcell's claim.

One can admire the beauties of the *Macbeth* music *per se*, and fight vigorously in support of the truth, without approving of the old managerial taste that could so disfigure the tragedy. Within the memory of the middle-aged the interpolation still held its place, but its disappearance a score of years ago marked the dawn of a truer culture. Only the dawn indeed, for Shakespeare is still encumbered with many scenic excrescences. For generations previously Matthew Lock had enjoyed posthumous honours and suffered posthumous abuse, both equally undeserved. Let us hope that the one has now cancelled the other. The hour has come to attach whatever meed of praise is due to the memory of the right man. The sum total of our musical heritage will be none the less for this tardy readjustment, and the eternal cause of truth and justice will have been maintained.

New Facts about the Blackfriars : Monsieur Feuillerat's Discoveries

New Facts about the Blackfriars : Monsieur
Feuillerat's Discoveries

ONE of the prime vexations of Elizabethan research is that it has absolutely no finality. Since opinions cannot be kept perpetually in solution where progress has to be made, earnest workers have to ignore this patent fact or risk paralysis of their activities. Some take refuge in dogmatism, only to be brought face to face at the end with the limitations of their horizon. One is moved to these reflections by the disturbing circumstance that Professor Feuillerat's modest preliminary announcement [1] of his important discovery of a series of documents in the Loseley MSS. proving the existence of an earlier and but dimly suspected [2] theatre in the Blackfriars, demands an immediate re-adjustment of our historical perspective with regard to the evolution of the Elizabethan playhouse. Enough has already been revealed to show that, within a period of two years from the building of the first public theatre in the fields, the principle of the private theatre was well established. What that principle was, *ab initio*, I shall strive later on to determine : it needs first to recapitulate the absorbing story of the earlier Blackfriars.

In December, 1576, Richard Farrant, master of the Children of Windsor and deputy-master of the Children of the Chapel, already favourably known as a playwright and composer, [3] took a twenty-one years' lease of the old Blackfriars monastery in the Liberties, and, pulling down

---

[1] See his article, "Shakespeare's Blackfriars," in *The Daily Chronicle* of December 22, 1911.

[2] Cf. Collier's *Annals* iii. 273.

[3] For fuller details concerning Farrant, see the *Dict. Nat. Biog.* and *Grove's Dict. of Music, sub nomine.* Various payments for the acting of Farrant's boys at court from 1568 to 1578 are recorded in the acts of the Privy Council. It is noteworthy that on Twelfth Night, 1576–7, the Children of Windsor and the Children of the Chapel appeared unitedly before the Queen at Hampton Court in *The Historie of Mutius Scevola.*

the partitions of its second story, proceeded to construct on that elevation a small theatre, ostensibly for the rehearsal of new court plays. In time, under conditions not readily ascertainable, certain select members of the public were permitted to be present at these "rehearsals." But the pretext under which the theatre was first opened about the close of 1577, with the Children of the Chapel, was that of a practising-place " for the better trayning them to do her Majestie service." One has some reason to believe that the Paul's boys were also acting in the city about this period, or at least very shortly afterwards. The earliest recorded court plays whose preliminary performances can be safely inferred to have been given at the Blackfriars were *The Historie of Loyaltie and Bewtie* and *A History of Alucius*, both of which were acted by the Children of the Chapel at Whitehall, the former on Shrove Monday, 1579, and the latter on St. John's Day, 1580. [1]

After Farrant's death in November, 1580, [2] his widow let the theatre to William Hunnis, master of the Children of the Chapel, who rendered his period of management memorable by producing in 1581-2 the *Campaspe* and *Sapho and Phao* of Lyly. By this time the Blackfriars had proceeded far beyond the stage of a mere rehearsal-theatre, for, notwithstanding that court performances by the Children were comparatively few, we learn in Gosson's *Plays Confuted in five Actions* [3] of the "great many comedies" that had recently been acted there. Among other plays given, in all likelihood, under Hunnis were Peele's *The Arraignment of Paris* and a Moral entitled *A Game of the Cards*, the latter of which was acted at Windsor by the Chapel Children on St. John's Day, 1582. In 1583 [4] the Chapel Children fell into disfavour at court and, as a consequence, the popularity

---

[1] Cunningham, *Revels Accounts*, pp. 142 and 154.

[2] I base here on Prof. Feuillerat. The *Dict. Nat. Biog.* gives the date as 1585.

[3] Published without date, but entered at Stationers' Hall on April 16, 1582.

[4] It is noteworthy that the boys of Merchant Taylors' School, under Richard Mulcaster, acted *A Historie of Ariodante and Genevora* before the Queen at Richmond on Shrove Tuesday, 1582-3. Mulcaster's boys had given court performances as early as 1574 (Collier, *Annals*, I, 208-9). *Quære*, might there not have been a rehearsal-theatre in the School?

of the Blackfriars waned. Owing probably to the double loss sustained (for we must remember that a charge of £6 13s. 4d. was usually made for each performance before the Queen), Hunnis made petition in the same year for an extra allowance for the upkeep of the twelve Chapel boys, in supplement of the annual grant of £40.[1] He had already surrendered the Blackfriars to its owner, the widow Farrant, who let the house in quick succession to one Newman and to Henry Evans, "the very man," writes Prof. Feuillerat, "who was to lease the Blackfriars Theatre started by Burbage in 1597." At this juncture that "passing singular odd man" Edward, the 17th earl of Oxford, who had been a patron of the drama from his youth, had a troupe of boy-players which had already acted before the Queen, and which, on and off from 1580, had been performing in the country.[2] For their better establishment in London, Oxford secured a sub-tenancy of the Blackfriars from Evans, and housed the children there under the control of his sometime private secretary, John Lyly. Seeing that Puttenham in his *Art of English Poesy* (1589) praises the earl for his writing of "comedy and interlude", it may be that most of his lost plays were written for performance by his Blackfriars boys. But all that can be arrived at regarding their doings is provokingly slight. In 1584 they gave three performances at court, the last at Greenwich, on St. John's Day, when *The History of Agamemnon and Ulysses* was presented.[3] In all probability, the anonymous comedy *The Weakest goeth to the Wall*, published in 1600, as "acted by the Earl of Oxford, Lord great Chamberlain of England, his servants", belongs to this period. This play was based on a story in Barnaby Rich's *Farewell to Military Profession* (1581), and in act ii, scene 1, allusion is made to Oxford's players as "pigmies." Another piece called *The True History of George Scanderbage*, entered by

[1] Cf. *The Athenaeum* of March 31, 1900, art. "William Hunnis" by Mrs. C. C. Stopes.

[2] Cf. John Tucker Murray's *English Dramatic Companies*, 1558–1642, i. 344 and ii. 62. Oxford's boys had acted several times at court before June, 1580. When at Bristol in September, 1581, they were nine in number.

[3] Cunningham, *Revels Accounts*, p. 188.

Edwarde Alde on the books of the Stationers' Company on
July 3, 1601, "as it was lately played by the Right Hon.
the Earle of Oxenforde his servants" but not published,
cannot be readily associated with the boy-players.[1] After
the closing of the Blackfriars in 1585 under circumstances
presently to be related, Oxford lent his countenance to a
troupe of adult-actors whom we find playing somewhere
in London late in 1586.[2] The boys went at once on tour,
but apparently did not long survive.[3]

At the conclusion of his terse account of the rise and
progress of the first Blackfriars, Prof. Feuillerat writes :

> But Sir William More [the landlord] was now getting restive
> at all these changes of tenancy, and he turned against Ann Farrant
> prepared "to take forfeiture against her", the conditions of the
> lease not having been fulfilled. She applied for protection to Sir
> Francis Walsingham, the Queen's secretary, but his intervention
> was ineffectual, for Sir William More, making up a list of his
> tenants in the Blackfriars in 1585, did not include Ann Farrant's
> name. This date, therefore, can be taken as indicating the moment
> when the Blackfriars theatre came to a premature end. The play-
> house was again divided into rooms, and it was to be remodelled
> into a theatre only in 1597, when Burbage bought the house from
> Sir William More.

To speak by implication of Farrant's house as the first
private theatre, as I have already done at the beginning of
this commentary, is, in a sense, to beg the question, seeing
that no positive evidence exists to show that the earlier
Blackfriars was known and recognised by that designation.
The point admits, however, of *a posteriori* reasoning. Most
of the distinguishing characteristics of the later private

---

[1] Cf. Fleay's *Biog. Chron. Eng. Drama*, ii. p. 64, No. 16. Also *Marlowe's* Works
(edit. Bullen), introduction, p. lxv.

[2] See the reference to them in the anonymous letter to Walsingham, under date
"25th January, 1586 [7]," cited by Collier (*Annals* i. 263) under a wrong period.
Fleay (*Chron. Hist.* 88) conjectures that Oxford's men were at the Curtain in 1586-8,
but Mr. J. Tucker Murray, (op. cit.) effectively traverses this.

[3] Early in the summer of 1585 they were acting at Bath, where they had been
about a year earlier. (Cf. Belville S. Penley, *The Bath Stage*, p. 12). The later references to Oxford's players in the country, traced by Mr. J. Tucker Murray (c. 1589-90)
evidently deal with visits from the adult company.

theatres can be shown to have existed, or may be rationally supposed to have existed, in the first Blackfriars. [1] The era of the small roofed theatre, with the seated pit, permanent stage devoid of "heavens" and with artificial lighting, undoubtedly began with that house. Precedent for the copious interspersion of music, dance and song which individualised the performances of the second Blackfriars was certainly established by Farrant's boys, whose master, we must recall, was primarily organist and composer. [2]

Apart from all this, by solving an allied and considerably more difficult problem, one can readily show that the earlier Blackfriars was clearly recognised as the first private house. Time out of mind, antiquaries and commentators have been much puzzled to determine how the epithet "private" came to be applied to a place of performance where admission could be obtained by anybody having money to burn. Thanks to Prof. Feuillerat's vital discovery, I am now in a position to clear up the mystery. In the "Act of Common Council" for the regulation of acting within the city, passed on December 6, 1575, the final clause runs :

Provydid allwaie that this Acte (otherwise then touchinge the publishing of unchaste, sedycious, and vnmete matters) shall not extend to anie plaies Enterludes Comodies, Tragidies or shewes to be played or shewed in the pryvate hous, dwellinge, or lodginge of anie nobleman, citizen, or gentleman, wch shall or will then have the same thear so played or shewed in his presence, for the festyvitie of anie marriage, assemblye of ffrendes, or otherlyke cawse, wth owte publique or comen collection of money of the auditorie, or beholders theareof ; referringe alwaie to the Lorde Maior and Aldermen for the tyme beinge the Judgement accordinge to equitie, what shalbe counted such a playenge or shewing in a pryvate place, anie thinge in this Acte to the contrarie notw^th standing. [3]

---

[1] Much of what has already been said at pp. 16–21 of the physical disposition and conventions of the second Blackfriars applies readily to its predecessor. For the differentia note what now follows.

[2] The evidence is a trifle more definite in the Hunnis period. Three songs were rendered in *Campaspe* and four in *Sapho and Phao*. In the former there was also dancing and tumbling.

[3] Collier, *Annals* i. 214, sqq.

There is not the shadow of a reason for doubting that Farrant had already determined, when he set about building his rehearsal-playhouse some twelve months after the passing of this act, to keep within the spirit of its final clause. He had only to live on the premises [1] and to avoid the collection of money at the door or "gathering" inside, to constitute the Blackfriars a "private house" within the meaning of the act. Publicity, of course, had to be shirked. No flag could be raised, no bills posted. [2] Here it is necessary to anticipate the argument that Farrant was under no necessity to indulge in this subterfuge, seeing that the Common Council had no jurisdiction in the liberties of the Blackfriars. In 1577 that was a point of law as yet unsettled, and Farrant had good reason for entertaining doubts. [3] A little better than a year after the opening of the theatre, the Lord Mayor laid claim to the exercise of authority within "the precinct of the late dissolved Monastery of the Blackfriars." But the Chief Justices delayed in giving judgment, and on May 15, 1580, the Privy Council issued an order that, pending their decree, things should "remain *in statu quo prius,* and that the Lord Mayor should not intermeddle in any cause within the said Liberties, saving for the punishment of felons as heretofore he hath done." [4] This rebuke was practically the last word on the subject, and dissipated all fears. Hunnis, in succeeding Farrant as manager a few months later, had consequently his standing better assured. From that onwards money could have been taken at the doors, or gathered inside, instead

---

[1] We have no evidence that Farrant had apartments in the Blackfriars (perhaps Prof. Feuillerat will inform us on the point later), but Lyly, a few years later, had.

[2] Posters were probably issued at a subsequent period, but the flag was never a characteristic of the private theatre. Malone in this connection cites from Middleton's *A Mad World, My Masters :* "The hair about the hat is as good as a flag upon the pole, at a common playhouse, to waft company."

[3] The Privy Council, in issuing instructions to the Lord Mayor on December 24, 1578, for permission to be granted to various companies "to exercise plays within the city", by way of rehearsing what they had arranged to present at Court at Christmas, included the Children of the Chapel in the list. (Fleay, *Chron. Hist.* p. 52). And yet it must have been about this time that the Children were established at Blackfriars.

[4] Cf. C. W. Wallace, *The Children of the Chapel at Blackfriars,* p. 154 note 1. Also Collier's *Annals,* iii. 273 note.

of relying upon the subscriptions or uncertain gifts of the house's patrons. One cannot say exactly when the change came, but when it did we may take it that the theatre ceased to be "private" in the old legal sense without losing its designation. That was to become the inheritance of its enfranchised successors, much to the mystification, be it said, of a long line of future antiquaries.

Everything tends to show that the first Blackfriars was a very simple building and not at all elaborately furnished. To begin with, Farrant was of little means and without subsidy. Even if he could have raised the necessary money, he is not likely to have constructed a sumptuous playhouse at a time when the Common Council were particularly restive regarding playing within the city precincts, and when, as we have seen, the Lord Mayor claimed jurisdiction within the Liberties of the Blackfriars. So quietly and unostentatiously was the house conducted that the inhabitants of the district scarcely recognised they had a theatre in their midst. This is shown by the fact that when the residents in the Blackfriars precinct petitioned the Privy Council in November, 1596, to restrain Burbage from constructing "a common playhouse" on this selfsame second floor of the old monastery, it was urged that the Liberties had thitherto remained unpolluted, that "there hath not at any tyme heretofore been used any Common Playhouse within the same Precinct."[1] This latter statement was, of course, strictly accurate, the word "common" as applied to theatres then being used in the sense of "public". But the inhabitants knew very well that Burbage was unable to construct an ordinary public theatre within the narrow limits of an upper storey. His intention was merely to reconstitute the old private playhouse with closer approximation to the public theatre type of auditorium. The natural inference is that the earlier Blackfriars was hardly recognised as a theatre at all.

It is on this showing that I am in opposition to Prof. Feuillerat in his view that "it seems pretty certain that

---

[1] Collier's *Annals* i. 227–8. See also C. W. Wallace, *The Children of the Chapel at Blackfriars*, pp. 17 and 18, notes 5 and 1.

Farrant erected galleries all round the room, as was generally practised when Royal or private halls were temporarily converted into playhouses." Even the latter part of this statement may be seriously queried. My own opinion is that the auditorium in the first Blackfriars merely consisted of the area, used as a pit and provided with stools or benches. In this connection it may not be unprofitable to examine Prof. Wallace's estimate [1] of the seating capacity of the second house, seeing that it occupied approximately the same space as the first. All told, he conjectures that its pit and three galleries held about 530 spectators. Of this total 96 are allotted to the pit. In Farrant's Blackfriars, however (if I may proceed on the strength of my own hypothesis), the pit space cut off in Burbage's house by the lowermost gallery would be at the disposal of the audience. Still basing on Prof. Wallace's estimate, I calculate this to represent an addition of 144 to the holding capacity of the first theatre, or a total of 240 in all. One can readily surmise that when the house was in the meridian of its prosperity, say in 1582, when Gosson speaks of " a great many comedies " being acted there, the supply of pit-seats would often be considerably less than the demand. Surely we have in this a clue to the origin of sitting on the stage. It seems reasonably well assured that that custom began in the private theatre, and it has already been demonstrated that it was in existence before the erection of the second Blackfriars. [2] We have, therefore, fair grounds for assuming that it first came into force at Farrant's house. If this assumption could be taken as a certainty, it would of itself prove the absence of galleries in the earlier Blackfriars, as, most indubitably, it can only have been under the severest pressure that the custom was allowed to spring into existence. It will not be difficult to show that in the beginning it proved a serious obstruction to the traffic of the stage, and that its persistence led to some modification of the ruling conventionalities.

---

[1] op. cit. p. 50, conjectural plan.
[2] Cf. C. R. Baskervill, *The Custom of Sitting on the Elizabethan Stage* (*Modern Philology*, viii. No. 4, 1911, pp. 581–3).

Since the earlier Blackfriars was primarily a rehearsal theatre for court plays, and as all the court plays of the period, excepting pastorals, were provided with scenery of the multiple order, it follows that to be properly rehearsed these plays must have been mounted at the Blackfriars in the same manner as they were to be given before the Queen. The scenery, costumes and properties required for court plays given by the Chapel boys were provided in the Revels office at the expense of the Crown. One can readily surmise that they would be lent for "rehearsals", but it is not so well assured that their use could be obtained for such performances as were given at the theatre after the plays were produced at court. There must have been many such performances, as well as performances of new pieces not intended for presentation before the Queen. The little theatre could not have been kept going for six months in the year simply as a court rehearsal-house. Under what conditions, then, were performances otherwise than "dress-rehearsals" given there? We do not know, and are not likely ever to be able to determine. It may be that they were given after the normal manner of the public theatre and that the earlier Blackfriars was furnished with a tiring-house façade, with the usual entering doors, and inner and upper stages. Such a disposition could frequently be turned to advantage, even when practicable scenery of the multiple order was utilised.

Excessive demand for seats is most likely to have occurred during the dress-rehearsals of court plays, the period when multiple scenery was certainly employed. Everybody would want to forestall the Queen in her Christmas enjoyment. But if sitting on the stage was permitted at such periods, it must have been within the zone of action, not at either end of the stage (the arrangement suggested by Prof. Wallace in his conjectural reconstruction of the later Blackfriars).[1] For the stool-holder

---

[1] op. cit. p. 46. In the absence of definite details as to the disposition of the early Blackfriars stage, it would be idle to speculate as to whether the Lords' room (in the tiring-house) was already in existence there.

to have planted himself outside the "apte howses of paynted canvas" and away from the traffic of the scene, would have been to lose sight of what was going on. Obviously, once the innovation grew into a habit drastic changes would take place. One has only to picture the stool-holders seated in the middle of the stage—an obstruction to the players and an eyesore to the audience—to see that, in time, the practice would lead to the abandonment of the multiple setting. It may be thought by some that a compromise was effected somewhat on the lines indicated by Percy a score of years later :

> Now if it so be that the Properties of any of These, that be outward, will not serve the turne by reason of concurse of the People on the Stage, Then you may omitt the sayd Properties which be outward and supplye their Places with their Nuncupations onely in Text Letters. [1]

But to this there are divers objections. Apparently the course proposed was even in 1600 very exceptional. Had it been the common practice under such conditions the instruction would have been superfluous. Moreover, the play with regard to which the option was given was a pastoral, and not therefore a strictly multiple (or heterogeneous) setting. It is vital to recognise this. Pastorals by their nature seldom outraged the Unity of Place, and although given a scenic background at court often arranged on the multiple principle, all the components of that background were strictly congruous. Take two court plays of this order that might possibly have been first performed at the early Blackfriars, *The Arraignment of Paris* and *Gallathea*. The setting required for Peele's play—Diana's bower in the midst of thickets—could be realised on the stage of to-day without evoking derision. Lyly's pastoral did not demand the use of even a single *mansion*. The scene was a simple landscape with a large oak tree in the foreground. The use of real trees was a marked characteristic of court plays of this order.

[1] Vide *supra* p. 60.

It is advisable that the student of Elizabethan drama
should make himself thoroughly conversant with the distinguishing characteristics of the multiple scene and the
conventionalisms its employment gave rise to, so that he
may readily recognise a play constructed strictly on its
principles, when he comes across it. With the hope of pre-
venting a perpetuation of the painful ignorance displayed
in this connection by certain recent (and otherwise learned)
commentators, I take leave now to expatiate on the subject.
In reading old plays, particularly of the historico-romantic
or narrative order, one may safely infer the employment
of a multiple setting in all cases where frequent changes of
scene take place while the characters remain. Other cor-
roborative signs and tokens may be found by the skilled
worker, but this, I think, is the unfailing test. It must be
noted, however, that solitary instances of this peculiarity
prove nothing. [1] They are merely graftings from the older
convention. By the employment of a strictly limited
number of symbolic *mansions* typifying certain widely
separated localities it was possible to make the characters
perform a journey in full sight of the audience by simply
walking across the stage from one figurative component of
the scene to another. In the French theatre of the early
seventeenth century the maximum number of *mansions*
utilised was five, but it would appear, from the evidence
of the Revels Accounts and a careful analysis of a variety
of court plays, that the normal number in English court
performances of c. 1570-1600 was three. [2] As a rule, only
one *mansion* existed for the spectator at any given moment,
the others being suppressed by conventional understanding.
But a few exceptions, confined, I think, to Lyly's plays,
are to be found. One of these occurs in *Sapho and Phao*,
v. 2, l. 45, where Venus seated in Vulcan's smithy spies
Cupid in Sapho's chamber on the other side of the stage.

[1] e.g., *Measure for Measure*, iii. 1–2, where the Duke remains while the change
takes place from the prison to the street.

[2] *The History of the Four Sons of Fabius* (1580) called for "a Cytie, a Mounte" and
a Prison. (Cunningham, *Revels Accounts*, pp. 155 and 161). For *the History of Serpedon*
(1580) "a great citie, a wood, a castell" were provided (ibid p. 156). See also *supra*
p. 66, *The Cuck-Queanes and the Cuckolds Errants*.

By way of giving pause to the Elizabethan commentator, who is usually obsessed by a mania for minute localisation, it is vital to point out that in many plays based on the multiple-scene principle not all the places of action were materially symbolised. This was due to the limited number of *mansions* [1] employed, and the dramatist had to write his play accordingly. In the printed copies one can readily distinguish the located (or visualised) scenes from the unlocated. Some reference to the place of action generally occurs in the located scenes, as in *The Woman in the Moone,* iv. 1, l. 292, when Stesias, on entering, says, " This is Enipeus' banke." In the others no clue whatever is presented. [2] Inconsistent and absurd as this arrangement may appear to us now, it created no confusion in the mind of the spectator when put into practice. This is accounted for by the fact that no interior scene was ever unlocated, the unlocated scenes passing in the street, or at any rate in the open. At these junctures the audience generally recognised that the place of action was near to the last located scene. [3] One remarks also that in the typical play of the multiple-scene order there is not only a conventional compression of space but an equally conventional compression of time. Admit the premiss and the one is a logical deduction from the other. Lyly's mind, for example, became so saturated with this associated principle that it influenced him even in the writing of pastorals. Hence Mr. Warwick Bond notes in his excursus on *Love's Metamorphosis,* that "there is visible an attempt at close continuity of action irreconcilable with the lapse of time which the plot requires."[4]

[1] The French term is used by me throughout in a broad technical scene to signify a component part of the multiple setting. It would comprise a cave, or a wood (as symbolised by a couple of trees).

[2] Thus all the scenes in *Endimion* placed by Mr. Warwick Bond (*Lyly's Works,* Vol. iii.) in the " Gardens of the Palace " are wholly unlocated. The multiple setting in this play was arranged in three parts, representing (1) The Lunary Bank, (2) The Castle in the Desert, (3) The Magic Fountain.

[3] For a clue to the origin of the unlocated scene, see C. F. Tucker Brooke, *The Tudor Drama,* p. 30. In the *Play of the Conversion of Sir Jonathan the Jew by Miracle of the Blessed Sacrament* (c. 1480), three *mansions* were employed, the rest of the stage being "unallotted territory" where the characters could meet to transact business, &c., &c.

[4] *Lyly's Works,* iii. 298.

It is noteworthy that " discoveries " could be made with the multiple scene almost equally as well as on the ordinary public stage and by a similar method. This lent illusion to the action, especially in bed-chamber scenes. Most of the *mansions* representing interiors such as shops, senate-houses and caves were provided with double front curtains working on poles and pulling back on either side. Consequently although all these "apte howses of paynted canvas " were *in situ* before the play began, some of them remained concealed from sight until the action called for the drawing of the curtains. [1] There can be little doubt that all the records to be found in the *Revels Accounts* of provision of material for curtains in connection with various plays refer to the curtains employed in front of the *mansions*. [2] Several years ago, I was mightily puzzled to know for what these curtains were used, and was half inclined to think some of them were placed at the front of the stage, to be drawn away at the beginning and to be closed at the end. [3] So much for viewing the past with a purely modern intelligence. It is time for us to recognise that no direct evidence exists of the employment of a front curtain in the court performances of Elizabeth's reign and that the principle of the multiple scene precluded the necessity of any such employment. [4] Apparently the front curtain came into vogue at a slightly later period, with the introduction of the proscenium arch and movable (i.e., successive) scenery.

It is apposite now to consider whether we have any definite evidence of the employment of the *décor simultané*, or multiple setting, on the stage of the first Blackfriars. Without beating about the bush I may say at once that we

---

[1] Cf. *Sapho and Phao*, iii. 3, and iv. 3 ; *The Woman in the Moone*, Act i. Abundant analogies can be traced on the later French stage. See Eugène Rigal, op. cit. pp. 252–3.

[2] Cunningham's *Revels Accounts*, pp. 56, 85, 168.

[3] See "Some characteristics of the Elizabethan-Stuart stage " in *Englische Studien*, Band 32 (1903), p. 40.

[4] Elsewhere, at private entertainments, front curtains were occasionally used. On January 3, 1593–4, when the Gentlemen of Gray's Inn presented a sort of masque in their Hall before the Queen, a curtain drew at the beginning, exposing the altar to the Goddess of Amity, and closed at the end. (Cf. *Gesta Grayorum ; or the History of the High and Mighty Prince Henry, Prince of Purpoole*, London, 1688, p. 56). In the same year *The Comedy of Errors* was acted in the same Hall.

have. Proof of the performance of Lyly's two court comedies, *Sapho and Phao* and *Campaspe*, at the Blackfriars is
afforded us in the printing of the prologues and epilogues
spoken there in the quartos of 1584.[1] By scenic analysis
it will not be difficult to show that both were constructed
on the principle of the compound simultaneous scene and
that one, at least, could not have been acted on any stage
without the use of a multiple setting.

In *Sapho and Phao* three *mansions* were evidently employed, representing (1) Sybilla's cave, (2) Sapho's chamber,
(3) Vulcan's forge. According to my reading all the scenes
unassociated with some one of these three *mansions* were
unlocalised. Act i. takes place in the open, near the ferry.
Act ii. 1, Sybilla's cave. At the close Sybilla goes off, leaving Phao to begin Scene 2, in the open; 3, unlocated; 4,
in the open near the cave. Phao goes to the cave and
calls and Sybilla answers without entering. Act iii. 1, unlocated; 2, in the open; 3, Sapho's chamber (with curtains
in front of the *mansion*). Sapho discovered in bed[2] . . . .
"Shee falleth asleepe. The curtaines drawne." . . . Subsequently the curtains must have been re-opened just
before Sapho's long soliloquy (no direction). Act iv. 1,
Sapho's chamber; 2, the open; 3, Sapho's chamber.
Seven characters on at the end but no direction for their
exeunt. *Quære* did they retire into the *mansion*? Sapho says,
"draw the curteine". Scene 4, Vulcan's forge (elaborately
arranged : note song while the arrows are being made).
Act v. 1, unlocated at the beginning; afterwards Venus
sends off Cupid, and, soliloquising, says she will await
his return at the forge, where she probably seats herself.

[1] In both quartos the prologues for the Blackfriars precede the prologues for the
court, a true indication of their correct chronological order. That even the newest of
new plays was almost invariably given in public before being acted at court is shown by
an order from the Privy Council to the Lord Mayor, under date November 18, 1581,
preserved among the City Records. Acting having been prohibited in the city in
the July previous, the Lords of the Council authorise its renewal, so "that the Players
may be in readiness with convenient matters for the Queen's solace at Christmas, which
they cannot be without their usual exercise therein." (Cf. *The Athenaeum*, January 23,
1869, p. 132, art. "Plays and Players," letter 295.)

[2] In scenes of this order on the ordinary public stage the bed was usually thrust
out from behind.

FRENCH MULTIPLE SCENE FOR DURVAL'S
TRAGI-COMEDY *AGARITE*.

Scene 2, Sapho's chamber, into which Venus (who speaks at line 45 without entering) can see from the forge, as she says, "I marvel Cupid cometh not all this while. How now, in Sapho's lap?" At the close of her speech Sapho replies. Sapho's chamber at end of scene was probably concealed again by the curtains. Sapho says, "Come, Milela, shut the door *(Exeunt)*". Scene 3, before Sybilla's cave. It is plain, I think, to be seen from this analysis that the fifth act could not have been given on any stage, public or private, without the conjunctive employment of two *mansions*. Hence we have reasonable proof of the use of the multiple setting at the early Blackfriars. As some doubts may be expressed as to the nature of the curtains employed in the scenes laid in Sapho's chamber, whether they were simply bed-curtains draped round a four-poster or traverses hanging in front of the *mansion*, I may say that I arrived at the latter opinion strictly through French analogy. At the Hôtel de Bourgogne at a slightly later period it was customary to stage all bed-room scenes, forming part of a *décor simultané*, in this way. Two examples will suffice. They are taken from the property-man's memoranda for the staging of the plays. "Au milieu du théâtre", we read of the *Agarite* of Durval, "il faut une chambre garnie d'un superbe lit, le quel se ferme et ouvre quand il en est besoin." Similarly the instruction regarding *La Folie d'Isabelle* of Hardy begins "il faut que le théâtre soit beau, et à un des côtés une belle chambre, où il y ait un beau lit, des sièges pour s'asseoir. Ladite chambre s'ouvre et se ferme plusieurs fois. Vous la pouvez mettre au milieu du théâtre, si vous voulez." [1]

In his recension of *Campaspe*, Mr. Warwick Bond (who has no suspicion of the existence of the multiple-scene principle and interprets Lyly's plays by the usages of the public theatre) places the action in Athens in four distinct scenes, representing (1) A Suburb, (2) Alexander's Palace, (3) The Market Place (with Diogenes' Tub), (4) Apelles' Shop. But according to my reading only three of the locali-

[1] Eugène Rigal, op. cit., pp. 248–9.

ties were materially symbolised, all the suburban scenes being unlocated. Hence the scene would be arranged somewhat after the following manner :

APELLES' SHOP.

PALACE.

TUB.

STAGE FRONT.

The Market Place was indicated simply by Diogenes' tub, which, so far from being thrust up a trap when required (as Mr. Bond surmises [1]) remained on the stage from first to last. Note that the tub stood on its end (at one juncture Diogenes pries *over* it), and that there was some means of getting into it unseen at the back. Diogenes sometimes departs from the stage in the ordinary way, only to emerge later from his tub. Without full conception of the multiple-setting it is impossible to visualize all the various mutations in the third act. That the action in the opening scene oscillates rapidly from the inside to the outside of Apelles' shop is indicated in Psydus' speech. The shop, or studio, must have been a fairly solid construction with a curtain in front of it, the necessity for the latter being indicated by the discovery at the opening of scene 3, as well as by the situation in act iv. 4, where Apelles is found painting Campaspe. Here the direction "Campaspe alone" does not signify that Apelles goes off (as Mr. Bond implies), but that Campaspe emerges into the street and soliloquises.

---

[1] Cf. C. F. Tucker Brooke, *The Tudor Drama*, pp. 173 and 432. It is painful to find Mr. Brooke, not only accepting Mr. Bond's view, but going so far as to say that in Lyly's court plays no effort was made to visualize the scene. How then would he explain away the strong collateral evidence of the *Revels Accounts* ?

Immediately after her departure, the page enters and addresses Apelles, showing that the artist has been all the time in his studio. Apart from these denotements, the transfers of scene while the characters remain prove the multiple-setting. Unlike *Sapho and Phao, Campaspe* would have admitted, at a pinch, of staging by the ordinary public theatre method, presuming the addition of a tub to the conventional resources of the tiring-house façade. But it would have been at best a clumsy alternative, and my own opinion is that both plays were given at the Blackfriars exactly as they were represented at court.

BIBLIOGRAPHY

BIBLIOGRAPHY

Actors' Remonstrance, The, or Complaint : for the silencing of their profession and banishment from their severall play-houses. 4to, 1643. (E. W. Ashbee's facsimile reprint, 1869.)

ADEMOLLO, A. — *I Primi Fasti del Teatro di via della Pergola in Firenze* (1657-61). Milano, Ricordi (no date).

ALBRIGHT, VICTOR E. — *The Shaksperian Stage*, New York, 1909.

ALGAROTTI, COUNT—*An Essay on the Opera*, London, 1767.

Apollo's Banquet for the Treble Violin, London, 1669.

ARCHER, WILLIAM—*The Theatrical World of* 1897. "The Growth of the Playhouse," art. in *The Tribune* of August 17, 1907. "The Elizabethan Stage," art. in *The Quarterly Review*, April, 1908. "The Fortune Theatre, 1600," in *Shakespeare Jahrbuch*, 1908, pp. 159-66.

ARIOSTO, LODOVICO—*Orlando Furioso*, folio, Milano, 1818.

BAKER, DAVID ERSKINE — *Biographia Dramatica, or A Companion to the Playhouse*, 2 vols., 1782.

BAKER, G. P. — *The Development of Shakespeare as a Dramatist*, 1907.

BAKER, H. BARTON—*The London Stage*, 2 vols., 1889.

BASKERVILL, C. R.—"The Custom of Sitting on the Elizabethan Stage." (*Modern Philology*, Chicago, VIII, No. 4, April, 1911).

BEAUMONT AND FLETCHER'S WORKS, folio, 1647.

BELLAMY, GEORGE ANNE—*An Apology for the Life of*, 2 vols., Dublin, 1785.

BERNARDIN, N. M.—*La Comèdie Italienne en France*, 1902.

BOADEN, JAMES—*Memoirs of Mrs. Siddons* (Memoir Library Series), 1896.

BOZ—*Memoirs of Joseph Grimaldi*, 2 vols., 1838.

BRADLEY, A. C.—*Oxford Lectures on Poetry*, 1909.

BRERETON, AUSTIN—*The Lyceum and Henry Irving*, 1903.

BROADBENT, R. J.—*Stage Whispers*, 1901.

BROOKE, C. F. TUCKER—*The Shakespeare Apocrypha*, 1908. *The Tudor Drama*, 1912.

BROTANEK, RUDOLPH—*Die Englische Maskenspiele*, Vienna, 1902.

BURNEY, CHAS.—*History of Music*, 4 vols., 1789.

Calendars of State Papers, Domestic Series, temp. Charles I and II.

Calendars of State Papers, Venetian.

CAMPORI, GIUSEPPE—*Notizie inedite di Raffaello da Urbino*, (Atti e Memorie di storia patria, Modena, 1863, vol I.)

CELLER, LUDOVIC—*Les Décors, les Costumes, et la Mise en Scène au Dix-Septième Siècle*, 1869.

CHALMERS, GEO.—*A Supplemental Apology for the Believers in the Shakespeare Papers*, London, 1799.

CHAMBERS, E. K.—*The Mediæval Stage*, 2 vols., 1903.

CHAPPUZEAU, S.—*Le théâtre français divisé en trois livres*, Lyon, 1674.

CHARDON, HENRI—*La Troupe du Roman Comique dévoilée et les Comédiens de campagne au 17ᵉ Siècle*, 1875.

CHETWOOD, W. R.—*General History of the Stage*, London, 1749.

CIBBER, COLLEY—*An Apology for the Life of*, London, 1826.

COLLIER, J. PAYNE—*The History of English Dramatic Poetry to the time of Shakespeare ; and Annals of the Stage to the Restoration*, 3 vols., 1831.

Connoisseur Magazine, The—Vols. xv and xviii (1906-7).

Cook, Dutton—*On the Stage*, 2 vols., 1883.

Coryat's Crudities—2 vols., Glasgow, 1905.

Cotgrave, R.—*A Dictionarie of the French and English Tongues*, folio, 1611.

Cox, Robert—*The Wits, or Sport upon Sport*, 1662.

Cummings, W. H.—"Purcell's Music in Macbeth." In *The Musical Times*, xxiii (1882), p. 471.

Cuningham, Henry — *Macbeth* (Arden Shakespeare Series), 1912.

Cunningham, Peter — *Extracts from the Accounts of the Revels at Court in the reigns of Queen Elizabeth and King James I* (Shakespeare Society, 1842). *Inigo Jones* (Shakespeare Society, 1848).

D'Avenant, Sir William—*Dramatic Works*, edited by James Maidment and W. H. Logan, 5 vols., 1872-4.

Dekker, Thomas—*The Non-Dramatic Works of*, edited by the Rev. A. B. Grosart, 5 vols., 1884-6.

Description of the Great Machines of the Descent of Orpheus into Hell. Presented by the French Commedians at the Cockpit, in Drury Lane, 1661.

Dibdin, James C.—*Annals of the Edinburgh Stage*, Edinburgh, 1888.

Dispatches of William Perwich, The—Camden Society, 1905.

Dodsley's Old English Plays—Fourth edition, edited by W. Carew Hazlitt, 15 vols., 1874-6.

Donaldson, J. W.—*The Theatre of the Greeks*, 1875.

Dörpfeld and E. Reisch — *Das Griechische Theater*, Athens, 1896.

Downes, John—*Roscius Anglicanus*, London, 1708.

Drama, or Theatrical Pocket Magazine, The—Vols. i-iv (1821).

Dryden, John—*Works*, edited by Sir Walter Scott and G. Saintsbury, 14 vols., 1883-9.

DUNLAP, WM.—*Memoirs of George Fred. Cooke*, 2 vols., 1813.

DUNTON, JOHN—*The Dublin Scuffle*, London, 1699.

D'URFEY, TOM—*Collin's Walk Through London*, 1690.

ELTON, C. I.—*William Shakespeare, his Family and Friends*, 1904.

Era Almanack, The, 1891.

EVANS, HERBERT A.—*English Masques* (Warwick Library Series), 1897.

FEUILLERAT, A.—*Documents relating to the Office of the Revels in the time of Queen Elizabeth*, 1908. "Shakespeare's Blackfriars," art. in *The Daily Chronicle*, of December 22, 1911.

FIELDING, HENRY—*The Complete Works of*, with notes and introductions by James P. Browne, M.D., 11 vols., 1902.

FITZGERALD, PERCY—*A New History of the English Stage*, 2 vols., 1882.

FITZJEFFREY, H.—*Notes from Black-fryers*, 1620.

FORESTIER, A.—"The Fortune Theatre reconstructed" (designs). In *Illus. London News*, Aug. 12, 1911.

FOSTER, FRANCES A. — "Dumb Shew in Elizabethan Drama before 1620," *Englische Studien*, band XLIV (1911), heft i.

FOURNEL, V.—*Curiosités Théâtrales*, 1878. *Le Vieux Paris*, Tours, 1887.

FURNESS, HORACE HOWARD — *New Variorum Edition of Shakespeare*, 15 vols., Philadelphia, 1871-1907.

FYVIE, JOHN—*Comedy Queens of the Georgian Era*, 1906.

GARNIER, CHAS.—*Le Théâtre*, 1871.

GAYTON, ED.—*Pleasant Notes upon Don Quixot*, 1654.

Gentleman's Magazine, The, for 1813, p. 220, art. on "Dorset Gardens Theatre."

Gesta Grayorum ; or the History of the High and Mighty Prince Henry, Prince of Purpoole, London, 1688.

GHERARDI, EVARISTO—*Le Théâtre Italien*, Amsterdam, 1721, 6 vols.

GILDON, CHAS.—*A Comparison between the two Stages*, 8vo, 1702.

GILLILAND, THOS.—*The Dramatic Mirror*, 2 vols., 1808.

GLAPTHORNE, HENRY—*The Ladies' Privilege*, a Comedy, 4to, 1640.

GODFREY, WALTER H.—"An Elizabethan Playhouse," *Architectural Review*, April, 1908.

GOSSE, EDMUND—*Seventeenth Century Studies*, 1883.

GOSSON, STEPHEN—*The Schoole of Abuse*, edit. Arber, 1868. *Plays Confuted in Five Actions* [1582].

GREETING, THOS. — *The Pleasant Companion; or New Lessons and Instructions for the Flagelet*, 1680.

GROBERT—*De l' Exécution Dramatique, considérée dans ses rapports avec le matériel de la Salle et de la Scène*, 1809.

Grove's Dictionary of Music and Musicians, edited by J. A. Fuller Maitland, 5 vols., 1904, &c.

HALLIWELL-PHILLIPPS, J. O.—*Outlines of the Life of Shakespeare*, 3rd edit., 1883.

Harlequin Horace; or the Art of Modern Poetry, third edit., 1735.

Hatton Correspondence, The, 2 vols., Camden Society, 1878.

HAWKINS, F.—*Annals of the French Stage from its origin to the Death of Racine*, 2 vols., 1884. *The French Stage in the Eighteenth Century*, 2 vols., 1888.

HECKETHORN, C. W.—*Lincoln's Inn Fields and the Localities Adjacent*, 1896.

Henslowe's Diary, edited by W. W. Greg, M.A., 2 vols., 1904-8.

HENTZNER, PAUL—*Itinerarium Germaniae, Angliae, Italiae, cum indice locorum, rerum atque verborum commemorabilium*, Noribergae, 1629.

Historical Manuscripts Commission Reports, various.

HOLBROOK, RICHARD—*The Farce of Master Pierre Patelin,* Boston, Mass., 1905.

JACKSON, JOHN—*History of the Scottish Stage,* 1793.

Jonsonus Virbius, London, 1638.

JORDAN, THOS.—*A Royal Arbour of Loyal Poesie.* No date [c. 1662]. *A Nursery in Variety of Poetry.* No date [c. 1665].

JUSSERAND, J. J.—*Shakespeare in France,* London, 1898.

KELLY, MICHAEL—*Reminiscences of,* 2 vols., 1826.

KILLIGREW, THOS.—*Dramatic Works,* folio, 1664.

KOMENSKY, J. A.—*Orbis Sensualium Pictus,* London, 1659.

LACROIX, PAUL—*Le 17ᵉ Siècle, Lettres, Sciences et Arts,* 1882.

LAFONTAINE, H. C. de — *The King's Musick,* no date [1909].

LAMBARD, WM.—*A Perambulation of Kent,* second edit., 1596.

LEE, SIR SIDNEY — *The French Renaissance in England,* Oxford, 1910.

Letter Book of Gabriel Harvey (1573-80), Camden Society, 1884.

Letters to Sir Joseph Williamson at Cologne, Camden Society, 2 vols., 1874.

LOWE, ROBERT W.—*Thomas Betterton* (Eminent Actors series), 1891.

LUTTRELL, NARCISSUS—*A Brief Historical Relation of State Affairs, from Sept.* 1678 *to April,* 1714, 6 vols., Oxford, 1857.

Lyly's Works—Edited by R. Warwick Bond, 3 vols., 1902.

LYONNET, HENRY—*Le Théâtre en Espagne,* 1897.

MAGALOTTI, LORENZO—*Travels of Cosmo III, Grand Duke of Tuscany, through England during the reign of King Charles II* (1669), 4to, 1821.

MALONE, EDMOND—*Shakespeare's Works*, 11 vols., Dublin, 1794. *Shakespeare Variorum*, edit. Boswell, 21 vols., 1821.

MANTZIUS, KARL—*A History of Theatrical Art*, 5 vols., 1902, &c.

Marlowe's Works—Edited by A. H. Bullen, 3 vols., 1885.

MARTIN, WILLIAM—*The Site of the Globe Playhouse of Shakespeare*, 1910.

MAU, AUGUST—*Pompeii, its Life and Art*, 1902.

Middleton's Works—Edited by A. H. Bullen, 8 vols., 1885.

MONCONYS, M. de—*Journal des Voyages*, Lyon, 1666.

MONKEMEYER, PAUL—*Prolegomena zu einer Darstellung der englischen Volksbühne zur Elisabeth- und Stuart-Zeit*, Hanover, 1905.

MÓRICE, EMILE—*Histoire de la mise en scène depuis les Mystères jusqu'à Cid.* 1836.

MOYNET, GEORGES—*Trucs et Décors*, Paris, no date.

MURRAY, JOHN TUCKER—*English Dramatic Companies*, 1588-1642, 2 vols., 1910.

Musick's Delight on the Cithren, London, 1666.

NASHE, THOS.—*Works of*, edited by Ronald B. McKerrow, 5 vols., 1904-10.

NICHOLS, JOHN—*The Progresses, Processions, &c., of King James I*, 4 vols., 1828.

NUITTER, CHAS. AND THOINAN, E. — *Les Origines de L'Opéra Français*, 1886.

ORDISH, T. F.—*Early London Theatres*, 1894.

Oxford History of Musick, The—Vol. VII.

PENLEY, BELVILLE S.—*The Bath Stage*, 1892.

Pepys' Diary, edited by H. B. Wheatley, 10 vols., 1897-9.

PERCY, WILLIAM—*Plays*, Roxburghe Club, 1824.

PLAYFORD, JOHN—*Musick's Recreation on the Viol, Lyra-way*, 1682.

"Plays and Players," art. in *The Athenaeum*, January 23, 1869, p. 142.

Prölss, R.—*Von den altesten Drucken der Dramen Shakespeares*, 1905.

Prynne, W.—*Histrio Mastix, The Players Scourge ; or Actors Tragaedie*, 1633.

Puttenham, Geo.—*The Arte of English Poesy*, edit. Arber, 1869.

Rennert, H. A.—*The Life of Lope de Vega*, Glasgow, 1904.

Reynolds, G. F.—*Some Principles of Elizabethan Staging*, Chicago, 1905 (Reprinted from *Modern Philology*). "What we know of the Elizabethan Stage," in *Modern Philology*, ix, No. 1, July, 1911.

Rigal, Eugène—*Le Théâtre Français avant la Période Classique*, 1901.

Rimbault, E. F.—*Ancient Vocal Music of England*, 1847.

Rye, W. B.—*England as seen by Foreigners in the days of Elizabeth and James I*, 1865.

Sabattini, Nicolo—*Pratica di fabricar scene e machine ne' Teatri*, Ravenna, 1638.

"Scale Model of the Fortune Theatre, The "—Illustrated Article in *The Architectural Review*, vol. xxxi (January, 1912), p. 53.

Scaliger, Julius Cæsar—*Poetices Libri Septem, &c.*, folio, Lyons, 1561.

Schelling, Felix E.—*Elizabethan Drama*, 1558-1642, 2 vols., Boston, 1908.

Scientific American, The, vol. l, No. 14, issue of April 5, 1884. Illustrated Article on the Madison Square Theatre, New York.

Scott, Clement—"The King of Clownland," art. in *The English Illus. Magazine*, Christmas, 1898, p. 271.

Secret Service Accounts of Charles II and James II, 2 vols., Camden Society, 1851.

Serlio, Sebastian—*Architettura*, Paris, 1545.

SETTLE, ELKANAH—*The Empress of Morocco*, a tragedy, 4to, 1673.

SHADWELL, CHAS. — *Dramatic Works*, 2 vols., Dublin, 1720.

SHIRLEY, JAMES—*Narcissus; or the Self-Lover*, 1646.

SIDNEY, SIR PHILIP—*Astrophel and Stella*, edited by A. W. Pollard, 1888. *Apologie for Poetrie*, edited by E. S. Shuckburgh, 1891.

SMALL, R. A.—*The Stage Quarrel between Ben Jonson and the so-called Poetasters*, Breslau, 1899.

SMITH, HORACE AND JAMES—*The Rejected Addresses*, 1813.

SMITH, JOHN STAFFORD—*Musica Antiqua*, 2 vols., 1812.

SORBIERES, SAMUEL DE—*Relation d'un voyage en Angleterre où sont touchées plusieurs choses qui regardent l'estat des sciences et de la religion et autres matières curieuses*, Paris, 1664. *A Voyage to England*, London, 1709.

SPEED, JOHN—*The Theatre of the Empire of Great Britain*. 1611.

SQUIRE, W. BARCLAY—" Purcell's Dramatic Music," art. in *The Quarterly Magazine of the International Society of Music*, Year v (1904), Pt. 4.

STOPES, MRS. C. C. — " William Hunnis," art. in *The Athenaeum* of March 31, 1900.

SYMONDS, J. A.—*Shakspere's Predecessors in the English Drama*, 1884.

Tarleton's Jests and News out of Purgatory, with Memoir by J. O. Halliwell. Shakespeare Society, 1844.

Term Catalogues, 1668-1709, edited by Edward Arber, 3 vols., 1903-6.

[VASARI, GIORGIO]—*Descrizione dell' apparato della Comedia et Intermedii d'essa recitata in Firenze il giorno di S. Stefano l'anno* 1565, &c., &c. Florence, 1565. (British Museum, press-mark " 604 b 20.")

VICTOR, BENJAMIN—*History of the Theatres of London and Dublin*, 2 vols. London, 1761.

WALKER, ERNEST—*History of Music in England*, 1907.

WALKER, J. C.—*Historical and Critical Essay on the Revival of the Drama in Italy*, 1805.

WALLACE, C. W.—*The Children of the Chapel at Blackfriars, 1597-1603*, 1908. "The Swan Theatre," art. in *Englische Studien*, band 43, pp. 340 ff.

WARD, A.W.—*English Dramatic Literature*, 3 vols., 1899.

WEGENER, RICHARD—*Die Bühneneinrichtung des Shakespeareschen Theaters nach den Zeitgenössischen Dramen*, Halle, 1907.

WHITELOCKE, BULSTRODE—*Memorials of the English Affairs, &c.*, folio, 1682.

WILKES, S. [SAMUEL DERRICK]—*A General View of the Stage*, 1759.

WILKINSON, TATE—*Memoirs of his own Life*, 4 vols., York. 1790.

WILSON, J. D.—*Life in Shakespeare's England*, 1911.

WINSTANLEY, WM.—*Lives of the Famous English Poets*, 1687.

WINWOOD, SIR RALPH—*Memorials of Affairs of State*, folio, 1725.

WOTTON, SIR HENRY—*Reliquiae Wottonianae*, 1685.

WRIGHT, JAMES—*Historia Histrionica : an historical account of the English Stage : shewing the ancient use, improvement, and perfection of dramatic representations in this nation. In a dialogue of Plays and Players*, 1699. (Reprinted in *Dodsley's Old Plays*, 1744, vol. XI.)

WYNDHAM, H. SAXE—*The Annals of Covent Garden Theatre*, 2 vols., 1906.

YOUNG, K.—"The Influence of French farce upon the Plays of John Heywood." (*Modern Philology*, June, 1904.)

INDEX

INDEX